FUNDAMENTALS OF
MENU
PLANNING

Paul J. McVety

Bradley J. Ware

VNR VAN NOSTRAND REINHOLD COMPANY
———————————————— New York

To Andrea, Brian, and Daniel McVety, and
Sheila I. Thompson-Ware

Copyright © 1989 by Van Nostrand Reinhold
Library of Congress Catalog Card Number 88–31556
ISBN 0–442–26492–5

Printed in the United States of America

Designed by Beehive Production Services

Van Nostrand Reinhold
115 Fifth Avenue
New York, New York 10003

Van Nostrand Reinhold (International) Limited
11 New Fetter Lane
London EC4P 4EE, England

Van Nostrand Reinhold
480 La Trobe Street
Melbourne, Victoria 3000, Australia

Nelson Canada
1121 Birchmount Road
Scarborough, Ontario M1K 5G4, Canada

16 15 14 13 12 11 10 9 8 7 6 5 4 3 2 1

Library of Congress Cataloging-in-Publication Data
McVety, Paul J.
    Fundamentals of menu planning/Paul J. McVety, Bradley J. Ware.
        p.   cm.
    Bibliography: p. 299
    Includes index.
    ISBN 0–442–26492–5
    1. Menus.   2. Foodservice.   I. Ware, Bradley J. (Bradley John), 1953–   . II. Title.
TX911.3.M45M38   1990
642'.5—dc19   88–31556

Contents

Foreword

The popular approach to menu satisfaction is that "people eat with their eyes." Present the customers with food that is attractive, and it usually satisfies their desires.

I am sure this concept is true today, but with advances in science, changing market practices, and the sophistication of the customer, many more complicated factors must be considered. The customers' knowledge about nutrition and caloric content of various foods, seasonal fluctuations in food supply, changing eating patterns due to fads and to more healthful eating, technical advances in the production of food, and the vast variety of foods available make menu planning a very difficult task. There are also a wide group of variables that must be considered in planning a menu to satisfy all needs: ease of reading, size of menu, size of print, menu format and content, proper wording, menu standardization, regional preferences, and employee skills. Certainly one of the latest considerations must be "truth in menu." Determining the cost of all menu items and then arriving at a feasible selling price is paramount in menu presentation.

All the above considerations have been discussed by Paul McVety and Brad Ware in *Fundamentals of Menu Planning*. An easily understandable approach to menu planning is presented. The text has been designed with one thought in mind: to make it easy for the educator, entrepreneur, and student to face and satisfy all the various factors in menu planning.

RICHARD BONIN
Associate Professor
Johnson and Wales University
Culinary Division
Foodservice Related Studies Department

Preface

The menu is the backbone of a foodservice operation. Developing a workable, quality menu is an important step in planning a *profitable* operation. The purpose of this book is to provide basic information about foods, management, and financing for today's menu planner. Numerous tables, forms, and sample menus are used to instruct the reader in nutrition; in costing, marketing, merchandising, and analyzing a menu; and in selecting equipment.

Fundamentals of Menu Planning is intended for foodservice students in culinary school programs in universities and in high-school settings. It is also intended to assist foodservice managers in developing new menus.

Grateful acknowledgment is extended to everyone who contributed ideas, materials, and assistance in the preparation of this text. We especially wish to thank John Bowen, Vice-President, Administration, Johnson and Wales University; Andrea McVety; Sheila I. Thompson-Ware; Rosemary DePetro, Associate Professor, Johnson and Wales University; Jennifer Schlitzer, Associate Professor, Johnson and Wales University; Richard Bonin, Associate Professor, Johnson and Wales University; Robert Ulm; and Agnes Manoogian.

1

Institutional, Industrial, and Commercial Menus

To plan a profitable menu in the foodservice industry, the menu planner must be knowledgeable about foods, management, and financing. This chapter discusses facts and practical work experiences that are essential in planning a profitable menu in the commercial, industrial, and institutional segments of the foodservice industry.

OBJECTIVES

1. To give the student an understanding of the type of knowledge a menu planner must have to write menus in each of the three foodservice segments.
2. To help the student effectively apply the knowledge of planning menus to writing menus.
3. To identify special characteristics in each of the foodservice segments.

BACKGROUND OF A MENU PLANNER

Who can plan a menu? Anyone can plan a menu in the simplest form. The definition of a menu is simply "a listing of foods." If people are hungry, they can mentally plan a menu by choosing the foods they would like to eat. To plan a simple menu does not take years of experience and education.

Menus planned for a commercial foodservice operation are different from those planned for an institutional or industrial foodservice operation. To plan a successful and profitable menu for a public foodservice operation does take foodservice work experience and a culinary education.

The person planning menus for a commercial, institutional, or industrial foodservice operation must be knowledgeable of many aspects of the foodservice industry. A professional menu planner is knowledgeable in foods, finances, and management.

The menu planner must have a good understanding of all three areas to plan a profitable menu. For a person to acquire enough knowledge in the three subjects requires a combination of educational theory (the know-how) and practical working experience (the how-to) in each area.

When planning a menu, it is helpful and important to categorize the information into the following categories: (1) necessary information and (2) helpful information.

Information not necessary in menu planning for a commercial foodservice operation might be very necessary in menu planning for an institutional foodservice operation. For example, it is not essential to know the sodium diet needs of the customers when planning a menu for a commercial foodservice operation. This information *would* be necessary when planning a menu for a patient in an institutional foodservice operation.

FOOD

In addition to knowing the type of market (customer) that will be patronizing the foodservice operation, the menu planner needs to be aware of the areas of food, finances, and management when planning a menu.

In the area of food, the menu planner must

1. Know the customer's likes and dislikes regarding food. Knowing which foods are preferred definitely helps the saleability of a product.

2. Be able to identify the various food products that are available in the markets.

3. Be able to explain the different criteria that establish the quality grades of food products.

4. Know the availability of the food products. Knowing when the food product is available helps keep the food cost down and the profit up.

5. Know how the food items are prepared, produced, plated, served, and consumed by the guest. This information will allow the menu planner to specify what type of equipment will be necessary to produce the food product. This knowledge will also indicate what level of skill is necessary for the cooks.

6. Know how the food product is packaged, shipped, received, and stored, and know the shelf life of the product. This information helps the menu planner establish a quality menu within the foodservice operation.

7. Know which foods are complementary to each other for proper garnishing of dishes and for achieving an aesthetic and nutritionally balanced menu.

8. Know the yields of the food products to help set up recipes.

9. Know how to do recipe conversions, how to merchandise, and how to market the food product.

10. Know cross utilization. Cross utilization refers to using a menu product in more than one menu or in more than one product. For example, if a chef placed baked scallops with buttered bread

crumbs on the menu, scallops should also appear in at least one or two more entrees such as fried scallops or scallops in a casserole with cheese sauce. Just having scallops once would present product and cost problems unless scallops were extremely popular and the amount purchased was used for one meal. Cross utilization should be followed throughout the menu, not just in the entrees. Most institutional menus use cross utilization of the food product exceptionally well.

This list is a sampling of the knowledge a professional menu planner must obtain.

FINANCES

The menu planner must understand the relationship between food cost and other expenses such as labor and overhead.* The menu planner must be able to produce a menu that is profitable. Thus, the menu planner must be able to understand how the portion cost affects the selling price. The price of the menu must be appealing to the customer, yet still allow for profit for the foodservice operation.

The menu planner needs to know how to do recipe costing. Portion cost and markup must be related to volume to make a profit. Recipe costing is essentially finding a portion cost and marking it up to a selling price that the market will accept. Awareness of how a sales history forms and the sales mix or scatter sheet used in forecasting is needed by the menu planner.† Knowing how to establish a check average and how to project for annual sales is essential financial information for a menu planner. The menu planner must understand financing as it applies to the foodservice industry as a whole and to the menu in particular.

---

*Overhead refers to all costs not included in payroll costs or food and beverage costs. Overhead costs include fixed expenses and variable expenses. Salary is an example of a fixed overhead expense because it does not fluctuate according to sales. No matter how much business a foodservice operation does, salary stays the same. Equipment needs can vary with the amount of business done and would therefore be a variable overhead expense.

†A scatter sheet is a record of the menu items that have been sold. Check average is the average amount of money a person or group of people will spend for a meal. Sales mix is a record of which menu items have been sold during a particular period of time.

MANAGEMENT

The menu planner must take into consideration personnel skills when designing a menu. To be able to successfully plan a profitable menu, it is important for the menu planner to be aware of the foodservice owner's wants and needs in the following areas: profit, check average, style of operation, style of menu, theme of foodservice operation, type of service to be used, atmosphere, that is, total environment of the dining room, mood that is to be achieved, skill level of personnel, and market to be established. The menu planner must know as much as possible about the customer including food preferences and the price the customer is willing to pay. For more information about the customer, see Chapter 2.

The menu planner, like the architect, must be able to design on paper what the owner dreams about. The how and the what must come together to form the type of menu the owner would like.

INSTITUTIONAL FOODSERVICE

The institutional foodservice category is composed of

- ♦ Grade schools
- ♦ High schools
- ♦ Community colleges
- ♦ Private colleges
- ♦ Residential colleges
- ♦ Private and federally funded hospitals
- ♦ Nursing homes
- ♦ Psychiatric hospitals
- ♦ Armed services

Each one of these operations has its own dietary requirements that must be followed on the menu. The most important factor in planning an institutional menu is that it must be nutritious. All institutional menus should include the four basic food groups: the meat group, cereal group, fruit and vegetable group, and dairy group.

The meat group includes roast beef, chicken, bacon, and pork. The cereal or bread group includes various breakfast cereals, oatmeal, whole wheat bread, and white bread. The fruit and vegetable group includes various fruits such as citrus oranges, grapefruit, and apples and vegetables such as corn, carrots, and green beans. The dairy group includes eggs, milk, cheese, and butter.

When planning a menu for any institution, the following factors must be taken into consideration:

1. Type of operation and the diet required by its patrons
2. Budget restrictions
3. Ages of the patrons
4. Food preferences of the patrons
5. Type of service needed
6. Hours of feeding
7. Storage area
8. Equipment needed to produce the menu
9. Government regulations
10. Religious and ethnic backgrounds of the patrons

Type of Operation and Required Diets

The menu will depend on the type of institutional operation. In a hospital setting the menu planner must follow strict dietary regulations that have been set by the certified dietician.

The seven main diets of a hospital are as follows:

1. Regular diet—includes salt and pepper along with other spices. The patient can usually have as much as he or she desires. Nothing on this diet has to be weighed except on rare occasions; for example, when a patient needs to watch his or her calorie intake.
2. Bland diet—includes salt but not pepper or other spices. The food must be weighed in most cases. The patient who receives this diet usually has a digestive ailment such as a stomach ulcer.
3. Soft diet—includes salt and pepper but no other spices. The food is usually weighed. This particular diet includes pureed foods for the elderly.
4. Low sodium—includes pepper but not salt. The food must be weighed.
5. Calculated diet or diabetic diet—includes salt and pepper. No sugar is allowed in this diet. The food must be weighed.
6. Low sodium or calculated diet—includes pepper but no salt. Sugar is not allowed in this diet. The food has to be weighed.
7. Clear liquid diet—includes salt and pepper but the patient cannot have solid foods. Persons with a nervous ulcer condition or patients who have had orthodontic surgery follow this diet.

It is vital that a patient's meal be planned very carefully for a faster recovery. If these diets are not followed as prescribed, illness or accidental death could result.

Budget Restrictions

Most institutional foodservices today are operated by large foodservice companies such as Saga, Daka, ARA, and Servomation. The hospital, nursing home, or school will establish a one sum per day food allowance per customer. For example, $1.90 per day might be the sum with which the company has to operate. The menu does not have to stay within this sum every day; rather it must stay within this budget over an accounting period, thus allowing the menu planner some flexibility in meal planning.

In most cases institutional cafeterias are set up on a break-even basis or on a 1 percent to 2 percent profit. The institution itself is not in business for the purpose of making a large profit in the foodservice operation. Thus, many institutional facilities charge very little for their food items.

Ages of Patrons

When a menu planner decides to plan a particular menu, the ages of the people who will consume the food must be considered. As we continue to grow older our bodies require and are able to handle different foods. At infancy our digestive systems are very delicate and are able to digest only delicate foods. As our digestive systems mature we are able to digest a much larger variety of foods. When we grow older our digestive systems become frail and we can digest less of a variety of foods. Age will have a direct effect on what items will be selected for a particular menu. Since hospital patients vary in ages, the menu planner must have food items on the menu that appeal to all age groups as well as making sure that these items together comprise a nutritionally balanced menu.

In an elementary or secondary school setting, the menu planner does not have to take into consideration as many age groups as in a hospital. Therefore, planning menus for elementary schools is a much simpler task than planning menus for hospitals.

The college or university presents more of a challenge to the menu planner. The ages may vary from young adults to much older adults. College students also tend to be more demanding than young school children. Many students today are paying high tuition costs and they expect to get adequate menu selections and quality food.

Food Preference

The menu planner must take a careful look at what the patient or patron wants to eat within the institution. This process can be accomplished by a number of different methods.

A survey can be taken to determine what foods are popular. A survey could also help to determine what foods one might hope to see on the menu in the future. The menu planner can look over the surveys and make important evaluations that could help improve future menus. If possible, the menu planner should eliminate those foods that prove to be unpopular.

Another method of determining food preferences is to put suggestion boxes in the cafeteria. This idea does not work as well as the food survey. People will take a survey more seriously than placing suggestions in a box. Many times an employer will make it mandatory to fill out the survey when it is entirely optional for the employee to put suggestions in a box.

In many cases, institutions such as hospitals and schools are under strict dietary regulations or government regulations.

Type of Service Needed

In most institutional settings, the service is cafeteria style, which encompasses a tray line. Another popular service system is the scatter system. This system allows large volumes of people to move quickly, bypassing food stations from which they do not want to select food. This system allows for much more customer involvement.

It is important to serve food that has good holding qualities, both hot and cold. In many institutions, hot food is served in steam tables and allowed to continue to cook or to evaporate excess moisture. Stews, casseroles, and quiches are good examples of foods that have good holding qualities and do not become overcooked or dried if the temperature is properly set at a steam table. Items such as fried fish or roast beef can be served on a steam table but only a few orders can be cooked or sliced at a time. Fried fish becomes soggy on the line if a cover is put over it. Roast beef tends to dry out and shrink when a cover is left on for a long period of time.

Cold items placed on a cafeteria service line should be placed on a bed of ice. Salads and dairy desserts require refrigeration units. It would be unwise to serve oysters or clams on the half shell because of their poor holding qualities; they lose their freshness when served at room temperature.

In a hospital, food is cooked and plated in the kitchen, placed in a refrigerated or heated cart, and transported to the patients' rooms.

Another method of serving hot foods is to precook the food in the kitchen and finish cooking the food in a prep kitchen on the individual floor. In a hospital, it is very important to be accurate with serving foods at their proper temperatures to avoid the development of foodborne diseases, such as salmonella.

Note: Overall, when planning menus for institutional foodservice operations, the menu planner must look at the type of service to be used to maintain a quality food product.

Hours of Feeding

Within the institutional framework, hours of feeding will help determine the types of items that the menu will offer. If the hours of feeding are from 8:00 A.M. to 4:00 P.M., the menu planner only has to plan menus for breakfast and lunch. If an institution is operating a 24-hour feeding system, then breakfast, lunch, and dinner menus have to be planned.

Storage Area

In an institutional setting, the storage area available helps determine the type of food offered on the menu. In many cases, institutions have limited walk-in freezer space. Limited freezer space indicates that many items on the menu must either be fresh foods that require refrigerated space or canned foods that require storeroom facilities. The menu planner must take into consideration the amount and type of storage area available and balance the variety of food products on the menu accordingly.

Equipment Needs

Many institutions purchase their equipment first and then set up the menu. It is only afterward that the management realizes that some of the equipment they procured is not necessary for the production of the menu. Always plan the menu first; then analyze it to decide what type of equipment is needed to produce the menu. This part of the planning process is called a *foodservice equipment analysis*.

Most institutions have limited equipment because of budget restrictions. This fact makes menu planning even more important in the institutional setting.

Government Stipulations

In most institutional facilities, the government plays an important role in menu planning. In elementary and secondary schools, the foodservice systems must follow the pattern A—school lunch requirements set up by the United States Department of Agriculture (USDA).

All branches of the armed services and veterans hospitals fall under strict government stipulations as well. It is important to keep abreast of the laws set by our governments (state and federal) that enact guidelines to be followed. Government financial aid may be suspended if certain laws or regulations are not followed when planning menus for institutions.

Religious and Ethnic Backgrounds

In institutional foodservice operations, religious and ethnic backgrounds of the people being served play an important role in the planning of menus. For example, in a Jewish hospital strict cultural dietary requirements must be followed: dairy and meat products cannot be mixed and have to be kept in separate reach-ins; eggs, fish, and vegetables are considered pareve and pareve products can be used with dairy or meat meals; lard or any other animal fat cannot be used, but soybean, palm, or vegetable oils are acceptable.

All nationalities have their own favorite foods. The Italian culture offers a variety of sausages, pasta products, and pastry products. The Irish culture offers a variety of Irish stews, sauces, and dessert coffees. It is important to offer employees or patients their favorite food items on the menu.

INDUSTRIAL FOODSERVICE

The industrial segment of the foodservice industry is composed of

♦ Corporations
♦ Companies
♦ Factories

and any other type of business that employs enough people to warrant the need for an in-plant foodservice operation.

For a menu planner to plan a successful menu within the industrial segment of the foodservice industry, the following factors must be taken into consideration:

1. Management's reasons for having a foodservice operation
2. Food preferences of employees to be fed
3. Type of work the employees are doing
4. Time allotted for meals
5. Amount that employees have to spend on meals

Profit

Management will spend money to make money. How does an industrial foodservice operation make a profit for management?

An industrial foodservice operation makes a profit by keeping employees at or near their working stations during their meal period. Most employees are given a half hour or an hour for their meal period. Employees will slow down or quit production five to ten minutes before eating and many workers are five to ten minutes late in returning from eating when a business does not have a cafeteria or a foodservice operation in-house. Keeping the employees on the grounds of the business for meals helps to reduce the number of workers getting back late from lunch, which increases production, which in turn increases profits.

Operating Methods

The two methods of operating an industrial foodservice operation are for management to contract a professional foodservice company to manage the operation, or to take full responsibility of controlling the feeding system as a part of the business.

Contracting outside professional foodservice companies to handle the responsibilities of feeding employees is a popular one and, in most cases, a profitable one. There are several methods of feeding employees for which management may contract:

1. Computerized vending units
2. Full table service
3. Cafeteria service
4. Coffee–deli shops
5. Fast food style

The two most important factors in choosing industrial foodservice establishments are that they must offer fast service and the menus must fit the needs of the employees.

Pricing

When pricing an industrial foodservice menu, management has a choice of setting the price in one of three ways.

1. Setting a large profit percentage, that is, 10 percent to 15 percent.
2. Setting a small profit percentage, that is, 1 percent to 2 percent.
3. Setting a break-even price, that is, food is sold at a price that covers only the cost of the food, labor, and overhead and does not make a profit.

Food Preferences

The menu planner needs to know food preferences of the employees to be able to plan a successful menu. A food survey should be conducted to determine employees' preferences in foods. Some employees may prefer a nutritional menu with poultry, fish, salads, fruits, and vegetables rather than a menu that serves hamburgers, hot dogs, sandwiches, and french fries. The survey should be conducted every three months because attitudes and tastes can change over time, and to accommodate employee turnover.

Type of Work

The menu planner needs to know what type of work employees do. Are employees involved in physical activity or are they sitting at desks all day? This information helps to determine food portions, amount of variety in the foods selected, and if the food items should be of a hearty, heavy calorie count. With physical jobs, employees are burning large amounts of calories and the menu should offer a selection of foods that will replace lost calories. When employees do not do much physical work, the menu selections should be light in calories and smaller in portion size.

Time

Knowing the amount of time allotted for the meal period is necessary for the menu planner so that a food item taking a long time to produce will not be put on the menu. Most employees are given only one half hour to one hour to eat. If the items take too long to produce, employees will not have enough time to finish their meals and will feel rushed. Thus, employees will be dissatisfied with the foodservice operation.

Price

The amount of disposable income an employee has or is willing to spend for a meal on a daily basis may be limited. Disposable income is income that is available for the employee's use after federal, state, and city taxes and personal bills have been paid. The menu planner should not select foods that have a high food cost and offer them at an even higher cost because the average employee cannot afford to buy that product on a daily basis. The average employee does not want to spend $5 or more on each meal. The menu planner needs to offer food items that are of good quality and that are reasonably priced.

COMMERCIAL FOODSERVICE

The commercial segment of the foodservice industry includes

- ◆ Hotels
- ◆ Restaurants
- ◆ Clubs
- ◆ Diners
- ◆ Fast food operations
- ◆ Specialty shops
- ◆ Cafeterias
- ◆ Catering businesses
- ◆ Vending businesses
- ◆ Dinner theaters
- ◆ Delicatessens

In each of the foodservice operations, the menu planner must know management's point of view on the following:

1. How the operation is to be operated
2. Type of clientele that management would like to attract (also known as the market)
3. Check average
4. Decor

5. Profit margin
6. Competition
7. Food markets

How the Operation Is to Be Operated

There are many different philosophies on how to operate a foodservice operation but there are three basic approaches: fast food, family, and classical. Management must recognize and have a full understanding of the philosophy to be operated in for maximum profit. Management needs to be completely dedicated to the philosophy selected and should not mix the different philosophies, which would result in confusing the market.

Fast Food Operation.   Characteristics of the fast-food philosophy and operation are

- Low check average: $4.00 to $8.00
- High turnover of capacity and high volume of sales: the National Restaurant Association indicates a $1,000.00 to $5,000.00 sales per hour as high volume
- Limited square footage per person for dining: 7 to 9 square feet
- Bright lights: almost a shadowless lighting scheme
- The use of bold, bright, and loud primary colors: red, blue, yellow
- Rapid employee movement: tends to make the customer move quicker
- Limited seat comfort: the use of plastic nonmoveable seats gives less comfort than a cushioned, unfixed seat
- High noise (decibel) level: the use of nonacoustic material (materials made from a hard substance such as stone, brick, ceramic tile, stainless steel)
- The use of styrofoam cups and plates and paper napkins
- Limited menu: the selection of food items on the menu is a limited to no more than 30 items to reduce the time it takes for customers to read the menu and decide on their orders

The philosophy is to create an atmosphere that will allow the customer to eat and leave the foodservice operation as quickly as possible, usually within a 30-minute time period. Management must design the entire building (exterior and interior) to allow for rapid movement (flow) of customers. Every detail is geared toward getting the customer in and out of the foodservice operation as fast as possible, without making the dining experience an uncomfortable, rushed, or negative one for the customer.

Classical Operation. The classical philosophy is the opposite of the fast food approach. The objective of the classical philosophy is not to get the customer in and out as fast as possible but to provide a relaxing and pleasant dining experience. Characteristics of this philosophy are

- High check average: $45.00 to $100.00 per person is the cost of the entire meal
- A low turnover rate: a 100-seat capacity foodservice operation will have a three quarter to one and a half turnover of the capacity
- Square footage per person: 24 to 30 square feet because more room provides more privacy to make the customer feel more relaxed
- Illumination level (lighting): low
- Colors selected are of a relaxing shade: pastel and earth-tone colors, such as tan and beige
- Employee movement in the dining room is not so rapid as to give a rushed impression and not so slow as to suggest indifference.
- Seating is very comfortable: the use of fabric padded seats provides more comfort
- Noise (decibel) level: a quiet relaxing decibel level 30 to 70 decibels level, facilitated by the use of soft acoustic material (wood, plants, carpets, fabric wallpaper and other material that absorbs soundwaves)
- Menu selection can be extensive, 60 to 125 items, or limited, 20 to 45 items, with more of a description accompanying the food items to enhance a person's appetite (when done correctly)
- High quality interior decor: the atmosphere being created is to encourage the customers to relax, enjoy themselves, and spend money

Family Operation. The family philosophy objective is to appeal to the market that falls between classical and fast food. The term "family" indicates that management must take into consideration the desires of customers ranging from grandparents to grandchildren. Characteristics of the family philosophy are

- Moderate check average: $8.00 to $15.00 per person
- Moderate turnover rate: one and a half to two and a half times per hour with a 100-seat capacity

- ◆ Square footage per person: 12 to 14 square feet
- ◆ Illumination (lighting) level: balanced, not dim or bright, but adequate
- ◆ Color scheme that incorporates a blend of pastel and bright colors
- ◆ Employee movement: prompt, not slow or too rapid
- ◆ Seating is moderately comfortable, using good quality chairs
- ◆ Noise (decibel) level: will vary from 60 decibels (calm conversation) to 90 decibels (a loud argument), with a balanced use of acoustic and nonacoustic material
- ◆ Menu selection will vary from 45 to 150 items and takes the longest time to read of all the philosophies because graphics (such as photographs) accompany the descriptions of the food products

This philosophy incorporates objectives from both the fast-food and classical philosophies for example, the objective of not rushing customers is taken from the classical philosophy, while not allowing the customer to take two hours to dine stems from the fast-food philosophy.

It is essential that management chooses one of the philosophies and becomes committed to that philosophy. This committment means that if you are operating under a classical philosophy, you must provide everything from valet parking to fresh flowers in the rest rooms.

Do not try to operate a foodservice operation by combining all three or even any two of the philosophies, such as operating a family philosophy from 4:30 P.M. to 8:00 P.M. and offering a classical philosophy from 9:00 P.M. to 11:30 P.M. This approach will confuse the market and keep customers from understanding who and what you are all about. Very few foodservice operations can combine philosophies at a profitable margin.

Clientele

It is critical that the menu planner knows the type of clientele for whom the menu is being planned. In the commercial segment, the primary motive for going into business is profit. To obtain the maximum profit the menu must satisfy the clientele.

The menu is one of management's ways of meeting clientele demands. The menu needs to reflect the demands of the clientele through food selection, price, and creativity.

Check Average

The check average is used to indicate how much money people are spending. Foodservice managers will use this information in obtaining and setting financial goals. If a foodservice operation indicates a $12.50 check average per person as a goal prior to opening and, once opened, is achieving only a $9.50 check average, this information allows management to analyze why the check average is $3.00 short of the goal and make corrections. If management does not use this information, it will fall short of the financial goals, which could lead to indebtedness or failure.

Decor

The decor, or decoration, of the foodservice establishment should project an image with which your market can identify. All of the exterior and interior designing—such as landscaping, painting of the building, color of the menu, the type of art work, the wallpaper, the style of windows, the size and shape of the parking lot—must be designed according to the taste and style of your market. The first impression of the interior is gained through the exterior. A littered parking lot reflects a negative image, one of messiness and filth, that is certainly not appealing or attractive to the customer who has never been to your establishment. To know what your market is looking for, you must do a market survey (see Chap. 2).

Profit Margin

Profit margin is the amount of money to be made on a food or beverage product. All food and beverage products generally have different profit margins even if they have the same food cost percentage.

The profit margin is calculated when the food and beverage product is marked up from a preliminary selling price to a final selling price. For example, a slice of apple pie may cost $0.35 to make. To make a profit, you sell the slice of pie for $1.25. The difference between $0.35 and $1.25 is $0.90, which will pay for the ingredients, the cost of labor, the cost of the equipment, and the energy to make the pie, and will also contain a percentage for profit. When the price of the pie is increased to $1.45, the true margin of profit increases. When the price is lowered to $0.75, the margin of profit is lowered.

Management will always make a profit on the piece of apple pie if it is priced correctly. The question is, how much profit? The answer is determined by how much the market is willing to pay for the slice of apple pie. If the market will pay $2.50 for the slice of apple pie, then management can price it on the menu at $2.50. (This topic is discussed further in Chap 8.)

Competition

Competition in the foodservice industry, as in all business endeavors, keeps operations on the competitive edge. Management must keep its standards high or the customer will go somewhere else. Competition will also do the following:

> Keep the prices of menu items under control. One foodservice operation will not overprice a food product, such as coffee, that is common among all the operations.

> Decrease advertising cost. If an independent foodservice operation locates next to a national chain foodservice organization, the independent foodservice operation does not have to spend as much money on advertising. The chain operation brings customers into and next to the independent foodservice operation.

Food Markets

The market is always changing. To be successful, the menu in a commercial foodservice operation needs to keep up with the changes in the market. Therefore, the menu planner and management must accurately forecast the demands of the market. This task is not simple. It involves the following: (1) knowledge of new developments in food products, menu styles, decor concepts, menu analyzing, and marketing trends that are happening throughout the foodservice industry; (2) knowledge of the economy and how it is affecting your market; (3) knowledge of the social needs of your market.

REVIEW QUESTIONS

1. What is the most important factor in planning a menu for an institution?

2. List three major areas a menu planner must know in order to plan any type of menu.

3. Explain how foodservice managers will use the check average for determining financial goals.

4. List five elements that a menu planner must take into consideration when planning a menu for a commercial foodservice operation.

5. To accurately forecast the changes within the market, what three areas must the menu planner and management recognize?

Market Survey

Once an owner has established a foodservice operational concept, a market survey needs to be done. The market survey is a detailed study of the people, the community, and the exact location of the foodservice establishment. This chapter discusses the elements that must be analyzed in a market survey.

OBJECTIVES

1. To demonstrate what is in a market survey.
2. To identify how a restaurant owner should use a market survey.
3. To illustrate the steps one needs to take in order to complete a market survey.

PRELIMINARY STEPS

There are two basic steps to a market survey in the foodservice industry. The first step is to establish the style and type of the foodservice operation or concept. This planning should be done before any money is invested.

The foodservice planner needs to address many issues such as the following:

1. Style of menu
2. Type of clientele
3. Type of cuisine
4. Style of atmosphere
5. Style of interior decor
6. Expense of food labor and overhead
7. Desired profit
8. Amount of capital to be invested
9. Regulations for operating on a daily basis
10. Architect
11. Lawyer
12. Accountant
13. Chef
14. Staff
15. Other details

Information carefully collected and analyzed comprises a market survey. The market survey will indicate if the community possesses enough positive factors to support the investors' foodservice operation.

The second step is to analyze the market survey completed in the community. Analysis of the market survey will determine what the community's needs or demands are for a new foodservice operation. The investor then opens a foodservice operation according to the needs of the community.

The majority of people opening a foodservice operation for the first time only complete the first step. Most corporations, foodservice chains, and hotels also complete step two. In both steps the key element to lowering the risk of failure is completing and analyzing a market survey.

AREAS OF ANALYSIS

The market survey is defined as a detailed analysis of the following areas: the customer, the community, and the physical location of the foodservice operation.

The Customer

The customer is the most important element of a foodservice operation. The customer will ultimately make the operation a success or failure. Some key factors to know about the customer and how they affect foodservice operations are

1. Market or type of customer desired
2. Age group
3. Amount of disposable income
4. Food preferences
5. Social habits
6. Educational level
7. Religious orientation
8. Ethnic background
9. Predominant gender
10. Occupational background
11. Arrival patterns
12. Preferred day for dining out

The Market. The market or type of customers the foodservice planner desires must be taken into consideration. It is very important for a foodservice planner to establish a market. Once a market has been established, every aspect of planning the foodservice operation will be geared toward that market. The more the foodservice planner knows about the customer, the better the dining experience will be, resulting in a satisfied customer. Satisfied customers are the food-service planner's key to a longer and richer existence in the food-service industry.

Ages. Knowing the age group of your market will help determine the following factors to be used in the planning of your foodservice operation:

(a) Type of cuisine and food selections
(b) Prices
(c) Portion sizes
(d) Nutritional selection
(e) Style of atmosphere
(f) Lighting level in the dining room
(g) Texture of the functional and decorative materials to be used
(h) Style of entertainment
(i) Accessibility of the operation and movement within it
(j) Intensity level of music
(k) Type of music
(l) Size of the printed letters on the menu

Disposable Income. Disposable income is the amount of income that is left after federal, state, and city taxes and personal bills have been paid. Other names for disposable income are entertainment, fun, and luxury money. The greater the income your market has, the greater amount of disposable income will be available for dining in your establishment.

Food Preference. Knowing the types of cuisine and the food selections within the cuisine that your market desires will save the operation money by not buying unnecessary foods. It will allow management more free time to be creative with food items.

Social Habits. Knowledge of how your market likes to socialize aids the investor in determining the type and style of entertainment to be used in the foodservice operation.

Educational Level. The higher the education level of your market, the more open it will be to trying new foodservice operations. People who have a higher level of education tend to have a higher level of disposable income and tend to dine out more often.

Religion. Some religious cultures have laws indicating how and what food items are to be consumed. Knowing customers' religious denominations can build up sales. An example would be having a fish special on Fridays during Lent if the foodservice operation is located in a predominantly Catholic community.

Ethnic Background. It is important to recognize the market's ethnic backgrounds because the investor does not want to miss having the market's favorite national dishes on the menu. It is not a realistic goal to open an Italian specialty restaurant in a heavily populated Chinese community. In all probability the rate of success would not be very high.

Gender. The knowledge of whether your market is predominantly male or female will aid you in choosing the types of cuisine on the menu, the portion sizes, the balancing of calories and nutritional elements on the menu, and the decor. These factors aid in determining the marketing and merchandising methods that are to be used in increasing sales.

Occupation. The type of work your market will be doing throughout the day will help to establish guidelines in the selection of foods to be placed on the menu and in the portion sizes. For example, if you are feeding people who do a lot of physical work, the food items and portion sizes should be heartier. Customers who are doing less physical work may prefer a food selection that has fewer calories and smaller portions. Other factors to be considered are the time allotted for the luncheon period and the type of foodservice system to be used.

Arrival Patterns. Knowing the number of single people, couples, and parties of three or more and the time of day these various groups will be dining will aid your maitre d' in setting up the dining room appropriately. Families with children tend to dine from 4:30 P.M. to 7:00 P.M. Large groups without children tend to dine from 7:00 P.M. to 9:00 P.M. and couples tend to dine from 8:00 P.M. to 11:00 P.M. The proper arrangement of tables and chairs in the dining room for each of the groups will result in a high turnover rate, thus increasing sales.

Preferred Day for Dining Out. Knowing which days are the more popular ones and which days are the slower ones for dining will help the investor establish when to run merchandising and marketing programs for the slow days. Fridays, Saturdays, and Sundays are very popular days for dining because very often people are paid on Thursday or Friday and will have a greater amount of disposable income and time for going out. Mondays are usually the slowest days because people have little if any disposable income left from the weekend and very little time for dining.

These factors are only a sampling of the information the foodservice planner should know about the market. The more factors known about the market, the easier it becomes to satisfy the customers' demands.

Customers expect the same treatment we all like when we dine in a restaurant. Go one step further and give each customer a greater dining experience than you have ever had.

The Community

The geographic region, district, city, or town from which the majority of the foodservice operation's customers come is known as the community. Elements to study within the community include

1. Growth rate
2. Availability of liquor licenses
3. Existence of competition
4. Public services provided
5. Requirements of the State Board of Health
6. Number of families
7. Possibilities for advertising

Growth Rate. If a community has a declining population it would be wise to find the reason and to think twice about building or operating an establishment there. For example, it would be a mistake to build in a location where the unemployment rate is high. High unemployment means that businesses are closing and people are moving away to find work elsewhere. Other reasons not to choose a location include a high crime rate, high rents, and high taxes. The investor must take into consideration the amount of time it takes to collect data and to analyze the market survey, which is approximately six months to two years. It then takes another six months to nine months to build the operation.

Liquor Licenses. Alcoholic beverages are one of the most profitable commodities the foodservice industry has to sell. Obtaining a liquor license in some communities is a very expensive and difficult task. Each state and community has its own laws and procedures.

The majority of the foodservice planners start the process of obtaining a liquor license by completing the proper application. The foodservice planner is then placed on a waiting list. Once there is an opening for a license and the foodservice planner is next on the list, he or she will be called to go before a committee that regulates the license. The committee interviews the candidate and if the committee gives its approval a license will be issued.

Most communities, depending on state law, have a limited amount of licenses to be issued. The supply is low and the demand is high, thereby making the value of the license high.

The second method of obtaining a liquor license is to buy a foodservice operation that already has a liquor license. When the foodservice planner buys an establishment, the liquor license is sometimes transferred to the new owner. The transferal of the license must be approved by the committee that regulates liquor licenses. All liquor licenses have to be renewed on an annual basis and may be revoked at any time if the foodservice planner is breaking the law.

It is pertinent to check with local and state laws on liquor liability and costs.

Competition. There are two basic types of competition the market survey must take into consideration: direct and indirect. Not all foodservice operations fall into these broad categories. Direct competition includes the foodservice operations that are directly related (similar) to your operation. They have a similar cuisine, decor, check average, capacity, turnover rate, and so forth. For example, if the investor wants to operate a steak house, the survey should indicate how many other steak houses are in the community that would be considered competition.

Indirect competition consists of foodservice operations that are not similar to the investor's but are competing for the same customers.

The main analysis is to determine if the community will profitably support another operation.

Public Services. As a tax-paying business, and to help calculate overhead expenses, the foodservice planner needs to find out what public services are included in his or her tax dollars. The planner needs to learn which services will cost additional money. Services paid by tax dollars are police protection and fire protection. Every community will differ in the types of services offered.

State Board of Health. The Board of Health is in business to protect the public from circumstances that may place the public's health in danger. When the Board of Health inspects a foodservice operation it is doing a public service for the community. If there is evidence of food contamination in a restaurant, the Board of Health may cite the operator or even shut down the operation.

Before any money has been invested in the project the Board of Health and the local fire department must look at the blueprints of the restaurant. Both departments can save time and money by indicating where there are violations in the project. Each community or state has different laws pertaining to the health and fire codes. It is important to be aware of the laws of your state and community.

Families. The number of families in a community usually indicates whether the community has a stable and/or growing population. When there are many families with children in a community there is usually a large school system. The school system is a good source for an effective merchandising program. For example, if the investor's market is families, then one effective merchandising program is to run a favorite dessert contest. The students in grades four, five, and six draw posters of their favorite desserts and give each dessert a name. The foodservice chooses the winner at the restaurant and everyone who participates is given a prize.

Advertising. One of the key elements to having a successful advertising program is to communicate on the same level as your customers. For example, if the investor is trying to attract business executives, the restaurant may place an ad in the *Wall Street Journal*. This ad would not be effective if the foodservice planner were trying to attract a different type of clientele.

The second point is to analyze the community's newspapers, radio stations, periodicals, and television stations. The amount of exposure or circulation each advertising method gives is important.

Always set aside enough money in the budget to run an effective advertising campaign. Planning ahead for advertising allows for many promotions throughout the year without going over the budget.

The Location

One of the first steps in choosing a location is to determine what the foodservice's needs are for the next two years, five years, and ten years. Planning for the future is vital when choosing a location. The needs of a foodservice operator who wants to establish a chain of operations differ from those of a foodservice operator who wants to open a single operation. Knowing what you want and need to buy before looking for a location helps eliminate much wasted time and frustration. Knowing your needs for the future is important when selecting real estate for the operation. If the land, developed or undeveloped, is available and you have the funding to purchase it, then do so. The land may not be available if and when you want to expand.

Another important point to keep in mind when selecting a location is that an excellent location alone will not make your foodservice operation a success. It is also true that a poor location does not mean that your operation will be a failure. The entire operation must be first-rate, in order to be successful, regardless of the location.

When selecting a location it is important to analyze the population of the state, city, and suburban communities before arriving at a decision. Population trends may shift drastically in a city if the city is dependent on a particular industry for its financial survival. When a factory or company goes out of business, the people in that city or community must travel elsewhere for work. The foodservice operation that depends on these people will also be closing its doors. It is important to note how fast or slow a state, city, or suburban community is growing. Refer to Figure 2-1 for other points in analyzing the location of a foodservice operation.

Zoning. There are three types of zones: residential, industrial, and commercial. Each zone has zoning ordinances that must be obeyed. One cannot freely erect any type of building in a residential zone. This zoning restricts business developments for the safety of the residents who live in the zone.

Industrial zones are established for large-volume companies and commercial zones are established for small-volume companies.

Always check the zoning board to find out what types of restrictions are placed on the land on which you plan to operate your business. You must comply with the zoning board regulations before opening your operation. As the population changes in a community, so will the zones.

Area Characteristics. The type of neighborhood in which your establishment is located will have a great effect on your business. If the neighborhood has a high crime rate, if pollution is evident, or if your neighbors oppose development, you will find it difficult to succeed.

Physical Characteristics. Analyzing the land (soil) will give you an idea of how much development is needed and what it will cost. Have the topsoil of the property analyzed for nutrient/mineral content for landscaping purposes. Take note of the slope of the land for proper drainage. Also note large rocks and trees that might have to be cleared, which can be a very costly project.

Always have a percolation test done on the land. The purpose is to see how long it takes for water to be absorbed into the soil for proper drainage. It is done by drilling small holes throughout the lot below the frost line (6 feet to 10 feet), filling them with water, and timing how long it takes the water to be absorbed into the soil. If it takes more than twenty minutes, usually the land will not pass its percolation test. The foodservice operator will not be allowed to obtain a building permit because the land is deemed unsafe for building. The percolation test will also indicate the type of soil, rock, clay, and so on that exists under the topsoil.

Figure 2-1. Checklist for analyzing the location of a foodservice operation. (*From E. A. Kazarian, 1983, Foodservice Facilities Planning, 2d ed. Van Nostrand Reinhold, New York, pp. 72 and 73; copyright © 1983 by Van Nostrand Reinhold.*)

(1) Zoning
　Current zoning of site
　Use permits needed
　Height restrictions
　Front line setback
　Side yard requirements
　Back yard requirements
　Restrictions on signs
　Parking requirements
　Other restrictions
(2) Area characteristics
　Type of neighborhood
　Type of businesses
　Growth pattern
　Proposed construction
　Other available sites
　Zoning of adjacent sites
(3) Competition
　Number of food facilities in drawing area of site
　Number of seats
　Type of menu offered
　Method of service
　Check averages
　Number of cocktail lounges
　Quality of drinks
　Bar service available at tables
　Annual sales
(4) Physical characteristics
　Type of topsoil
　Type of subsoil
　Depth of water table
　Presence of rocks
　Load-bearing capacity
　Direction of slopes
　Surface drainage
　Percolation test results
　Natural landscaping
　Other features
(5) Size and shape (including sketch)
　Length
　Width
　Total square feet
　Square footage needed for building
　Square footage needed for parking
　Space for other requirements
(6) Costs
　Cost per front foot
　Cost per square foot
　Total cost of site
　Cost of comparable sites nearby
　Costs for land improvements
　Real estate taxes
　Other taxes
(7) Utilities
　Location, cost, and size or capacity of Storm sewer

Sanitary sewer
Gas lines
Water lines
Electricity
Steam
(8) Streets
　Basic patterns
　Width or lanes
　Paved
　Curbs and gutters
　Sidewalks
　Lighting
　Public transportation
　Grades
　Hazards

(9) Positional characteristics
Distance and driving time to

	Distance	Driving Time
Central business district		
Industrial centers		
Shopping centers		
Residential areas		
Recreational areas		
Sporting events		
Educational facilities		
Special attractions		
Other activity generators		

(10) Traffic information
Distance to nearest intersection
Traffic characteristics

		Day	Time	Count
Traffic counts				
Site street				
Adjacent streets				

(11) Visibility
　Anticipated changes
　Distances of sight from
　　Left
　　Right
　　Across
　Obstructions
　Location of signs
(12) Services
　Quality of police protection
　Quality of fire protection
　Location of hydrant
　Availability of trash pickup
　Availability of garbage pickup
　Other services required
(13) General recommendations
　Suitability
　Desirability
　Other recommendations

Size, Shape and Costs. The Department of Health and the zoning board will need to see blueprints of the building you wish to build or renovate. The blueprints must be printed by a registered architect for them to be approved. Both departments will want to check and make sure that all of the building material and the total square footage meet their regulations. The architect will also see that all the materials are purchased at the lowest prices and are of the best quality.

Utilities. To help plan your budget, you must know the location, cost, size, and capacity of all the utilities. It will cost extra money to bring the utilities to your land if they are available.

Streets and Traffic Information. Street patterns, such as one-way streets, should be noted. Usually foodservice operations located on one-way streets do not do as much volume as operations located on two-way streets. The driver usually has better access to your operation if it is on a two-way street. Note the width of the street and the width of the driveway. Make sure delivery trucks can enter and exit your establishment easily.

Intersections always slow down potential customers. When people are stopped at an intersection for the traffic light or stop sign, they have time to look around and notice your business.

The slower the speed limit, the more opportunity a person has to observe your operation. Traffic counts of how many cars pass the location of your establishment can be obtained through the city transportation office. The more cars, the greater potential for customers.

Sales Generators. Places that can generate sales are civic centers, theaters, shopping malls, and so on. The more people that are around or in your location, the more potential customers.

Visibility. The higher visibility of the foodservice operation, the less money you have to spend on advertising. If the location is in a city and is hidden by a building, you must advertise more to let people know where you are located.

Parking. Provide adequate parking to attract customers. The parking area must be designed to accommodate the following:

Customers

Employees

Lights

Dumpsters

Delivery trucks

Landscaping

Snow and Trash Removal.   Removal of snow and trash is expensive. It is best to check local rates and methods of removal.

OBTAINING INFORMATION FOR THE MARKET SURVEY

The information for completing a market survey should be collected from the following sources:

- National Restaurant Association
- Chamber of Commerce
- Better Business Bureau
- Small Business Association (SBA)
- Public library
- Economic Development Department of your city or state
- City Hall
- Tourist Information Bureau
- United States Census
- Banks and financing corporations
- Real estate agencies
- Surveying the community and location yourself

REVIEW QUESTIONS

1.   What is the purpose of a percolation test?

2.   What is disposable income?

3.   What is a market survey?

4.   What are the two methods of obtaining a liquor license?

5.   What are three elements to be analyzed in the community?

3

Nutrition
and
Menu Planning

This chapter* examines the role of nutrients in food, and their relationship to health. The planning of therapeutic diets is discussed. Methods to improve the nutrient quality of foods offered in a foodservice institution are suggested.

OBJECTIVES

1. To provide an understanding of the basics of nutrition.
2. To discuss the relationship of nutrition to health.
3. To illustrate how menus can be nutritious and still be profitable for the foodservice operation.

NUTRITION BASICS

Nutrition is the study of how food is used by the body. Food is composed of *nutrients*, which are chemical compounds needed for survival. Some of these are *essential* nutrients, which cannot be made in the body and must be supplied by food or supplements. Examples of essential nutrients are minerals, such as iron and calcium, vitamins, and certain amino acids that combine to form protein. Without a source of these essential nutrients, good health cannot be maintained. There are other nutrients that are equally important for survival, but these can be synthesized in the body, provided that the raw materials are available. Examples of this type of nutrient are the fatty substance, lecithin, and the nonessential amino acids.

The six major nutrient groups are

1. Proteins
2. Carbohydrates
3. Fats
4. Vitamins
5. Minerals
6. Water

Proteins provide calories, synthesize new body tissue during growth, and replace worn-out cells. Proteins also form hormones, enzymes, and antibodies, which are required for performing numerous bodily processes and maintaining immunity to diseases.

---

*This chapter was contributed by Jennifer Schlitzer, M.S., R.D.

Carbohydrates, which include sugars, starches, and fiber, are most important as an energy source for the body, particularly the nervous system. Dietary fiber, which is mostly indigestible carbohydrates, helps to regulate the movement of food through the digestive tract.

Fats are a very concentrated energy source, providing more than twice as many calories as an equal amount of protein or carbohydrate. Some fats are *saturated*, which means that their chemical structure contains the maximum number of hydrogen atoms (i.e., they are saturated with hydrogen). These fats are solid and tend to be found in animal products. *Unsaturated fats* are missing some hydrogen atoms in their chemical structure and are liquid at room temperature. The missing hydrogens are replaced with chemical structures called double bonds. If a fat has one double bond, it is a *monounsaturated* fat; if it has two or more double bonds, it is a *polyunsaturated* fat. A commonly used monounsaturated fat is olive oil, and corn, soybean, and sunflower oils are examples of polyunsaturated fats. As a rule, fats that come from plants are unsaturated; however, two exceptions to this rule are coconut and palm oils. Unsaturated fats can be turned into solid, saturated fat by a process called *hydrogenation*. Unsaturated fats that have been hydrogenated, and therefore made more saturated, convey many of the same health risks as fats that are naturally saturated.

Vitamins are chemical compounds that are involved in various metabolic reactions in the body. (Table 3-1). They are divided into two groups.

1. Fat-soluble vitamins: vitamins A, D, E, and K.
2. Water-soluble vitamins: B vitamins and vitamin C

Minerals are crystalline chemical elements that comprise about 4 percent of a person's weight. Like vitamins, they perform various functions (Table 3-2). Calcium, phosphorus, sodium, potassium, magnesium, sulfur, and chlorine are considered macronutrients, because they are present in the body in relatively large amounts. The micronutrients, or trace minerals, are thus named because of the extremely minute quantities found in the body. These micronutrients include iron, zinc, selenium, manganese, copper, iodine, and fluorine, to name a few. Altogether, there are twenty-two minerals known to be required.

Water, often taken for granted, is perhaps the most vital nutrient. While a person can survive for weeks or months without the other essential nutrients, a complete deprivation of water would cause death in a few days. Water dissolves and transports nutrients into, throughout, and from the body. It also regulates body temperature, lubricates joints, is involved in chemical reactions, and helps cells retain their shape.

Table 3-1. Vitamins

Vitamin (Chemical Name) Food Sources	Functions	Deficiency
Vitamin A (retinol, carotene) liver, butter, carrots, pumpkin	Enables eyes to adjust to changes in light; maintains cells of skin, eyes, intestines, and lungs	Night blindness; keratinization (formation of thick, dry layer of cells on skin and eyes)
Vitamin D (ergocalciferol, cholecalciferol) fortified milk, fish livers	Enhances calcium and phosphorus absorption	Rickets in children; Osteomalacia in adults
Vitamin E (alpha-tocopherol) vegetable oils	Acts as antioxidant, protecting substances damaged by exposure to oxygen	Rare, but may cause hemolytic anemia in premature infants
Vitamin K (phylloquinone menaquinone) dark green leafy vegetables, liver	Essential for blood clotting	Rare, causes hemorrhaging
Vitamin B1 (thiamin) pork, whole grains	Part of coenzyme, thiamin pyrophosphate, which is needed for metabolism of carbohydrates and fat	Beriberi, which results in appetite loss, nausea, vomiting, impaired heart function
Vitamin B2 (riboflavin) milk, green vegetables, cheese	Part of coenzymes, flavin mononucleotide and flavin adenine dinucleotide, which aid in the release of energy from fat, protein, and carbohydrate	Ariboflavinosis, with symptoms of cracked and dry skin around nose and mouth
Vitamin B3 (niacin) milk, whole grains, nuts	Part of nicotinamide adenine dinucleotide and nicotinamide adenine dinucleotide phosphate, which are needed for energy release in cells	Pellagra, causing dermatitis, diarrhea, dementia
Vitamin B6 (pyridoxine) liver, bananas, wheat bran	Vital for amino acid synthesis and breakdown	Abnormal protein metabolism, poor growth, convulsions, anemia, decreased antibody formation
Vitamin B12 (cobalamin) almost all animal products (none in plant products)	Aids in formation of nucleic acids; needed for proper red blood cells development	Pernicious anemia, which causes megaloblastic anemia and spinal cord degeneration
Folic acid dark green, leafy vegetables	Needed for cell growth and reproduction and amino acid metabolism	Megaloblastic anemia, which is characterized by abnormally large red blood cells that have failed to mature properly
Biotin egg yolk, liver, nuts	Part of enzyme system, acetyl coenzyme A, which is necessary for producing energy from glucose, and forming fatty acids, amino acids, nucleic acids, and glycogen	Very unlikely, but could cause dermatitis, fatigue, loss of appetite
Pantothenic acid liver, eggs, peas, peanuts	Part of coenzyme A, which is involved in releasing energy from carbohydrates, fat, and protein; also part of enzyme needed for fatty acid synthesis	Unlikely; causes fatigue, headaches, muscles cramps, poor coordination
Vitamin C (ascorbic acid) citrus fruits, broccoli, strawberries	Needed for formation of collagen, which binds cells together; maintains elasticity and strength of blood vessels	Scurvy, with symptoms of bleeding and swollen gums, poor wound healing

Table 3-2. Minerals

Mineral/Food Source	Functions	Deficiency
Calcium milk, soybeans	Forms bones and teeth; essential for blood clotting; involved with nerve stimulation, muscle contraction, and good muscle tone	Osteoporosis, causing bones to become brittle and break easily; most likely to occur in postmenopausal women
Phosphorus meat, poultry, carbonated drinks	Combines with calcium to form bones and teeth; part of nucleic acids; part of substances that store and release energy	Unlikely, but can cause weakness, appetite loss, bone pain
Sodium table salt, cured meats, processed foods	Dissolved in the water outside cells where it maintains osmotic balance and regulates water balance; aids in transmitting nerve impulses	Very unlikely; causes cardiac arrest, convulsions
Potassium oranges, bananas, winter squash	Dissolved in water inside cells to maintain osmotic balance and regulate water balance; aids in transmitting nerve impulses	Irregular heart beat
Magnesium milk, whole grains, nuts	Needed to conduct nerve impulses; catalyst in many energy transfer and release reactions	Nerve tremors, convulsions, behavioral disturbances
Sulfur Eggs, cabbage, meat	Component of several amino acids and vitamins	Extremely unlikely
Chlorine table salt, meat, milk, eggs	Part of hydrochloric acid in stomach, which aids in digestion and absorption; when bound to sodium or potassium, involved in maintaining water balance in cells	Loss of appetite, poor growth, weakness
Iron liver, nuts, meat, spinach	Part of hemoglobin that carries oxygen in the blood; part of myoglobin that transfers oxygen from hemoglobin to muscle cells	Anemia that causes low hemoglobin levels and fatigue
Zinc meat, fish, milk	Needed for collagen formation; component of insulin	Impaired growth, wound healing, sexual dysfunction and taste dysfunction
Selenium meat, seafood, wheat	Antioxidant	Not observed in humans
Manganese cereal, legumes	Needed for bone development	No deficiency observed in humans; in deficient animals it causes slowed growth, deformities, and interferes with reproduction
Copper nuts, dried beans, liver	Needed for hemoglobin and connective tissue formation	Anemia
Iodine saltwater fish and shellfish, iodized salt	Part of thyroid hormones that regulate basal metabolism	Goiter
Fluorine fluoridated water, sardines, tea	Stengthens bones and teeth	Teeth less resistant to decay

Meeting Nutrient Needs

In order to receive adequate supplies of all the essential nutrients, it is important to eat a variety of foods. The *Four Food Group Plan* (or the Basic Four Food Groups) was developed as a convenient method for ensuring that this goal is met. It divides foods into four groups based on their nutrient content and recommends the number of servings from each group. The Four Food Group Plan is detailed in Table 3-3. Note that there is no food group for fats and oils and for many sweets.

Following the Four Food Group Plan in the strictest sense could provide a nutritious diet with as few as 1,000 calories. Many people have higher calorie needs that can be met by increasing the number of servings from the groups or by adding foods that are not part of this food plan.

Recommended Dietary Allowance

More specific than the Four Food Group Plan, the *Recommended Dietary Allowance* (RDA) is the suggested level of daily consumption for protein, ten vitamins, and six minerals. The RDA is developed by the Food and Nutrition Board of the National Research Council-National Academy of Sciences and is intended to be a generous recommendation that should meet the nutrient needs of practically all healthy persons. The RDA is grouped by age and sex, and also makes recommendations for pregnant and lactating females. Recommendations for calorie intake and a range of estimated safe and adequate levels for additional vitamins and minerals are also included in the RDA. The RDA is revised approximately every five years, at which time changes in the suggested nutrient intake levels might be made, based on recent research findings.

U.S. Recommended Daily Allowance

The *U.S. Recommended Daily Allowance* (U.S. RDA) was developed by the Food and Drug Administration to provide a basis for listing nutrient levels on nutrition labels. The U.S. RDA is based on the 1968 revision of the Recommended Dietary Allowances. Unlike the RDA, there is only one value for each nutrient in the U.S. RDA; this value is the highest RDA level for all age and sex groups (excluding the values for pregnancy and lactation). The U.S. RDA is most commonly used on nutrition labels, where the amounts of protein and several vitamins and minerals are expressed as a percentage of the U. S. RDA.

Table 3-3. The Four Food Group Plan

Food Group	Servings Per Day	Serving Size
Milk and milk products calcium, vitamin D, riboflavin, vitamin A, protein	Under 9 years old: 2–3; 9–12 years old: 3–4; teenagers: 4 or more; adults: 2 or more; pregnant women: 3–4; lactating women: 4 or more	1 cup milk; 1 ounce cheese, 1 cup yogurt
Meats, fish, poultry, eggs, nuts, legumes protein, iron, B vitamins	2 or more	2–3 ounces cooked beef, pork, poultry, lamb, fish; 2 eggs; 1 cup cooked legumes; ¼ cup peanut butter
Fruits and vegetables vitamin A, vitamin C, iron, fiber	4 or more	½ cup fruit or vegetables; 1 piece fruit; ½ cup fruit juice
Grains carbohydrates, B vitamins, iron, some protein, fiber if whole grain	4 or more	1 slice whole grain or enriched bread; 1 ounce cereal; ½ cup cooked grain

THE RELATIONSHIP OF NUTRITION TO HEALTH

Americans are becoming increasingly aware that nutrition has a strong impact on health. Not only will adequate amounts of nutrients promote good health by preventing deficiencies, but good nutrition may also help one avoid chronic diseases and increase longevity.

Preventing Deficiencies

Fortunately in the United States, our abundant food supply makes it possible for most individuals to be well-nourished. However, obtaining enough of certain nutrients may still be a problem for some groups of people. Females of reproductive age often receive too little iron in their diets, making iron-deficiency anemia the most common nutrient deficiency in this country. In addition, females are frequently victims of osteoporosis, which develops after menopause, usually after years of a chronically low calcium intake. Other vulnerable groups include

♦ The elderly, whose physical and economic restrictions often limit their ability to eat a nutritious diet

♦ The poor, because they often cannot afford an adequate diet

♦ Chronic dieters, whose goal of thinness often precludes eating nutritiously

Avoiding Chronic Diseases

Many chronic diseases in this country are the result of a combination of overnutrition and the advances in technology that make our lives easier. A good case in point is cardiovascular, or heart, disease. Although deaths from heart disease have declined since the 1960s, it is still the number one killer in the United States, causing about a half million deaths every year. The underlying condition that causes heart disease is *atherosclerosis,* or hardening of the arteries. Atherosclerosis is characterized by the presence of fatty deposits, called *plaques,* in the arteries. As these plaques develop, they progressively increase blockage in the arteries, causing chest pain (angina pectoris), heart attacks, and strokes. Extensive research has identified high blood cholesterol levels, cigarette smoking, high blood pressure, obesity, and physical inactivity as some of the major contributors to the development of atherosclerosis.

Risk of heart disease is increased when blood cholesterol levels are above 200 mg per 100 ml of blood. As well as total blood cholesterol, it is important to know the amounts of "good" (HDL) and "bad" (LDL) cholesterol in the blood. A high proportion of LDL cholesterol increases one's risk whereas a high proportion of HDL lowers the chances of cardiovascular disease. To lower blood cholesterol, the American Heart Association recommends a diet providing less than 300 mg of cholesterol per day, and no more than 30 percent of the calories coming from fat. Of this fat allowance, less than one-third should be saturated. Recent research has also suggested the possibility that various other dietary changes may lower cardiovascular disease risk. These include the highly unsaturated fatty acids (omega-3 fatty acids) found in salmon and other fatty fish, dietary fiber (particularly oat bran and pectin), and monounsaturated fats such as olive oil.

Some forms of cancer have been linked to diet. Research studies abound suggesting that a high-fiber diet prevents cancer of the colon. The risk of lung cancer may be reduced by eating generous amounts of foods containing vitamin E and beta-carotene (the orange pigment in vegetables that is converted to vitamin A). A high-fat intake has been implicated as a risk factor for breast, colon, and prostate cancers. The National Cancer Institute has released dietary guidelines designed to reduce the incidence of cancer and cancer-related deaths. These recommendations include raising fiber to 20–30 g daily, eating more fruits and vegetables, and lowering fat and alcohol consumption.

A medical problem that plagues approximately 20 percent of adult Americans is *high blood pressure* or *hypertension*. Called the silent killer, because it usually has no symptoms, high blood pressure can cause strokes, heart attacks, and kidney failure. A high sodium intake is frequently linked with high blood pressure and diet therapy often includes sodium restriction. Most people consume far more sodium than they need; one reason is the prevalence of sodium in our food supply. Some foods naturally contain a lot of sodium, but the vast majority of it comes from processed foods that have salt and other sodium-containing ingredients added for flavor. The American Heart Association recommends a maximum of 3,000 mg of sodium per day, which can easily be exceeded by a person who uses processed foods or eats frequently in restaurants and other foodservice institutions.

Obesity is a problem that afflicts approximately one-fourth of adults in the United States. Not only does it cause numerous social problems, but it contributes to myriad health problems as well. These health problems include heart disease, diabetes, high blood pressure, and even cancer. There are numerous causes for obesity, both physiological and environmental. A sedentary life-style combined with a high calorie intake most certainly contributes to the development of obesity in many individuals. Unfortunately, in this country, people are constantly bombarded with calorie-laden meals and snacks. This, combined with the conveniences of modern life, creates a vicious cycle that increases calorie intake and decreases calorie expenditure, resulting in obesity. A good treatment plan not only includes a lower-calorie, nutritionally balanced diet, but also changes an individual's eating behavior and encourages physical activity.

NUTRITIONAL IMPLICATIONS FOR MENU PLANNING

When planning the menu for an institutional, industrial, or commercial foodservice operation, it is beneficial to the clientele when their nutrient needs are considered. Even though some people are unconcerned about nutrition, an ever-growing number want the opportunity to select nutritious foods.

If a foodservice operation offers nutritious food, it is advantageous to heighten the patrons' awareness of nutrition. Including a nutrient breakdown of the menu items, printing general nutrition information on the menu, circulating a health-oriented newsletter, and offering nutrition seminars are just a few ways to increase interest in healthful eating. The staff should also possess some knowledge about nutrition, so they are able to answer questions about the foods they are serving.

Educating foodservice personnel about nutrition can be achieved by organizing seminars and encouraging employees to take courses in this subject.

Institutional Food Service

In some cases, the foodservice operation must follow strict guidelines when planning the menu. For instance, the United States Department of Agriculture National School Lunch Program delineates a meal pattern that must be followed in all public elementary and secondary schools. For example, the meal pattern for high school students must provide three ounces of meat or meat alternative, two slices of bread or one-half cup of another grain, three-fourths of a cup of fruit or vegetable, and eight ounces of milk. While this meal pattern provides many essential nutrients, it can also be high in fat, sodium, and sugar, depending on how the food is prepared. By offering broiled chicken, baked potatoes, a salad bar, fresh fruit, and low-fat milk instead of fried chicken nuggets, french fries, canned vegetables, cake, and whole milk, a school lunch program can provide students with a healthful midday repast. While both these meals are similar in calorie content, the former provides much lower amounts of fat and sodium, as well as higher levels of protein, fiber, vitamins, and minerals.

While the government has not set guidelines for college foodservice organizations, it is the responsibility of these organizations to provide nutritious meals for students, especially since the cafeteria is the sole provider of food for many of them. The Four Food Group Plan is a good foundation for planning a college menu, as well as taking care to provide a wide variety of foods that are low in fat, cholesterol, sodium, and sugar. Some college and university foodservice organizations set a good example by offering vegetarian or ethnic fare to their students.

A hospital also is not subject to governmental regulations when planning patients' menus. However, it is influenced by the patients' dietary restrictions, which may vary from mild to severe. Some of the diets served in a hospital include

> Regular or house diet—a patient on this diet faces no restrictions and can choose freely from the menu. Offering a variety from the four food groups helps to ensure that the patient will receive adequate amounts of nutrients.

> Liquid—A clear liquid diet is usually the first nourishment a patient receives postoperatively. It is used in preparation for bowel surgery or examination as well as when there is an acute disturbance in gastrointestinal function. It is not nutritionally balanced; thus, it should not be used for an extended period of time unless supplements are

added. The foods allowed on this diet include broth, bouillon, gelatin, strained fruit juices, coffee, tea, carbonated beverages, and sugar. A full liquid diet is much more nutritionally balanced because it includes a much wider variety of foods. All items on a clear liquid diet are allowed, as well as all other beverages, strained cream soups, eggs, certain hot cereals, ice cream, sherbet, custards, puddings, margarine, butter, and all spices. This diet is indicated if there is difficulty with chewing or swallowing and is also used postoperatively.

Mechanical soft diet—This diet is useful for chewing or swallowing problems, or if there is narrowing of some part of the gastrointestinal tract. It provides more variety than a full liquid diet, making it more palatable and nutritious. Foods excluded from a mechanical soft diet are nuts, seeds, raw vegetables, and fruits with skins. Depending on the reason for which this diet is prescribed, certain spices and caffeine may be restricted.

Low sodium diet—a diet low in sodium is indicated for congestive heart failure, liver and kidney failure, and in the management of high blood pressure. The degree of restriction may vary from a "no-added-salt" diet (about 4,000 mg), which eliminates very salty foods and the salt shaker, to a 250-mg sodium diet, which is extremely restrictive and requires the use of special low-sodium foods.

Diabetic diet—A diabetic diet is necessitated when an individual does not produce enough insulin, and blood sugar levels become dangerously high. This diet restricts the use of sugars, fat, and cholesterol and encourages a high-complex carbohydrate intake. The diet plan usually consists of three meals and two snacks each day. To allow variety in the diet, permitted foods are divided into the following exchange groups: starch/bread, meat and meat substitutes, vegetables, fruit, milk, and fat. If, for example, a diabetic is allowed a starch/bread exchange at a meal, he or she may choose one slice of bread, one-half cup of rice, or a small potato. Because this diet is well balanced and provides a good deal of variety, some hospitals use it for planning weight loss regimens as well.

Cardiac diet—The purpose of this type of diet is to lower the levels of cholesterol and fat in the blood. In general, cholesterol and total fat are reduced. The proportion of unsaturated compared to saturated fat is raised. In some cases, sodium, sugar, and alcohol might be restricted. Foods usually avoided in this diet include egg yolks, fatty meats, most cheeses, whole milk products, fried foods, and high-fat sweets such as cakes and cookies.

Industrial Foodservice

Because it is often more convenient and inexpensive for employees, an industrial foodservice organization is usually serving a "captive" audience. The nature of the work being performed plays a role in determining the menu. For example, if many of the employees have desk jobs that require little physical exertion, foods lower in calories and less filling, such as salads and soups, may be preferred. If, on the other hand, employees are engaging in heavy physical labor, high-calorie foods will be required to provide the necessary energy. In this case, offering meals such as stews and substantial sandwiches would be in the best interest of the employees. A variety of foods that are low in fat and high in complex carbohydrates should be adequate to meet the needs of both sedentary and physically active employees.

Commercial Foodservice

It is profitable for a commercial foodservice operation to offer nutritious menu items because many patrons are demanding dishes that are lower in calories, fat, cholesterol, and sodium. A commitment to healthful food is demonstrated by the concept of "Spa Cuisine," which was developed by New York City's Four Seasons Restaurant and the Columbia-Presbyterian Medical Center. Spa Cuisine selections are made with less oil, salt, and sugar and offer the customer a delicious meal that is lower in calories and more healthful. Other restaurants, from the expensive and exclusive to the fast food operations, have followed suit and now it is no longer unusual to find a selection of nutritionally balanced dishes on a restaurant's menu.

Even when a restaurant does not offer its own version of Spa Cuisine, it is still possible for that establishment to cater to a customer's special needs or preferences. Serving sauces or dressings on the side, decreasing the amount of butter and salt added to vegetables and broiled items, and offering fresh fruit as an alternative to rich desserts are just a few of the many ways a restaurant can accommodate its patrons without having to revamp its cooking methods or menu.

Ingredients and Preparation

The ingredients and preparation methods a foodservice operation uses will have a vast effect on the food's nutrient content. It is desirable to maximize the amount of vitamins, minerals, and fiber and minimize calories, fat, cholesterol, sodium, and sugar.

Vitamins are very fragile substances that can be destroyed by exposure to acid, alkali, heat, light, and air. The enzymes naturally present in foods can cause destruction, and the water-soluble vitamins can leach into the cooking water and be lost when that water is discarded. Frozen fruits and vegetables are generally higher in vitamins than their fresh or canned counterparts, due to the fact that they are usually frozen immediately after harvesting and have undergone minimal processing. Fresh foods, on the other hand, may travel great distances to the market and it can be days or even weeks before they are sold "fresh." During this lag time, a large percentage of vitamins may be lost. Canned foods experience harsher processing conditions and might not be eaten for months or years after harvesting.

Tailoring a foodservice operation's cooking methods to minimize vitamin loss can be achieved by adhering to the following guidelines:

1. Avoid overcooking food.
2. Steam, stir-fry, or microwave foods instead of boiling. If cooking in water cannot be avoided, use as little as possible and reuse that water in a soup stock or gravy.
3. Keep food wrapped to prevent oxidation.
4. If appropriate, keep foods cool to decrease the activity of enzymes.
5. Do not add baking soda to green vegetables to give them a bright green color.
6. Store foods in the dark or in opaque containers.
7. Cut food into medium-size pieces for cooking. Large pieces usually cook too slowly and very small pieces promote oxidation and loss of vitamins into the cooking water.
8. Avoid holding food at serving temperature for a prolonged period, such as on a steam table. This procedure not only increases vitamin loss, but also affects texture and increases the risk of food poisoning.

Compared to vitamins, minerals are relatively indestructible, although they can be lost in the cooking water and drippings from roasted or broiled meats. Precautions such as reusing the cooking water and the defatted drippings can help retain the mineral content.

The fiber content of a meal can be raised by using high-fiber ingredients and by not removing the peel from some fruits and vegetables. Serving whole-grain breads and rolls, incorporating legumes into the menu, and using unpeeled potatoes in soups and stews are just a few ways to increase a meal's fiber level.

Lowering the fat content of a food can usually be achieved with little change in flavor. Simply decreasing the amount of butter, margarine, or oil for sautéing can greatly reduce fat, and therefore calorie content. Using lower-fat ingredients will have the same effect; some examples of these are fish, skinless poultry, lean meats, and low-fat milk products. Broiling, steaming, or poaching foods will produce a final product that is lower in fat than fried foods. Instead of using the traditional fat and flour roux for thickening, flour can be mixed with a cold liquid and heated until thickened, omitting the fat completely. Chilling stocks and soups, then removing the fat that has hardened on top, is also an effective way to decrease fat calories.

When fat levels are lowered in a food, cholesterol is often reduced at the same time. One of the most common high-cholesterol ingredients used in many foods is egg yolk. It is often effective to substitute two egg whites for one whole egg, or use a cholesterol-free egg substitute. Decreasing saturated fat in foods and raising the proportion of unsaturated fat may help to reduce blood cholesterol levels. This process can be achieved by using liquid oils instead of solid fats; in particular, most animal fats should be avoided as well as highly saturated vegetable fats such as coconut and palm oils.

Salt is an expendable item in most recipes; the lost flavor can be enhanced with herbs and spices. Cooking with fresh or frozen ingredients is preferable, as most canned foods contain high levels of sodium.

Replacing rich, sugary desserts with fresh fruits and lighter, low-fat choices on a menu will help patrons lower their sugar and calorie intake. While dessert is often an opportunity to indulge, a delicious fruit sorbet or light soufflé can be satisfying without a high-sugar and high-calorie intake. Reducing the amount of sugar in a recipe often requires experimentation. Compensating for the loss of sweetness can be done by adding chopped fruit, extra spices, and extracts.

CONCLUSIONS

Nutritious foods can be incorporated into almost every menu. The benefit to the consumers is the possibility of enjoying better health. It is also profitable for the foodservice operation to modify its menu and make it more attractive for a wider variety of patrons.

REVIEW QUESTIONS

1. What are the six groups of nutrients?

2. How can the Four Food Group Plan provide a nutritious diet?

3. Which groups of people are likely to be deficient in nutrients?

4. Which dietary changes can help prevent heart disease?

5. How can a foodservice operation offer more nutritious foods to its customers?

4

Foodservice Characteristics of a Menu

A menu is a list of food and beverage items. In order to plan a successful menu, a foodservice professional needs to be able to define the three main styles of menus: a la carte, semi a la carte, and table d'hôte. Once the individual knows the style of menu he or she desires, a study of the general foodservice characteristics of the menu should be analyzed. The foodservice characteristics of a menu are broken into eight elements: menu, food availability, equipment, expense level, atmosphere, proficiency, customer makeup, and service. These elements can be applied to any menu such as a breakfast or ethnic menu.

Identification and understanding of the foodservice characteristics of different menus are vital to the general comprehension of menu planning within the foodservice industry. Once the individual masters this area, the foodservice characteristics of a menu will be applied to various foodservice menus throughout the country.

OBJECTIVES

1. To define the three styles of menus: a la carte, semi a la carte, and table d'hôte.
2. To enable the student to have a general understanding of the foodservice characteristics as they relate to the thirteen menus discussed.
3. To define American, French, and Russian service.
4. To explain and discuss how the foodservice characteristics of a menu apply to various foodservice menus.

MENU STYLES

In the foodservice industry there are three styles of menus as follows:

A la carte menu—Everything on the menu is priced separately from appetizer to dessert.

Semi a la carte menu—A menu in this category usually prices appetizers and desserts separately. The entree will include salad, potato, vegetable, and sometimes a beverage. This style of menu is the most popular in today's restaurants.

Table d'hôte menu—This type of menu offers a complete meal at a set price.

Breakfast, luncheon, dinner, specialty, and ethnic menus can be a la carte, semi a la carte, or a combination of both.

The eight important foodservice characteristics (Table 4-1) of a menu are as follows:*

1. Type of menu
2. Food availability
3. Equipment
4. Expense level
5. Atmosphere
6. Proficiency
7. Customer makeup
8. Type of service

We discuss thirteen menus in regard to the foodservice characteristics:†

- Breakfast
- Luncheon
- Dinner
- Children's
- Special occasion
- Twenty-four-hour or California
- Club
- Banquet
- Institutional
- Room service
- Ethnic
- Specialty
- Standard

BREAKFAST MENU

Type of Menu. Most breakfast menus are a combination of both a la carte and semi a la carte sections. The a la carte section offers juices, fruits, cereals, eggs, meats, bakery goods, and sometimes beverages. The semi a la carte section offers a wide variety of combinations. For example, (1) two eggs any style with bacon or sausage served with toast or (2) three pancakes with syrup and bacon or sausage served with home fries.

---

*The authors wish to express thanks to Professor Lothar A. Kreck, author of *Menus: Analysis and Planning*, Second Edition (1975, 1984), for the outline of foodservice characteristics of menus.

†Actual menus are reproduced as examples at the end of this chapter.

Table 4-1. Foodservice Characteristics of Menus

	Type of Menu	Food availability	Equipment	Expense level
Breakfast	Combination of a la carte and semi a la carte	Procure from local purveyor	(Compact) Broiler, oven, griddle, grill, and toasters	Low to moderate
Lunch	Combination of a la carte and semi a la carte	Procure from local purveyor	Ovens, broiler, steamer, grill, and top of range	Low to high
Dinner	Combination of a la carte and semi a la carte	Procure from local purveyor	Soup kettle, ovens, broilers, steamers, grill, and top of range	Moderate to high
Special Occasion	Table d'hôte	Procure supplies on time	Equipment for most part will already be within the establishment	Most often high
Twenty-four-hour or California	A la carte or semi a la carte; serves breakfast, lunch, or dinner	Supplies easy to obtain; have enough on hand to handle peak hours	Can be extensive to only a broiler, grill, ovens, and toasters	Low to moderate
Club	A la carte, semi a la carte, or table d'hôte	No problems; order in advance for parties	Full range of equipment	Moderate lunch; expensive dinner
Banquet	Comes in two forms: 1. No choice; 2. Choice	Allow enough time to obtain items	No problem	Cost depends on items served
Institutional	Cycle menu for the most part	Procure through local purveyor	Can be difficult to obtain because of strict budgets	Set sum per customer or student per day
Room Service	A la carte, semi a la carte, or table d'hôte	No difficulty in obtaining food supplies	Service table with heating units	Expensive
Ethnic	A la carte, semi a la carte	Supplies can be a problem	Make sure the equipment can handle the different items on the menu	Low to high
Specialty	A la carte, semi a la carte, offers seafood, beef, or chicken	Supplies must be fresh	Full range when dealing with seafood; less for steak or chicken	Moderate to high
Standard	A la carte, semi a la carte, offers lunch and dinner	Easy to obtain; have enough supplies on hand to cover busy periods	Fully equipped for the most part	Low to moderate

Food Availability. For the most part, food for the breakfast menu can be purchased from local purveyors. Items should be taken off the menu if they are not available or if they don't sell.

Equipment. When you plan a breakfast menu, careful attention should be given to purchasing and placing of equipment. The equipment usually consists of a broiler, flat top, griddle, convection oven, conventional oven, plate warmers, toasters, and microwave ovens.

Table 4-1.   Continued

Atmosphere	Proficiency	Customer makeup	Type of service
Fit menu	Somewhat skilled; fast	In a hurry for hot food	American
Fit menu	Culinary background helpful	In a hurry	American
Fit menu	Strong culinary skills	Couples, business people, leisurely paced	American, French, or Russian
Fit the occasion	Average culinary background	Good food, good service	American
Simple and basic	Quick and well organized	Business people, young couples, elderly people, students	American
Fit menu	Highly skilled in front and back of house	Members want convenience	American, French, or Russian
Menu should fit the theme	Good culinary background	Customer interested in good food and good service	American, French, or Russian
Decor should play more important role than currently	Chef must have a good background in special diets	Young children to elderly	Tray service or cafeteria style, self-service
Should fit the decor and theme of the hotel	Strong skills in front and back of the house	Good service and food	Trays are delivered to individual's room
Most important to fit menu and enhance theme of country	Service personnel should speak language of country represented as well as English	Tourists, business people, ethnic groups	American or French
Fit menu	Skilled in front and back of the house	Tourists, business people, couples, and families	American or Russian
Simple, not elaborate	Vary in culinary skill; front of house personnel should be quick and organized	Couples, elderly, tourists, and business people	American

Equipment should be located in a logical and compact fashion to aid employees in cooking and serving food promptly. The most common complaint of breakfast customers is being served lukewarm food when it should be served hot.

Expense Level.   The prices of food items on a breakfast menu are low to moderate. Most people do not expect to pay much for breakfast. However, large hotels can and do charge more for this meal than other foodservice establishments.

Atmosphere. A breakfast menu should reflect the decor of the operation. For example, if the tablecloth, carpeting, and napkins are white and the flowers on the table are yellow, the menu should be light in color also.

Proficiency. All breakfast items generally are cooked to order. Therefore, the cooks must be quick and well organized. One does not need to be a master chef to handle the items on a breakfast menu. The service personnel also have to be quick and efficient because of the high turnover rate during the breakfast service.

Customer Makeup. The customer who is having breakfast is often in a hurry, perhaps on the way to work. The patrons are tourists, business people, and people who work third shifts and leave work at 7:00 A.M. or 8:00 A.M.

Type of Service. For the most part the service is American, that is, one waiter or waitress takes the order and brings it to the table. The table is then cleared by a dining room attendant.

LUNCHEON MENU

Type of Menu. A luncheon menu can be a la carte or semi a la carte. A la carte items include appetizers, salads, cold and hot sandwiches, entrees, desserts, and beverages. The semi a la carte section includes entrees with salad, vegetable, and potato. Many luncheon menus offer daily specials as well. Specials are usually presented the following three ways:

1. On a blackboard at the entrance of a restaurant.
2. Inside the menu as a clip-on.
3. Verbally by the waiter or waitress.

Food Availability. Any food supplies for a luncheon menu can be obtained easily through local purveyors. If a food item is hard to obtain or if it does not sell it should be taken off the menu.

Equipment. Broiled, baked, braised, fried, poached, and roasted items on the luncheon menu require a full range of equipment. Specific equipment needed will depend on menu items.

Expense Level. Prices for a luncheon menu will depend on the menu items and the location of the establishment. The prices can range from low to high.

Atmosphere. The luncheon menu should reflect the decor of the operation. In a seafood restaurant, for example, the tablecloths might be light blue with white napkins. The menu cover might be light blue with a blue anchor on the cover, symbolizing the logo or design of the restaurant. The inside might be light blue and the printing might be dark blue to match the cover.

Proficiency. Preparing and serving a luncheon menu requires professional cooks, waitresses, and waiters. Many times, luncheon items such as appetizers, soups, entrees, and desserts are made from scratch, requiring a culinary background. The waiters and waitresses might have to describe specials and other dishes in detail to the customer, which would require some culinary aptitude as well.

Customer Makeup. The clientele can be tourists or business people.

Type of Service. The type of service is most often American—quick and efficient. Most people have only one-half hour to one hour for lunch, and they expect fast service as well as good food.

DINNER MENU

Type of Menu. A dinner menu is usually a combination of both a la carte items and semi a la carte items. The dinner menu has more appetizers and entrees than a luncheon menu. The dinner menu is often the most expensive type of menu.

Food Availability. Most supplies are not hard to obtain. Items difficult to get should be eliminated from the menu.

Equipment. The menu determines the equipment needed to produce items effectively and efficiently. For example, a specialty restaurant featuring steak and seafood needs broilers, deep-fat fryers, steamers, steam kettles, ovens, and flat ranges for sautéing.

Expense Level. Pricing will depend on the restaurant and what items are featured on the menu. However, dinner items are usually expensively priced compared to luncheon and breakfast items.

Atmosphere. The menu should be a reflection of the decor. For example, a French restaurant might have red carpeting, gold napkins, and red tablecloths. The menu cover could be red with the name of the restaurant in gold print. The inside of the menu could have a light gold background and red printing.

Proficiency. The food items on the menu will again determine the degree of skill needed by the staff. For instance, dinner menus can list ham that requires sauces. Sauces require a skilled kitchen staff. The waiter or waitress should also be aware of preparation methods of food items.

Customer Makeup. Clientele may be couples and working people who come to enjoy a leisurely dinner.

Type of Service. The type of service can range from American to French to Russian. In American service there is one waiter or waitress who takes the order and brings it to the table. The table is then cleaned by a dining room attendant.

French service takes place when there are two waiters: a captain and a secondary waiter. The captain takes the order, does the tableside cooking, and brings the drinks, appetizers, entrees, and desserts to the table. The secondary waiter gets bread and water, clears each course, crumbs the table, and serves the coffee.

In Russian service, the entree, vegetables, and potatoes are served from a platter onto a plate. In modified Russian service, which is found in seafood or specialty houses, the waiter or waitress serves the main entree from a casserole using a serving spoon and fork.

CHILDREN'S MENU

The main purpose of the children's menu is to help keep children occupied while parents are dining by providing some sort of activity for children to entertain themselves with. A children's menu therefore can be in the form of a toy or a puzzle. The menu should be table d'hôte in nature and offer a limited amount of choices in order not to confuse children. It is also important to call items on the menu in terms familiar and entertaining to children such as "Texas chili," "round-up steak," or "warpath stew." Prices should be low to moderate.

SPECIAL OCCASION MENU

Type of Menu. The special occasion menu is table d'hôte in style and often includes alcoholic beverages with the price. For the most part, the special occasion menu should display the theme or season on the cover of the menu and the food items and/or garnishes should be typical of that particular season.

Food Availability.   Menu planners should procure supplies early so there will be no problems at the last minute.

Equipment.   For the most part, the function will take place in an already established club or restaurant, so equipment will be available. A menu planner will ensure that the equipment needed for any special items on the menu is available.

Expense Level.   In many cases, entertainment is included in the price of the special occasion menu, often making special occasion menus expensive.

Atmosphere.   It is important that the menu carry the theme of the special occasion whether it be Easter, Mother's Day, Thanksgiving, or Christmas. For example, cornucopias can be displayed for Thanksgiving or poinsettias for Christmas.

Proficiency.   Skills needed for a special occasion menu are average. The cooks should know some time in advance what will be on the menu. Waiters and waitresses need to know how to wait on customers arriving at different times, which takes organizational skills on the part of the service staff.

Customer Makeup.   The clientele who attend these special occasions expect good food and good service. At holiday times, especially, customers can be far from home and family and usually appreciate extra attention.

Type of Service.   Style of service is American. The waiter or waitress may have to contend with the entertainment along with extra tables and chairs. As a result, the food quality of a special occasion menu is usually better than the service quality.

CALIFORNIA MENU OR TWENTY-FOUR-HOUR MENU

Type of Menu.   The California or twenty-four-hour menu offers three main meals throughout the day. Breakfast, lunch, or dinner can be purchased at any time. The menu can be a la carte or semi a la carte. Most twenty-four-hour menus have breakfast items, appetizers, soups, salads, hot and cold sandwiches, entrees, desserts, beverages, and fountain items. Many twenty-four-hour menus have laminated covers and extensive clip-ons. Laminated menu covers are very expensive to produce. Clip-ons often cover up items found on the menu, which can frustrate the customer when trying to read the menu.

Food Availability.   All of the food supplies can be purchased through local purveyors. It is important for the menu planner to have enough food on hand during the high-volume periods.

Equipment.   In some cases the equipment needed in a twenty-four-hour restaurant can be extensive. For some twenty-four-hour restaurants, however, the equipment can be a limited amount. For example, if only steaks and sandwiches are served, only a broiler, grill, toasters, slicers, and heat lamps are required.

Expense Level.   The patrons who frequent a twenty-four-hour establishment are usually concerned with price. The price is usually low to moderate.

Atmosphere.   The decor is usually simple and not as integral to the menu's success as in other types of restaurants.

Proficiency.   A person need not have great culinary skill in order to work in a twenty-four-hour operation. As with a breakfast menu, the kitchen staff has to be quick and well organized. Service personnel, because of high turnover of customers, need to be experienced in work organization.

Customer Makeup.   Customers may often consist of working people, young couples, elderly or retired couples, and college students.

Type of Service.   People who go to a twenty-four-hour restaurant expect fast service and good food. The service is American.

CLUB MENU

Type of Menu.   The club menu can come in three styles: a la carte, semi a la carte, or table d'hôte. Club menus usually serve lunch or dinner. The lunch menu usually consists of short-order items and a few specials. Club members expect full service for lunch. In contrast, dinner menus often offer a wide variety of appetizers, soups, salads, entrees, and desserts. Service is slower than at lunch and club members expect to pay more.

Food Availability.   For the most part, there are no problems in sources of supplies for club menu items. If you are having difficulty procuring a certain item, take it off the menu as soon as possible. When parties are scheduled and certain items may be hard to obtain, order items in advance to be prepared.

Equipment. Equipment needed for a club menu will again be determined by the items on the menu. In most cases, kitchens in clubs are fully equipped to accommodate the large variety of items on the menu as well as being equipped for parties and banquets that many clubs schedule.

Expense Level. Club members usually expect to pay little for lunch and to pay more for dinner. The menu planner must determine what members expect and what they are willing to pay. In most cases, food cost or profit is not the primary concern of dining clubs; the satisfaction of members is primary.

Atmosphere. The menu should fit the style of the operation. For example, if a club was established in the 1800s, the cover might be in leather and the logo in gold to accompany the old and lasting atmosphere.

Proficiency. In most dining clubs, kitchen and service personnel have to be well trained. In these clubs, culinary school backgrounds and many years of experience are not uncommon for kitchen staff.

Customer Makeup. Members have joined a club because they want convenience. They want to dine in a relaxed atmosphere where they can bring family and friends, often with little advance notice.

Type of Service. Service can be American, French, or Russian depending on the menu. Club members expect fast service during lunch; therefore, American service should be employed. More relaxed service during dinner allows the use of French or Russian service.

BANQUET MENU

Type of Menu. The banquet menu comes in two varieties. The first variety offers a succession of dishes without a choice for a set price. For example, you might select number three on a breakfast banquet menu that would include orange juice, fried eggs, ham, home fries, toast, and coffee, tea, or milk for $7.95. The second type of banquet menu is less popular than the first. In this variety, the customer is allowed to pick from a large variety of choices within each food group. For example, there might be seven different kinds of juices from which one is to be selected.

Food Availability. It is important that enough time is allowed to order all necessary food items.

Equipment. In most cases the banquet will take place within the hotel or restaurant so all the equipment will be on hand. It is wise not to include anything on the menu that requires special equipment.

Expense Level. The cost of a banquet menu will depend on what is being served, gratuity, catering transportation, and special equipment that is needed. If transportation and special equipment are necessary, it is up to the operation to charge enough to cover expenses and to make a profit.

Atmosphere. The menu should fit the theme or the special occasion. If the banquet theme is a spring wedding, the menu cover should be light in color, maybe blue or white, with some sort of flower arrangement in the center. The printing might be green or blue—something that is easy to read against a white background.

Proficiency. In most cases a good culinary background is needed to prepare banquet menu items. Serving personnel must be highly skilled. Planning is the most important skill needed for banquet menus, for example, ordering items ahead of time.

Customer Makeup. Banquet customers are invited guests usually at a wedding reception or other type of reception. These customers are interested in good food and drink and are less concerned about service than customers for other menu dining.

Type of Service. Type of service is American, French, or Russian. The guests usually sit at long tables. The first course, usually an appetizer, is placed on the table before the guests arrive. After everyone is finished with the first course, the second course is served, and so on.

INSTITUTIONAL MENU

Type of Menu. The institutional menu is used in correctional facilities, hospitals, elementary and secondary schools, and the armed forces. The institutional menu must be nutritionally sound, serving the four basic food groups at each meal: meats, cereals, vegetables and fruits, and milk.

Most institutions, especially hospitals, use a cycle menu to alleviate boredom for their clients. A cycle menu is one with different items on the menu each day for a period of three to five weeks, at which time the cycle starts again. Most hospitals have a three-week cycle menu, for example, and most schools or universities have a five-week cycle menu.

Food Availability. Procuring food does not present a problem for institutions because most foods can be purchased through local purveyors.

Equipment. Equipment can be difficult to obtain because of strict budgets that many institutions have to follow.

Expense Level. Today, a large number of institutional food operations are run by professional foodservice companies such as Saga, Daka, and Servomation. Institutions give the foodservice company one sum per customer or student per day. For example, $1.25 per employee per meal might be the figure the foodservice company charges to make a profit in a hospital cafeteria.

Atmosphere. In many institutions, dining room decor is not a priority budget item. Administrators often see no need to improve a hospital cafeteria, for example. After all, patients are in hospitals out of necessity and therefore hospitals will always have customers to feed. Recently, institutions such as hospitals are realizing that a nice decor, which may include paintings on the walls and flowers on the table, not only makes meals more enjoyable but also increases morale on the part of the employees, patients, and visitors.

Proficiency. The chef should have a culinary background and knowledge of special diets. The cooks can be less skilled. Most institutions encourage on-the-job training and in-service training to improve skills in kitchens and cafeterias where safety and sanitation are a must.

Customer Makeup. The clientele is dictated by the type of institution and can range from young children in schools to senior citizens in nursing homes.

Type of Service. Except for service to hospital rooms, the service is mostly cafeteria-style and self-service. Cafeterias require many types of food to be held for long periods of time. This food is kept warm in steam tables.

ROOM SERVICE MENU

Type of Menu.   The room service menu can be a la carte, semi a la carte, or table d'hôte. The menu can consist of a complete wine and liquor list, appetizers, soups, salads, hot and cold entrees, hot and cold sandwiches, vegetables, potatoes, and an assortment of desserts. It is important that room service items have good hot and cold holding qualities, for example, beef stew and a tossed salad.

Food Availability.   All food items on a room service menu are included in the main dining room menu; therefore, there is no difficulty obtaining food items.

Equipment.   The most important piece of equipment that all room service operations should have is a server table with adequate heating units. If hotels do not have adequate heating units, hot items should be removed from the menu.

Expense Level.   The room service menu is usually expensive because of the added service of delivering food to the rooms. Often a room service menu is more expensive than the regular dining room menu.

Atmosphere.   Room service menus will often look like miniature versions of the main dining room menu, fitting the decor and theme of the hotel.

Proficiency.   Many room service menus have very elaborate items that require special skills on the part of the kitchen staff. And in no other menu does skill play a more important role in regard to service personnel. The waiters or waitresses are completely on their own from the time they leave the kitchen until they arrive at the guests' rooms.

Customer Makeup.   Room service customers expect excellent food because of the high price of menu items.

Type of Service.   Orders are phoned in by the guests and are then placed on serving trays or tables and delivered to the guests' rooms.

ETHNIC MENU

Type of Menu.   An ethnic menu can be either semi a la carte or a la carte. In most cases, an ethnic menu offers food from a particular geographical area or a specific country. The appetizers, soups, salads, entrees, vegetables, potatoes, and dessert descriptions should be in the original language. There should also be a complete English translation explaining what the item is and how it is prepared.

Food Availability.   Food supplies can be problematic for ethnic menus. Before producing or printing the menu, the planner of an ethnic menu should ensure ability to purchase supplies at a reasonable cost and in a reasonable delivery time.

Equipment.   Assuring equipment can handle the different items is especially important in planning an ethnic menu. For example, Chinese restaurants must have woks; Italian restaurants will most likely have cappuccino makers.

Expense Level.   The cost of the meal will depend on the customers. Prices can range from low to high at ethnic foodservice establishments.

Atmosphere.   For no other menu will the decor be more enhancing than in an ethnic restaurant. In a Mexican restaurant the music played is Mexican. Waiters and waitresses are dressed in the appropriate costumes and the walls are decorated with brightly colored tiles.

Proficiency.   The cooks and the service personnel must be highly skilled in an ethnic restaurant. To make the food as authentic as possible, cooks or chefs from the particular country the restaurant is addressing should be employed. Service personnel should have a good understanding of the language of the restaurant's country and of English. Many customers will naturally ask questions about a particular food item and if the waiter or waitress cannot describe the dish adequately, the patron may be dissatisfied.

Customer Makeup.   The clientele consists of tourists, business people, and ethnic groups.

Type of Service.   Service in most ethnic restaurants is American. Of course, in French restaurants, the service should be French.

SPECIALTY MENU

Type of Menu.   The specialty menu is usually semi a la carte. Specialty houses offer steak, seafood, or chicken, for the most part. The specialty will be carried throughout the menu. For example, at a seafood specialty restaurant, seafood will be in the appetizers, soups, salads, and entrees. It is important to note that many specialty houses will use different cooking techniques as well. In seafood houses, entrees will be broiled, sautéed, poached, baked, steamed, or fried. In planning a menu for a specialty restaurant, other items should be included on the menu in addition to the specialty itself. For instance, a seafood restaurant should also cater to those who do not like seafood or who are allergic to it.

Food Availability. The most important factor for serving seafood is freshness. Seafood should be purchased on a daily basis, preferably from local fisheries if location permits.

Equipment. The size and complexity of the menu makes it necessary to have a fully equipped kitchen when specializing in seafood. Less sophisticated equipment is required when the specialty is steak or chicken.

Expense Level. The price depends on the menu items. Seafood and steaks are usually moderately to expensively priced.

Atmosphere. If a restaurant's specialty is seafood, the decor should be nautical in theme. Lobster traps, fish netting, and anchors create a seafaring atmosphere.

Proficiency. In most specialty houses, the wide range of dishes and preparation methods require that professional cooks be hired. Service personnel should be skilled in American and Russian service. Russian service is often used in seafood houses. The waiters and waitresses should be able to explain the preparation of dishes to guests.

Customer Makeup. The clientele consists of tourists, business people, couples, and families.

Type of Service. Service in a specialty house is usually American. However, in many seafood houses a number of dishes are served in casseroles, which is indicative of Russian service. Russian service requires that the waiter or waitress, using a serving spoon and fork, serve a portion of the casserole onto a dinner plate.

STANDARD MENU

Type of Menu. Most standard menus are a la carte or semi a la carte. These menus usually have lunch and dinner items on the menu.

Food Availability. Most standard menu items are purchased through local purveyors. It is important to remember that, as with the twenty-four-hour menu, the manager should order enough supplies so as not to run out during peak serving periods.

Equipment. The more items on the menu, the more complex the equipment will be. For the most part, standard menus have a fully equipped kitchen.

Expense Level. The price level is usually low to moderate depending on the location and the type of restaurant.

Atmosphere. In most cases, the decor is simple and does not overpower the guest (similar to the twenty-four-hour operation).

Proficiency. Personnel who work with a standard menu will vary in culinary skill depending on the difficulty of the menu items served. Service personnel, because of the high customer turnover rate, need to be skilled in work organization as in a twenty-four-hour operation.

Customer Makeup. The clientele consists of young couples, children, tourists, and business people.

Type of Service. The type of service is American. Similar to a twenty-four-hour operation, people expect fast service and good food.

REVIEW QUESTIONS

1. What is a table d'hôte menu?

2. What is a semi a la carte menu?

3. What are the major characteristics of the special occasion menu?

4. What are the major characteristics of the California menu?

5. Explain the two forms of banquet menus.

6. What are the major characteristics of an institutional menu?

7. What characteristics should an ethnic menu have?

8. What are the major characteristics of a specialty menu?

9. What is the main characteristic of a standard menu?

10. Discuss American, French, and Russian services.

EXAMPLES OF FOODSERVICE MENUS

Breakfast Menu

*STANFORD'S, Biltmore Plaza,
Providence, Rhode Island*

Type of Menu. The menu (Fig. 4-1) is a combination of a la carte and semi a la carte. The juices, fruits, cereals, bakery items, side orders, and beverages are a la carte. The club section on the semi a la carte section is made up of the Continental Breakfast and The All American. Most of the items on the menu are hot, such as omelettes, pancakes, steaks, eggs, and hot cereal.

Food Availability. The breakfast items are obtained through local purveyors.

Equipment. The top of the range is needed for poached eggs and hot cereals. Refrigeration is required for dairy products, meats, and juices. An oven or a steam table is used to keep the food items warm. A grill is needed for eggs, pancakes, and corned beef hash. A waffle iron is used for waffles. Sausage, bacon, home fries, and French toast are cooked on the grill and kept warm in the oven. A broiler is used for steaks. A baker's oven might be used for baked goods.

Expense Level. The expense level is moderate considering that the Stanford is in a major city hotel. The price range is from $1.00 for toast to $7.95 for the Biltmore petite steak and egg.

Atmosphere. This menu reflects a decor of elegance through its simplicity. The menu employs four colors that are relaxing to the eye: gray, pink, green, and beige. The headings and subheadings, that is, Fruits and Juices, Breakfast Specialties, and so forth are of a printing style that is light in character, adding to the simplicity of the menu.

Proficiency. The waiters, waitresses, and cooking staff have to be efficient and organized to serve a fast and hot breakfast. The cooks, for example, have to know various cooking techniques such as poaching, grilling, broiling, and sautéing. The waiters and waitresses have to know how certain items are prepared, such as eggs benedict.

Customer Makeup. Customers consist of business people, tourists, and families. The clientele is most likely in a hurry and expects fast and efficient service.

Type of Service. The type of service is American.

Figure 4-1. Breakfast menu—Stanford's. *(Courtesy of Omni Biltmore Plaza, Providence, RI.)*

FRUITS & JUICES

FRESHLY SQUEEZED ORANGE OR GRAPEFRUIT JUICE *1.75*

CRANBERRY, V-8, TOMATO OR APPLE JUICE *1.50*

CHILLED SEASONAL MELON *1.95*   FRESH BERRIES IN SEASON *2.95*

FRESH ONE-HALF GRAPEFRUIT *1.75*   FRUIT YOGURT *1.95*   FRESH FRUIT *2.95*

HOT & COLD CEREALS

CREAM OF WHEAT   OATMEAL   GRANOLA   RICE KRISPIES

SPECIAL K   CORN FLAKES

2.25

With Fresh Seasonal Fruits 3.25

THE ALL AMERICAN
Two Eggs, any style;
Bacon, Sausage, or Ham;
Home Fried Potatoes; Buttered Toast
Coffee, Tea, or Milk
5.50

CONTINENTAL BREAKFAST
Freshly Squeezed Juice;
Croissant, Danish and Toast
Coffee, Tea, or Milk
3.95

BREAKFAST SPECIALTIES

EGGS BENEDICT *6.95*   PETITE STEAK AND EGG, *any style 7.95*

THE NEW YORKER
Smoked Salmon with Toasted Bagel 7.50

OMELETTE   SPANISH OMELETTE *6.50*
With choice of Ham, Cheese, Onions, or Mushrooms 5.75

FROM THE GRIDDLE

BELGIUM WAFFLE   GOLDEN BROWN PANCAKES   FRENCH TOAST
Served with Vermont Maple Syrup and Whipped Butter 4.50

A LA CARTE

TWO EGGS, *any style*	*1.75*
BACON OR SAUSAGE	*2.00*
GRILLED HAM OR CANADIAN BACON	*2.25*
CORNED BEEF HASH	*3.25*
PETITE STEAK	*7.00*
HOME FRIED POTATOES	*1.00*

PASTRIES & BREADS

FRESHLY BAKED CROISSANT	*1.75*
FRUIT FILLED DANISH	*1.95*
FRUIT OR BRAN MUFFIN	*1.25*
COFFEE CAKE	*1.00*
BUTTERED TOAST	*1.00*
BAGEL AND CREAM CHEESE	*1.95*
TOASTED ENGLISH MUFFIN	*1.25*

BEVERAGES

FRESHLY GROUND AND BREWED GUATEMALAN OR
COLOMBIAN DECAFFEINATED COFFEE *1.00*

SELECTION OF STASH TEAS,
HOT CHOCOLATE, OR MILK *1.00*

All Prices Subject to State Tax.

OBH-GPS11686-1-87-1M

Luncheon Menu

TWENTY WATER STREET,
East Greenwich, Rhode Island

Type of Menu. The style of menu is a combination of semi a la carte and a la carte (Fig. 4-2). Soups, stews, and wines are a la carte. The salads, croissants, and house specialties are semi a la carte. Characteristic of a luncheon menu, Twenty Water Street has a large variety of house specialties such as Croque-Madame, Veal du Jour, Scallops Dijonaise, and Pasta de Jour. Along with specialties, the menu also includes a number of popular croissant items.

Food Availability. Food items are procured through local purveyors. The house specialties, consisting mostly of seafood, are obtained in Rhode Island.

Equipment. Soups and stews require a soup kettle or a stockpot. The croissant sandwiches require an automatic slicer. A broiler is needed for the London Broil and Broiled Flounder. The Baked Stuffed Shrimp and Baked Fish en Papillote require an oven. Vegetables require a steamer. Finally, pasta requires the top of the range.

Expense Level. The expense level is moderate to high for lunch. The Tuna Salad with Bacon croissant is $3.95 and the Veal du Jour is $8.95.

Atmosphere. The menu cover with the design of ships in blue and gray reflects the nautical atmosphere and decor.

Proficiency. The waiters and waitresses have to be knowledgeable about how certain items are prepared such as the Baked Fish en Papillote and the sauce bordelaise. The cooks are required to know a variety of cooking techniques such as broiling, sautéing, and steaming. They also have to know how to prepare various sauces and seafood dishes such as Scallops Dijonaise.

Customer Makeup. Business people, couples, and local merchants are the customers.

Type of Service. The type of service is American.

Soups & Stews

Soup du Jour	Cup 1.50	Bowl 1.95
New England Clam Chowder	Cup 1.95	Bowl 2.50
Lobster Bisque	Cup 2.50	Bowl 3.95
Baked French Onion Soup		2.50
Finnan Haddie Stew	made to order	3.95
Oyster Stew (6)	made to order	4.95
Seafood Stew	made to order	5.95

Salads

Spinach Salad 4.95
Artichoke hearts, fresh mushrooms, bacon, eggs, tomatoes and gruyere cheese

Lobster Salad 9.95
Made fresh daily, prepared with a mayonnaise dressing

Tuna Salad 4.95
Garnished with cottage cheese and fresh vegetables

Vegetable Salad 3.95
Today's fresh vegetables with tossed greens

Julienne Salad 5.95
Tossed greens topped with roast beef, ham, sliced chicken and cheese

Crabmeat Salad 8.95
Made fresh daily, prepared with a mayonnaise dressing

House Salad 1.95
Fresh greens garnished with tomato, mushrooms, cucumbers and fresh fruit

Salads served with choice of dressing and freshly baked breads.

Croissants

French Dip 5.25
Thinly sliced roast beef served au jus

Lobster Salad 8.95
Made fresh daily and prepared with a mayonnaise dressing

Baked Ham and Imported Cheese 4.75
Served hot upon request

Cold Sliced Chicken 5.25
Sautéed chicken breast served with lettuce and tomato

Tuna Salad with Bacon 3.95
Prepared with white albacore tuna

Crabmeat Salad 7.95
Made fresh daily and prepared with a mayonnaise dressing

Chopped Sirloin Croissant Club 4.95
Served with bacon, lettuce and tomato

Croissant with Soup du Jour .... additional charge 1.00

Croissants served with parsley-sautéed potatoes and fresh fruit.

Figure 4-2. Luncheon menu—Twenty Water Street. *(Courtesy of Twenty Water Street, East Greenwich, RI.)*

House Specialties

Croque-Madame 5.75
Sliced boneless chicken, french toasted with swiss cheese and dijon mustard

Baked Fish en Papillote 6.95
Fresh fish baked in parchment with lemon herbs and butter

London Broil 5.95
Sliced tenderloin with a mushroom bourguignonne sauce

Veal du Jour 8.95
Served with fettuccine noodles

Broiled Scallops 7.95
Tender scallops baked with wine and butter

Swordfish Steak .... priced to market
Broiled with lemon butter, fresh only

Baked Stuffed Shrimp 7.95
Prepared with sherry wine and fresh seafood stuffing

Quiche du Jour 5.50
Made fresh daily, served with salad

Chopped Sirloin 5.25
Broiled and served with sauce bordelaise

Scallops Dijonaise 8.95
Sautéed with sweet cream and dijon mustard, served over rice

Shrimp Scampi 7.95
Sautéed in a seasoned batter with shallots, garlic and sweet butter

Broiled Flounder 5.95
Seasoned crumb topping, garnished with lemon butter

Pasta du Jour .... priced daily
Served with house salad

All entrées include fresh vegetable, parsley-sautéed potatoes or rice pilaf,
salad and freshly baked bread.

International coffees of your choice are available upon request.

Ask your server about our assortment of home made desserts.

Due to the new laws regarding sales taxes,
we request that you do not put gratuities on credit card charges.

Figure 4-2.   Continued.

Wines by the Glass

RED   *Valbon rouge* 2.75
          Beaujolais-Villages 2.75
          Mouton-Cadet 2.75
          Krug Cabernet Sauvignon 3.00
          Deluze Classique 2.25

WHITE   *Valbon blanc* 2.75
          Pouilly-Fuisse 3.00
          Bolla Soave 2.75
          Zellar Schwartz Katz 2.75
          Blue Nun 2.75
          Mouton-Cadet 2.75
          Sakonnet America's Cup White 2.50
          Deluze Classique 2.25

CHAMPAGNE   *Paul Masson Splits* .... (6 oz.) 2.75

HOUSE   *Chablis, Rosé, Burgundy* ...... (By the glass) 2.00

Complete wine list available upon request.

We accept American Express, Mastercard or Visa.

Figure 4-2. Continued.

Dinner Menu

*L'APOGÉE, Biltmore Plaza,
Providence, Rhode Island*

Type of Menu. The style of menu (Fig. 4-3) is a combination of a la carte and semi a la carte. The a la carte items include Pâté of Duckling, Native Mussels, French Onion Soup, and Caesar Salad. Semi a la carte items include Filet of Salmon, Braised Pheasant Biltmore, and Veal a la Roma; they include vegetable and potato. The menu also offers a large variety of cold and hot appetizers characteristic of a dinner menu.

Food Availability. This menu calls for at least one purveyor who specializes in high-quality gourmet foods such as pheasant. Other food items can be obtained through local purveyors.

Equipment. Baked Stuffed Clams L'Apogée and Bay Scallops require an oven. The French Onion Soup and the Lobster Bisque require a stockpot or soup kettle. The Pasta du Jour needs a specialized heating unit called a *réchaud*, and the cart for the heating unit called a *guéridon,* used for tableside cooking. The new England Lobster requires a steam kettle or broiler. The Filet of Salmon and the Filet Mignon require a broiler. The Chicken L'Apogée and the Scalloppini of Veal Dijonnaise require the top of the range.

Expense Level. The price level is moderate to high, which is typical for a dinner menu. Prices range from $9.95 for Chicken Breast Estragon to $37.00 for Chateaubriand Bouquetière for two.

Atmosphere. The menu reflects a relaxing and elegant atmosphere. The style of printing and the use of gold and red reflects the Biltmore's rich, glamorous hotel decor.

Proficiency. The employees of the front and back of the house require an extensive culinary background. For example, Chateaubriand Bouquetière requires the cook and waiters and waitresses to work as a team because the dish is partially cooked in the kitchen and finished tableside. Caesar Salad also requires the skill of tableside preparation.

The cooks have to know how to braise, sauté, broil, poach, and prepare the various sauces. The cooks also need an understanding of the timing of the foods being cooked while using French service.

Customer Makeup. Customers of L'Apogée's dinner menu consist of business people, tourists, and couples sometimes celebrating special occasions in the luxurious atmosphere of the hotel.

Type of Service. The type of service is French.

Appetizers

Cold

AN ARRAY OF FRESH SEAFOOD
Clams, oysters and shrimp with horseradish and cocktail sauce
5.50

FRESH CLAMS OR OYSTERS
On the half shell
4.50

ICED SHRIMP COCKTAIL
From the Louisiana Gulf Coast
5.75

PÂTÉ OF DUCKLING
Duck, pork and veal seasoned with white wine and brandy
4.25

PROSCIUTTO HAM AND MELON
3.95

SMOKED NOVA SCOTIA SALMON
6.50

Hot

BAKED STUFFED CLAMS L'APOGEÉ
Little neck clams stuffed with bay scallops,
herbed butter and bacon
5.25

SHRIMP PERNOD
Sautéed shrimp with tarragon and pernod
finished with cream
6.25

PASTA DU JOUR
3.75

ESCARGOTS BOURGUIGNONNE
Baked in garlic butter
4.95

NATIVE MUSSELS
Steamed in white wine and seasoned with fresh herbs
4.50

Soups

SOUP DU JOUR
2.25

FRENCH ONION
Baked with gruyere cheese
2.75

LOBSTER BISQUE
Laced with cognac and cream
3.00

Figure 4-3. Dinner menu—L'Apogée. *(Courtesy of Omni Biltmore Plaza, Providence, RI.)*

Salads

GARDEN GREENS
An array of mixed greens with tomatoes, cucumbers, artichoke hearts,
and choice of dressing
1.95

BOSTON BIBB LETTUCE WITH BAY SHRIMP
Served with celery seed dressing
3.00

CAESAR SALAD
Prepared for two at your table
7.00

Artemisia
dracunculus

Pasta

Made fresh on premises with natural imported semolina and eggs

LINGUINI
With a white clam sauce
8.50

LINGUINI WITH MUSSELS
In heavy cream with tomato, garlic and herbs
9.25

FETTUCINE COLUMBUS
Fettuccine in a creamy sauce with mushrooms, prosciutto, topped with
freshly grated parmesan cheese
9.00

Entrees
Red Meats

NEW YORK SIRLOIN STEAK   14.00
Broiled, served with Café du Paris butter

FILET MIGNON   15.50
Filet of beef tenderloin, served with sauce Bearnaise

SURF N' TURF   15.50
A petit filet mignon with baked stuffed shrimp

ROAST PRIME RIB OF BEEF   13.75
Slowly roasted select cut of prime rib, au jus

BROILED DOUBLE LAMB CHOPS   16.50
Served with fresh mint sauce

CHATEAUBRIAND BOUQUETIÈRE   37.00
Double filet mignon for two with an array of fresh vegetables, sauce Bearnaise

Foeniculum
vulgare

Veal Dishes

BROILED VEAL CHOP   16.50
Fresh Provimi veal served with Maitre d'Hôtel butter

VEAL A LA ROMA   12.75
Sautéed scalloppini set on linguini, laced with a delicate wine sauce and
garnished with tomato, ham and mushrooms

SCALLOPPINI OF VEAL DIJONNAISE   12.75
Sautéed veal laced with a creamy Dijon mustard sauce

Rosmarinus
officinalis

Figure 4-3. Continued.

Entrees
Fish and Shellfish

NORTH ATLANTIC SWORDFISH   12.75
Broiled swordfish steak served with lemon butter

FILET OF SALMON   12.50
Poached or broiled, served with sauce Hollandaise or Maitre d'Hôtel butter

BAY SCALLOPS   12.00
Baked with lemon lime butter

BAKED STUFFED SHRIMP   14.00
Jumbo shrimp topped with crabmeat stuffing served with herbed butter

STUFFED FILET OF SOLE   11.00
Filet of sole rolled, with a crabmeat stuffing laced with lobster sauce

FRUITS OF THE SEA L'APOGEE   14.75
Scallops, shrimp and mussels in a white wine cream sauce with
a golden pastry shell

NEW ENGLAND LOBSTER   *Priced by the Tide*
Your choice - Boiled, Broiled or Baked Stuffed

Thymus
vulgaris

Poultry

CHICKEN BREAST ESTRAGON   9.95
Boneless double breast in a tarragon cream sauce

CHICKEN L'APOGÉE   13.50
Boneless chicken breast, sautéed with morels, chantrelles, and woodland
mushrooms, finished with a light wine sauce

BRAISED PHEASANT BILTMORE   19.75
Semi-boneless pheasant simmered in a rich game stock, finished with cream
cognac, mushrooms and goose liver pâté, topped with puff pastry

 OUR CHEF'S CREATIONS
Each evening we bring to you our Chef's creations
prepared especially for you. Your server for the evening will fully explain
these delectable and creative offerings.

Desserts

SELECT FROM OUR PASTRY CART
3.00

ICE CREAMS AND SHERBETS   **SEASONAL BERRIES**
2.50   3.00

SOUFFLE GLACE GRAND MARNIER
Iced Souffle Grand Marnier
3.50

All Prices Subject to State Tax.

Ocimum
basilicum

Figure 4-3. Continued.

Children's Menu

CHUCKY'S WAGON, St. Catherine Hospital,
East Chicago, Indiana

This menu (Fig. 4-4) is an excellent example of what a children's menu should contain. The cover design is the shape of a wagon in bright colors, sure to attract children. The use of cartoon terms, such as Buckaroo's Breakfast and Cowpoke Salad Corral, is entertaining for children. The food selection is marketed toward children's selections of foods such as Pecos Peanut Butter and Bronco Buster's Bologna.

Figure 4-4. Children's menu—Chucky's Wagon. *(Courtesy of St. Catherine Hospital of East Chicago, IN.)*

Buckaroo's Breakfast

Bust out of the bunkhouse with:

- Osage Orange Juice
- Sioux Warrior Strawberries
- Arapahoe Apple Juice
- Bow-legged Bananas
- Geronimo Grapes
- Navajo Nectars
- Fort Apache Applesauce
- Great Divide Grape Juice

- Silver Dollar Pancakes With Butter 'N Syrup
- Texas Toast With Powdered Sugar or Syrup
- Stampeded Eggs (Scrambled)
- Petrified Eggs (Hard Boiled)
- Saddle Up — Sausage Links, Bacon or Smoked Ham

Fer the Ask'n — Cereals, Toast, Tortillas, Biscuits With Butter and Jelly, Milk and Hot Chocolate

Wagon Full of Lunch and Supper

Cowpoke Salad Corral

- Loco Lettuce
- Round Redskins (Tomatoes)
- Carrot and Celery Spears
- Ranch Style Tuna Salad
- Gold Ore Eggs (Hard Boiled)

Hoot 'N Holler Fer:

- Wild West Spaghetti With Wrangler Sauce
- Rancher Pork Chops For Big Hands
- Cowhand Cheeseburger
- Cowboy Hot Dog
- Big West Fries to Beat All
- Whoopee! Mashed Potatoes 'N Gravy
- Corn on the Cob in a Heap of Butter
- Carrot Wheels

Have a Sandwich Hoedown With:

- Bronco Buster's Bologna
- Howdy Ham
- Chuckwagon Chicken
- Pecos Peanut Butter
- Chucky's Jelly or Cheese

Dessert Jamboree

- Buckboard Jello
- Campfire Chocolate 'N Vanilla Pudding
- Fruit Cocktail Roundup
- Sidekick Applesauce
- Herd-a-Cupcakes or Prairie Ice Cream Sundae

Fer the Ask'n — Bread, Biscuits, Tortillas and all the Fixins Not to Forget Milk and Hot Chocolate

CHUCKY SAYS: EAT GOOD FOOD and FEEL GOOD!

When ya got a hankerin' fer some grub, beat a trail to Chucky's Wagon.

Help yourself to a heap a breakfast and a wagon full a lunch 'n supper—

See ya'll there!

Figure 4-4. Continued.

Special Occasion Menu—New Year's Eve

L'APOGÉE, Biltmore Plaza,
Providence, Rhode Island

Type of Menu. The style of menu (Fig. 4-5) is modern table d'hôte, which offers a complete meal for one price with choices. This menu includes choices of hors d'oeuvres, soups, salads, entrees, and desserts for one price.

The artwork on the menu and the offering of a seafood dish, Baked Stuffed Shrimp, and a red meat dish, Roast Tenderloin of Beef, are typical of a special occasion menu for New Year's Eve.

Food Availability. It is important that all food items on a special occasion menu can be purchased in large quantities because of the large volume usually served. All the food items on this menu can be obtained through local purveyors.

Equipment. Mushroom Caps with Curried Crabmeat, Baked Stuffed Shrimp, and Roast Duckling require an oven. The soups require a stockpot or soup kettle. Veal Scallopini L'Apogée requires the top of the range. The vegetables require a steamer. An oven or top of the range are used for the potatoes and rice. The desserts require an oven, preferably a baker's oven.

Expense Level. The expense level is high on a typical New Year's Eve menu.

Atmosphere. A picture of the New Year's Baby is often found on this special occasion menu. The restaurant is adorned with New Year's decorations.

Proficiency. Both the front of the house and the cooking staff have to highly skilled to work a special dinner at L'Apogée. The waiters and waitresses not only have to know French Service but also have to be familiar with the various sauces and entrees on the menu. The cooks have to be skilled in all phases of cookery, including preparation of hors d'oeuvres, soups, and sauces and sautéing, roasting, and baking.

Customer Makeup. This menu attracts couples celebrating the New Year.

Type of service. The service is French.

Hors d'oeuvres

PATÉ OF DUCKLING
Duck, Pork and Veal seasoned with White Wine and Brandy

AN ARRAY OF FRESH SEAFOOD
Clams, oysters and shrimp with horseradish
and cocktail sauce.

MUSHROOM CAPS WITH CURRIED CRABMEAT

**PAUPIETTES OF SOLE WITH SALMON MOUSSE
AND LOBSTER SAUCE**

Soup

PETITE MARMITE HENRY IV
Double strength Consommé with Julienne of
Beef, Chicken and Vegetable

LOBSTER BISQUE
The Classic Cream based Bisque fortified with Cognac

Salad

Bibb lettuce and Radicchio Salad with Walnut Oil Dressing

New Year's Eve Specialties

**ROAST TENDERLOIN OF BEEF
SAUCE PERIGOURDINE**

VEAL SCALLOPINI L'APOGEE

BAKED STUFFED SHRIMP

**ROAST DUCKLING
CRANBERRY LEMON SAUCE**

———

All Entrees served with Chef's Special Selection
of Two Fresh Vegetables and Potato or Rice

Desserts

Selection of Continental Pastries

Soufflé Glace Grand Marnier   Strawberry Romanoff

Figure 4-5.   Special occasion menu, New Year's Eve—L'Apogée.
(Courtesy of Omni Biltmore Plaza, Providence, RI.)

California Or Twenty-Four-Hour Menu

Type of Menu. Brian's menu (Fig. 4-6) offers a variety of food items for breakfast, lunch, and dinner, which is the main characteristic of a twenty-four-hour menu.

Food Availability. All the food items on this particular menu can be purchased through local purveyors. It is extremely important to keep enough food items on hand during the peak hours of business, which most likely occurs on the weekends.

Equipment. The egg dishes require a grill and top of the range. The waffles require a waffle iron. Hamburgers require a broiler. The Chicken Cordon Bleu and Broiled Swordfish need an oven. The Fried Clams and Onion Rings need a fryolator. The Beef Stew needs a stockpot and the pies need a baker's oven.

Expense Level. The expense level is low to moderate.

Atmosphere. The decor is simple. Customers at Brian's expect fast service and food that is consistently good.

Proficiency. The front and back of the house need to be organized and efficient because of the high customer turnover rate. The cooks need to know the basic cooking techniques such as sautéing, broiling, frying, operating the grill, and baking.

Customer Makeup. Brian's customers are a mixture of families, young couples, working people, retired couples, and students.

Type of Service. The service is American.

Figure 4-6. California or Twenty-four-hour menu—Brian's.

BRIAN'S

EGGS	1.25
Two eggs in any style.	
EGGS BENEDICT	3.95
A poached egg on top of an English muffin with a slice of canadian bacon capped with our zesty hollandaise sauce.	

OMELETTES

WESTERN OMELETTE	2.50
A fluffy omelette consisting of three eggs with diced ham and onions.	
EASTERN OMELETTE	2.50
A fluffy omelette consisting of three eggs with diced ham, onions, and peppers.	
IMPERIAL OMELETTE	3.25
Fit for any emperor or empress, an omelette stuffed with cheddar cheese, crabmeat, and mushrooms and topped with sour cream.	

ROLLING IN THE DOUGH

FRENCH TOAST	2.75
Three slices of toast sautéed, then sprinkled with powdered sugar, covered in sweet maple syrup, with a dollop of whipped butter.	
PANCAKES	2.75
Three golden pancakes served with the toppings of your choice—blueberry, apple, maple, and cranberry.	
WAFFLES	2.25
Two hot, delicious waffles served with powdered sugar and butter.	

SIDE ORDERS

Bacon   Sausage   Toast   English muffins

ALL SANDWICHES COME WITH
STEAK FRIES AND SALAD

SANDWICHES — A choice of rye, white, or pumpernickle
bread.

BLT	2.25

The tallest bacon, lettuce, and tomato sandwich.

CHARBROILED HAMBURGER	3.25

½ lb ground sirloin with a generous portion of
cheddar or swiss cheese.

TURKEY CLUB	3.95

Tender slices of turkey with fresh lettuce, tomatoes,
and crisp bacon served on your choice of bread.

STEAK SANDWICH	4.50

A mile high of shaved steak with sautéed mushrooms,
onions, and melted cheese served on an open-face
bulky role. Comes with zesty barbecue sauce.

SEAFOOD SALAD ROLL	4.25

A delicate blend of crabmeat, lobster, and shrimp
stuffed inside a toasted roll.

ENTREES

All luncheon entrees come with salad.

BROILED SWORDFISH	8.50

8-oz portion grilled to perfection. Includes french fried
potatoes and cole slaw.

SIRLOIN STEAK	7.25

A broiled 8-oz portion of sirloin crowned with a
generous portion of sautéed mushrooms.

CHICKEN CORDON BLEU	6.75

A tender breast of chicken stuffed with ham, swiss
cheese, and deep fried and baked to a golden brown.

FRIED CLAMS	6.25

Clams fried in our own special beer batter. With
cornbread and cole slaw.

CHILI CON CARNE	4.95

Made the old-fashioned way with just the right blend of
spices with melted cheese. A touch of tabasco sauce
make ours special.

SIDE ORDERS

Tossed salad	1.25
Cole slaw	.75
Cottage cheese	.75
Onion rings	.75

DINNERS

All dinners include a choice of salad, potato, rice pilaf,
rolls and butter.
All children under twelve will receive half servings.

VEAL PARMESAN	8.50

Three slices of sautéed veal baked with a rich zesty
tomato sauce and melted cheese.

TEXAS STEAK	9.25

Only for the hungriest appetites. An 18-oz sirloin
broiled to perfection.

FISH & CHIPS	6.95

North Atlantic scrod deep fried to a golden brown with
crisp chips and a lemon wedge or homemade tartar
sauce.

SOUTHERN FRIED CHICKEN	7.25

Our chef's specialty of southern fried chicken from the
deep south.

PRIME RIB	9.95

12-oz portion of roast beef roasted in its natural juices.
Of course, with popovers.

LIVER AND ONIONS	7.50

Liver covered with onions and bacon.

BARBECUED CHICKEN	6.95

Three pieces of chicken done the old-fashioned way.

BEEF STEW	6.10

A generous portion.

QUICHE OF THE DAY	5.25

DESSERTS

Fruit pies	1.25
Cakes	1.25
Sundaes	.95
Puddings	.95

BEVERAGES

All beverages	.50

Orange juice, tomato juice, pineapple juice, cranberry
juice, coffee, tea, Sanka, iced tea, iced coffee, hot
chocolate, Coke, Sprite, Seven-Up, Root Beer, Diet
Sprite, Diet Coke.

Figure 4-6. Continued.

Club Menu

*BROWN FACULTY CLUB, Brown University,
Providence, Rhode Island*

Type of Menu. This menu (Fig. 4-7) is a la carte and semi a la carte. The a la carte dishes are listed in the appetizers, soups, salads, desserts, and beverages. The semi a la carte dishes are listed in the entrees.

Food Availability. This menu offers food available through local purveyors. When specialty food items are needed, the club manager orders them in advance.

Equipment. Major pieces of equipment needed to produce this menu are a range to sauté the shrimp for the Shrimp Casino au Pernod, a soup kettle or tureen, a charbroiler to broil the New York Sirloin Steak, a steamer for the fresh vegetables, and a salad bar unit for the salads.

Expense Level. This menu is moderately priced for a club menu with the Vegetable Platter at $6.95 and the New York Sirloin Steak at $14.95.

Atmosphere. The artwork of various food displays, the typeface, and the burgundy and black type reflect the richness of decor of the club.

Proficiency. The waiters and waitresses have to be trained in full table service to allow the patrons to be relaxed and unrushed. The food items are gourmet and service personnel need to know what the items are and how they are prepared.

The cooks must know a wide variety of cooking techniques such as sautéing, broiling, steaming, and preparing gourmet sauces.

Customer Makeup. The clientele is composed of faculty members, alumni members, and their guests.

Type of Service. The service is American.

*Brown
Faculty
Club*

*A gracious welcome.
Relax and enjoy your repast with us.
Our wishes for a wonderful evening which will
be a repeated pleasure.*

DINNER MENU

APPETIZERS

Escargots Bourguignonne $4.50
*The aromas of garlic, herb butter, wine
and escargots combine to be served on
croustades under a glass dome.*

Melon Ambrosia $2.50
*Assorted sweet melon with toasted
coconut, walnuts, flavored lightly with
Midori and Galliano liqueurs.*

Shrimp Casino au Pernod $4.95
*Jumbo shrimp sautéed with casino
butter, finished by a splash of Pernod.*

Market
Shellfish of the Day . . . . .Price
*The freshest ocean seafood prepared
in a special way daily to provide the
greatest variety and best quality.*

Pâté Maison $2.95
*Creamy chicken liver spread with a
hint of Cognac and served with crusty
warm bread.*

Gravlox $3.95
*Club cured fresh salmon with Cognac
and dill, served with Norwegian flat
bread, crisp cucumbers, tomato and
mustard sauce.*

SOUPS

Potage du Jour $1.50
*A special soup prepared daily with the
freshest ingredients to please every
palate.*

Chilled "Melon" Bisque $1.75
*A unique combination of fresh melon,
cream, zest of lemon for a refreshing
start of an evening.*

French Tomato Onion Soup, au Gratin . .$1.95
*Rich broth seasoned with herbs, sweet
onions and tomato, baked in a crock
with bubbling melted cheese.*

Figure 4-7. Club menu—Brown Faculty Club. *(Courtesy of Brown University, Providence, RI.)*

ENTRÉES

Chicken Céleste $9.95
A Club specialty which combines the flavors of mushrooms, cheese, a boneless breast of chicken, napped with Madeira sauce and glazed with a touch of Hollandaise sauce.

Dinner Souffle $6.95
A true French classic combining eggs, cream, and market fresh products to provide a different souffle nightly.

Canard de Maison $10.75
Duckling prepared in a special style to utilize the season's harvest and provide for changing tastes.

Filet of Sole, Amandine $8.25
Fresh ocean sole, sautéed, served with toasted almonds and lemon butter.

Shrimp Parisienne $12.95
Succulent shrimp, sautéed with white wine, garnished by a fine julienne of carrots and leeks, aromatic seasonings of fennel and Spanish saffron complete this unusual dish.

Veal Piccatta Basilico $11.50
Tender scaloppini of milk-fed veal, sautéed with select mushrooms, fresh sweet basil in a delicate lemon wine sauce.

Medallions of Beef, Financière $13.95
Three medallions of tenderloin cooked to your order, served with a truffle rich Madeira sauce.

New York Sirloin Steak $14.95
At its best, simple and pure, a char-broiled sirloin steak grilled to perfection.

Vegetable Platter $6.95
Variety of fresh market vegetables combined for a beautiful selection to entice the most distinguished vegetarian.

Entrées Accompanied by Fresh Seasonal Vegetables and Club Salad

Figure 4-7. Continued.

SALADS

Caesar Salad for One (or more) $2.75
*Crisp romaine lettuce, pure olive oil,
imported Parmesan cheese, fresh
lemon, anchovies and garlic combined
to produce the emperor of salads.*

Avocado and Crabmeat Salad $9.50
*Emerald ripe avocado, filled with
luscious crabmeat salad, garnished
with garden tomatoes, marinated
cucumbers and watercress.*

Hearts of Baby Bibb $1.95
*Tender crowns of baby bibb lettuce
with your choice of dressing.*

Fresh Fruit Salad Supreme $7.50
*Light and delicious combination of
melon, peaches, tropical and citrus
fruits, garnished with your choice of
yogurt, cottage cheese or sherbet.*

DESSERTS

Special daily selections from the Dessert Cart
Variety of pastries, fruits of the season, and sweets displaying the talents of the Club's chefs.

Coupé Elizabeth $2.25
*Häagen Daz ice cream, fresh whipped
cream, dark bing cherries, Cherry
Herring Liqueur with a dusting of
cinnamon.*

Peach Melba $2.50
*Classic combination of vanilla ice
cream, poached peaches, whipped
cream and rich raspberry sauce.*

Club Sorbet $2.75
*Freshly made citrus and fruit ices
of the day. A refreshing complement
to every meal.*

Brown "Brownie" Royale $2.65
*Rich, nutty, chewy, chocolate brownie,
covered with Häagen Daz ice cream,
homemade fudge sauce and fresh
whipped cream.*

BEVERAGES

Coffee . . . . $.60

Sanka . . . . $.60

Teas . . . . $.60
*Darjeeling
Earl Grey
Orange Spice
Herbal*

Please See the Back for Evening Specials and Coming Events.

*We will be pleased to assist you in any way possible.
Thank you for letting us serve you.*

*Peter L. Cooper
Manager
Brown Faculty Club*

Figure 4-7. Continued.

Banquet Menu

BILTMORE PLAZA,
Providence, Rhode Island

Type of Menu. The style of the banquet menu (Fig. 4-8) is different from any other menu because merchandising such a menu is a total package concept from appetizer to dessert. Modern table d'hôte is the typical style used in banquet menus.

The Biltmore Plaza Banquet Menu is a good example of the total banquet menu concept. The package offers menus for all occasions including breakfasts, luncheons, cocktail receptions, and dinners, and includes a beverage list and wine list.

There are two forms of banquet menus. The first is a table d'hôte menu, that is, a set price for the entire meal. There are no choices in a true table d'hôte menu. For example, a breakfast menu can consist of one fruit selection, one egg selection, one pastry selection, and one beverage selection. The second form of banquet menu is a modern table d'hôte, which offers either a limited or a variety of food selections. For example, the breakfast suggestions menu offers the Yankee, which includes a fruit selection, pancakes, choice of breakfast meats, assorted breakfast pastries, and a choice of beverages.

The Luncheon/Lite Luncheon Selections offers a larger selection of three appetizers, six soups and salads, fifteen entrees (priced accordingly), six desserts, and four beverages.

This banquet menu offers general information on gratuities and tax, price list, room rentals, billing and deposits procedures, function room arrangements, and food guarantees.

Food Availability. All the food items on the banquet menus are available through local purveyors. Ordering food for banquets requires orders in advance and in sufficient quantity.

Equipment. Banquet menus usually require some duplication of the standard production equipment such as a range, oven, and steamers. If a banquet room is located away from the main kitchen, it is necessary to have equipment such as heated food warmers that will reconstitute the food to serving temperature. A secondary production kitchen near the banquet room is sometimes employed.

The dining rooms will call for specialized equipment depending on the function. For example, for a wedding reception a champagne fountain may be needed.

Expense Level. This banquet menu is priced moderate to high. Breakfast items are priced from the American (scrambled eggs) at $5.95 to the breakfast buffet brunch at $15.00.

The lunch items are priced from Quiche du Jour at $7.00 to Petit Filet Mignon at $14.00.

The dinner items are priced from Roast Loin of Pork at $12.95 to Grilled Filet Mignon at $18.50.

Atmosphere. The decor of a banquet menu should fit the style and theme of the individual banquet rooms of the hotel.

The burgundy and gray of the Biltmore Plaza Banquet Menus support the rich and stylish decor exhibited in the Biltmore's banquet rooms.

Proficiency. The serving personnel need to be highly skilled because banquets require French or Russian service. The service personnel must be able to handle the heavy trays of food.

The cooks must have a strong culinary background to be able to prepare the variety of food items. For example, a cook must be able to know how to cook coddled eggs and how to roast and carve a suckling pig.

Customer Makeup. This banquet menu is marketed toward business personnel at conferences and the public when celebrating a special occasion.

Type of Service. American, French, and Russian services apply to this banquet menu.

Figure 4-8. Banquet menu. *(Courtesy of Omni Biltmore Plaza, Providence, RI.)*

GENERAL INFORMATION

THE BILTMORE PLAZA
BANQUETS AND MEETINGS

The Biltmore Plaza is very pleased to be of service to you. Based on our excellent reputation for providing the finest foods and beverages, superb service and superior facilities, we know you can be assured of a successful and memorable event.

The following information will be helpful to you in planning your banquet or meeting.

MENU SELECTIONS

Menu selections are to be submitted to us at least four weeks in advance; otherwise items selected cannot be guaranteed. Our banquet menus are merely a sampling of what we at the Biltmore Plaza can do for you. If you prefer, our staff would be more than happy to suggest interesting alternatives for any meal function.

FOOD GUARANTEES

You will be billed for the amount specified in your letter of confirmation unless the Catering Manager is notified 2 working days prior to your function. Your guarantee is a minimum charge. If an increased number of meals are served above your guarantee, this number will be charged.

ROOM AND RENTAL

Function rooms are assigned according to the anticipated guaranteed number of guests. If there are fluctuations in the number of attendants, the hotel reserves the right to accordingly reassign the Banquet Function Room. The hotel reserves the right to charge a service fee for set up of meeting rooms with extraordinary requirements.

BEVERAGES

Arrangements for beverage service are to be made four weeks prior to your event. All beverages must be purchased from the Biltmore Plaza. Bar set-up charges and minimum purchases are required.

FUNCTION ROOM ARRANGEMENTS

Arrangements are to be finalized with the Catering Manager two weeks prior to your function. Please advise us if you will require special arrangements such as special seating arrangements, award tables, decorations, floral arrangements, audiovisual equipment and any other needs.

LIABILITY

The Biltmore Plaza reserves the right to inspect and control all private functions. Liability for damage to the premises or equipment will be charged accordingly. We cannot assume any responsibility for personal property and equipment brought onto our premises.

GRATUITIES AND TAX

Gratuities for food and beverage service will be added to the account at 15% and also prevailing state sales tax will be added to the account.

BILLING AND DEPOSITS

Billing arrangements for all events must be made in accordance with hotel policies. All requests for direct billing must be authorized by our Catering Department. A determination of a deposit or payment in advance is predicated on information received from our Catering Department. If a deposit is required it becomes nonrefundable sixty days prior to the event.

COFFEE BREAKS & SPECIALTY BREAKS

CONTINENTAL BREAKFAST
Assorted Breakfast Pastries,
Chilled Fruit Juice,
Butter and Preserves.
Coffee, Tea, Decaffeinated Coffee and Milk
3.75

TEX A MEX BREAK
Nachos, Corn Chips and sliced fresh Vegetables
served with Cheese and Guacamole Dips.
Assorted Soft Drinks, Coffee,
Decaffeinated Coffee, Tea and Milk
4.50

SUNDAE BREAK
"Make Your Own Sundae", Choose from
Vanilla, Chocolate or Strawberry Ice Cream
with Assorted Toppings, Diced Fruit and
Whipped Cream. Assorted Soft Drinks,
Coffee, Tea, Decaffeinated Coffee and Milk
4.25

SAY CHEESE BREAK
A Selection of Domestic and Imported Cheese
served with Whole Fresh Fruit and an
Assortment of Crackers. Soft Drinks,
Coffee, Tea, Decaffeinated Coffee and Milk
3.75
With Wine   4.75

"THAT'S THE WAY THE COOKIE CRUMBLES" BREAK
Fresh Baker Shop Cookies and Brownies, Assorted Whole Fresh Fruit.
Soft Drinks, Coffee, Tea, Decaffeinated Coffee and Milk
4.50

NATURAL BREAK
Assortment of Sliced Fresh Fruit,
Fresh Yogurt, Nuts, Honey and Granola.
Assorted Soft Drinks, Perrier, Coffee,
Tea, Decaffeinated Coffee
4.25

CAPE CODDER BREAK
Chilled Cranberry and Apple Juice,
Cranberry Danish and Muffins. Coffee, Tea,
Decaffeinated Coffee and Milk,
Assorted Soft Drinks
3.75

Coffee, Tea, Decaffeinated Coffee	.95	Coffee, Tea, Decaffeinated Coffee	
Coffee, Tea, Decaffeinated Coffee		Assorted Muffins or Danish	2.75
Soft Drinks	1.95		

A 15% gratuity plus prevailing sales tax will be added to all prices.

PRICE LIST

BREAKFAST SELECTIONS

B-1	5.95	B-4	9.00	B-7	7.50	B-10	13.00
B-2	6.75	B-5	8.25	B-8	8.50	B-11	15.00
B-3	7.00	B-6	8.50	B-9	9.50		

LUNCHEON SELECTIONS

L-1	9.95	L-7	11.00	L-13	7.95	L-19	7.00
L-2	8.95	L-8	8.25	L-14	8.25	L-20	7.25
L-3	8.50	L-9	12.50	L-15	13.00	L-21	7.50
L-4	9.75	L-10	12.50	L-16	8.75	L-22	9.50
L-5	9.50	L-11	14.00	L-17	8.00		
L-6	7.95	L-12	10.50	L-18	7.25		

DINNER SELECTIONS

D-1	16.50	D-5	16.25	D-9	13.95	D-13	12.95
D-2	17.50	D-6	15.95	D-10	14.25	D-14	13.95
D-3	12.95	D-7	13.95	D-11	13.25		
D-4	18.50	D-8	16.00	D-12	14.95		

A 15% gratuity plus prevailing sales tax will be added to all prices.
A guaranteed count must be submitted 48 hours prior to function.
All menu selections must be made at least 4 weeks prior to function.

THE AMERICAN

Choice of Chilled Juice
Scrambled Eggs
Choice of Breakfast Meat
Assorted Breakfast Pastries
Butter and Preserves
Coffee, Tea or Milk
B-1

THE YANKEE

Fresh Melon in Season
Pancakes with Maple Syrup
Choice of Breakfast Meat
Assorted Breakfast Pastries
Butter and Preserves
Coffee, Tea or Milk
B-2

THE RHODE ISLANDER

Choice of Chilled Juice
or Half Grapefruit
Scrambled Eggs
 Choice of Breakfast Meat
Hash Brown Potatoes
Assorted Breakfast Pastries
Butter and Preserves
Coffee, Tea or Milk
B-3

THE KENNEDY PLAZA

Choice of Chilled Juice
or Melon in Season
6 Ounce New York Sirloin
Scrambled Eggs
Hash Brown Potatoes
Assorted Breakfast Pastries
Butter and Preserves
Coffee, Tea or Milk
B-4

BUFFET BREAKFASTS

THE BILTMORE
(50 Guests Minimum)

Chilled Fruit Juices
Assorted Fresh Fruit Sections On Ice
Hot and Cold Cereals
Fluffy Scrambled Eggs
Sausage, Bacon and Ham
Hash Brown Potatoes
Assorted Breakfast Pastries
Butter and Preserves
Coffee, Tea, Decaffeinated Coffee and Milk
B-5

THE FRENCH LIFT
(50 Guests Minimum)

Fresh Fruit Sections
Assorted Yogurts
Hot and Cold Cereals
Crepes filled with Cream Cheese
and Strawberries
Assorted Breakfast Pastries
Butter and Preserves
Coffee, Tea, Decaffeinated Coffee and Milk
B-6

THE EXECUTIVE
(15 Guests Minimum)

Chilled Fruit Juices
Fluffy Scrambled Eggs
Bacon, Ham or Sausage
Assorted Breakfast Pastries
Butter and Preserves
Coffee, Tea, Decaffeinated Coffee and Milk
B-7

Figure 4-8. Continued.

BRUNCH

Fruit Cup
Eggs Benedict
Asparagus
Red Grapes
Assorted Breakfast Pastries
Butter and Preserves
Coffee, Tea, Decaffeinated Coffee and Milk
B-8

Tropical Fruit Cup
Shrimp Quiche
Broccoli Polonaise
Red Grapes
Assorted Breakfast Pastries
Butter and Preserves
Coffee, Tea, Decaffeinated Coffee and Milk
B-9

BUFFET BRUNCH

Mixed Greens and Assorted Salad
Fruit Compote
Sliced Salmon with Bagels, Tomatoes,
Onions and Cream Cheese
Chicken a la Reine
Cheese Blintzes with Sour Cream and
Apricot Sauce
Fresh Vegetables of the Day
Saffron Rice
Assorted Luncheon Rolls
Coffee, Tea, Decaffeinated Coffee and Milk
B-10

Mixed Greens
Chilled Fruit Juices
Sliced Melon in Season with
Assorted Yogurts
Omelettes
Mushroom, Ham, Cheese, Western or
Spanish. Made to order.
Beef Strogonoff
Egg Noodles
Fresh Vegetable of the Day
Assorted Luncheon Rolls
Coffee, Tea, Decaffeinated Coffee and Milk
B-11

Figure 4-8. Continued.

APPETIZERS

Chilled Fruit Juices   Fresh Fruit Cup   Melon in Season

SOUPS AND SALADS

Biltmore Clam Chowder   Minestrone   Soup of the Day
Spinach and Mushroom Vinaigrette   Tossed Green Salad   Caesar Salad 1.50 *additional*

ENTREES

BREAST OF CHICKEN CORDON BLEU	L-1	BROILED SWORDFISH	L9
HAWAIIAN HAMSTEAK	L-2	ROAST LEG OF VEAL	L-10
CHICKEN A LA KING IN PATTY SHELL	L-3	PETIT FILET MIGNON	L-11
BREAST OF CHICKEN KIEV	L-4	LONDON BROIL	L-12
YANKEE POT ROAST JARDINIERE	L-5	CHOPPED BEEF STEAK	L-13
BOSTON SCHROD	L-6	BEEF BOURGUIGNONNE	L-14
FILET OF SOLE ALMANDINE	L-7	MINUTE STEAK	L-15
SEAFOOD NEWBURG	L-8		

May we Suggest our Executive Chef select the Potato
and Fresh Vegetable to best compliment your selection.

DESSERTS

Fresh Fruit Cup   Biltmore Mousse
Ice Cream or Sherbet   Parfaits   Plaza Ice Cream Pie   Pear Belle Helene
Fresh From the Biltmore Plaza Bakeshop
Freshly Made Cheese Cake   Freshly Made Apple Pie

BEVERAGES

Coffee, Tea, Decaffeinated Coffee and Milk

LITE LUNCHEON SELECTIONS

Minestrone
CHEF'S SALAD
Chocolate Mousse
L-16

Melon Wedge
STUFFED TOMATO
with Chicken and Tuna Salad
Sherbet
L-17

FRESH FRUIT PLATTER
Choice of:
Yogurt or Cottage Cheese
Ice Cream
L-18

Spinach Salad
QUICHE DU JOUR
Biltmore Mousse
L-19

Clam Chowder
ASSORTED SANDWICH PLATTER
Served Family Style
Fresh Whole Fruit
L-20

Soup du Jour
DELI PLATTER
Potato Salad and Cole Slaw
Apple Pie
L-21

Consommé
AVOCADO STUFFED WITH CRABMEAT
Sliced Tomato and White Asparagus
Sherbet
L-22

DINNER SELECTIONS

APPETIZERS

Shrimp Cocktail 3.50 *additional*   Fresh Fruit Cup   Coquille St. Jacques 2.50 *additional*
Crabmeat Remoulade 3.50 *additional* Melon in Season   Pâté of Duck
Melon with Prosciutto 1.50 *additional*

SOUPS AND SALADS

Clam Chowder   Minestrone   Onion Soup   Lobster Bisque
Spinach and Mushroom Vinaigrette   Biltmore Salad   Caesar Salad 1.50 *additional*

ENTREES

ROAST SIRLOIN OF BEEF	D-1	ROAST DUCK A L'ORANGE	D-8
NEW YORK SIRLOIN STEAK	D-2	BREAST OF CHICKEN KIEV	D-9
ROAST LOIN OF PORK	D-3	BREAST OF CHICKEN CORDON BLEU	D-10
GRILLED FILET MIGNON	D-4	FILET OF SOLE ALMANDINE	D-11
ROAST PRIME RIB OF BEEF	D-5	BROILED SWORDFISH	D-12
ROAST LEG OF VEAL MARSALA	D-6	FRESH BOSTON SCHROD	D-13
ROAST TOP SIRLOIN OF BEEF	D-7	STUFFED BONELESS HALF CHICKEN	D-14

May we Suggest our Executive Chef select the Potato
and Fresh Vegetable to best compliment your selection.

DESSERTS

Ice Creams or Sherbets   Kahlua Parfait   Biltmore Plaza Parfait   Plaza Ice Cream Pie
Strawberries Romanoff 2.50 *additional*   Raspberry, Lemon or Chocolate Mousse

Fresh From the Biltmore Plaza Bakeshop
Freshly Made Cheese Cake   Freshly Made Apple Pie   Baked Alaska

BEVERAGES

Coffee, Tea, Decaffeinated Coffee and Milk
A selection of House Wines are available to compliment your meal.
All Meals are served with Rolls and Butter.

A 15% gratuity plus prevailing sales tax will be added to all prices.

Figure 4-8.   Continued.

COCKTAIL RECEPTION

COLD HORS D'OEUVRES
(Per 65 Pieces)

Asparagus Points Rolled in Ham	75.00	Melon with Prosciutto	75.00
Smoked Salmon Points	95.00	Oysters on the Half Shell	80.00
Salami Cornets	67.50	Clams on the Half Shell	80.00
Turkey Canapés	67.50	Iced Gulf Shrimp	95.00
Crabmeat Canapés	75.00	Celery with Roquefort	55.00
Sardines on Toast	67.50	Deviled Eggs	65.00

HOT HORS D'OEUVRES
(Per 65 Pieces)

Chicken Livers Wrapped in Bacon	67.50	Fried Cauliflower	55.00
Stuffed Mushrooms Imperial	95.00	Deep Fried Gulf Shrimp	95.00
Scallops Wrapped in Bacon	90.00	Swedish Meatballs Bordelaise	67.50
Barbecued Spareribs	67.50	Prunes Wrapped in Bacon	55.00
Petite Fried Chicken	65.00	Oysters Rockefeller	90.00
Beef Brochettes	80.00	Quiche Lorraine	65.00
Chinese Egg Rolls	55.00	Clams Casino	90.00

FROM THE CARVING TABLE

Roast Suckling Pig	450.00	Country Style Bone-In Ham	125.00
Top Round of Beef	145.00	Steamship Round of Beef	420.00
Tenderloin of Beef	125.00	Roast Turkey	95.00
Steak Tartare, *per pound*	25.00	Mirror of Pâté Maison	125.00

Carving Fee 35.00

ASSORTED SNACKS
(Per 30 People)

Dry Roasted Peanuts, *per bowl*	8.50	Assorted Cheese with Fruit, Bread	95.00
Assorted Raw Vegetables with Dip	55.00	Chips, Pretzels, Tortillas, *bowl*	7.50

A 15% gratuity plus prevailing sales tax will be added to all prices.

Figure 4-8. Continued.

WHITE DINNER WINES

United States, Mirassou Chablis	10.50
United States, Mondavi White Table	9.75
Italy, Soave Bolla	9.75
Italy, Verdicchio, Battaglia	12.50
France, Mouton Cadet	14.00

RED DINNER WINES

United States, Mirassou Burgundy	10.50
United States, Mondavi Red Table	9.75
France, Mouton Cadet	14.00
France, Beaujolais Villages	13.50
Italy, Valpolicella, Bolla	9.75

ROSÉ DINNER WINES

United States, Mirassou Petite Rosé	9.50
France, Moe Baril Rosé d'anjou	10.50
Portugal, Lancers	10.50

CHAMPAGNES AND SPARKLING WINES

United States, Great Western Extra Dry	16.50
Spain, Frexinet Cordon Negro Brut	14.50
Italy, Asti Spumanti	15.00

Additional Wines Available Upon Request

A 15% gratuity and prevailing sales tax will be added to all prices
A guaranteed count must be submitted 48 hours in advance.

Figure 4-8. Continued.

BEVERAGE LIST

THE OPEN BARS

Unlimited Cocktails and Highballs with Liquors, Manhattans, Martinis and Whiskey Sours

HOUSE BRANDS		PREMIUM BRANDS	
4.50	per person for the first hour	7.50	per person for the first hour
2.75	per person for the second hour	4.50	per person for the second hour
2.25	per person each additional hour	3.75	per person each additional hour

CORDIAL CART
For After Dinner Drinks
3.00 *per Cordial*
Cigars 2.75 *each*

STANDARD BRANDS
6.25 per person for the first hour   3.75 per person for the second hour
3.25 per person each additional hour

BOTTLED BAR SUGGESTIONS

SCOTCH WHISKEY		GIN	
Johnny Walker Red Label	35.00	Beefeater	35.00
Johnny Walker Black Label	45.00	Tanqueray	35.00
Dewars White Label	35.00	House	28.00
J & B	35.00	**RUM**	
Cutty Sark	35.00		
Chivas Regal	45.00	Bacardi Silver	32.00
House	28.00	House	28.00

BLENDS - Irish, Canadian		BEER	
		Imported	2.50
Seagrams 7 Crown	32.00	Domestic	2.00
Canadian Club	35.00		
Seagrams V. O.	35.00	**PUNCH**	
Seagrams Crown Royal	42.00		*Per Gallon*
John Jameson	37.00	Champagne	75.00
House	28.00	Fruit	35.00

STRAIGHT WHISKEY		DRINKS	
Jack Daniels	35.00	Standard	2.25
Old Grandad 86	35.00	Premium	2.75
House	28.00	Soft Drinks	1.25
		Cordials	3.25
VODKA		Wine	2.00
Smirnoff Red	32.00		
House	28.00		

A 15% gratuity will be added to all prices.
A guaranteed count must be submitted 48 hours prior to function.

Figure 4-8.   Continued.

Institutional Menu

ST. CATHERINE HOSPITAL,
East Chicago, Indiana

Type of Menu. This institutional menu (Fig 4-9a, b, c) is unique in that it is in the style of a restaurant menu instead of an institutional menu.

A restaurant-style menu is a menu that offers a large variety of foods. This menu gives the patient a nutritionally balanced meal through the use of the four basic food groups. The menu also offers daily specials for patients.

Food Availability. All items on the menu can be purchased through local purveyors.

Equipment. Major pieces of equipment are required as follows: The hash browns and eggs call for a grill; the poached, soft, and hard-cooked eggs call for the top of the range; a slicer is needed for the assortment of sandwiches; a broiler is used for the hamburgers and lamb chops; an oven is used for the meatloaf; a fryolator is required for the fried shrimp; and a baker's oven is needed for the cheesecake and assortment of pies.

Expense Level. The expense is included in the total hospital bill. The food cost is usually a set sum per person per day.

Atmosphere. The menu is designed to boost morale and is set up for the patient to easily see and select items.

Proficiency. The chef should have not only a good culinary background but also a knowledge of special diets. The dieticians need an excellent knowledge of nutrition. Dietary aides need to know what the food items are and their method of preparation to answer any questions patients might have about their meals.

Customer Makeup. This menu caters to hospital patients.

Type of Service. The type of service is tray service.

Welcome

THIS IS YOUR PERSONAL MENU

The challenge of our times is one of change. St. Catherine Hospital has accepted this challenge. Through the efforts of our Dietetics Department, this unique V.I.P. menu has been created.

The menu corresponds with the diet your physician prescribed. Diet is essential to total well being. Planning meals from this extensive menu will prepare you to make wise choices at home or in a restaurant.

This is your personal menu, it is yours to keep. Each morning you will receive an **ordering sheet.** A member of the dietetics department will instruct you on the use of the menu and order sheet. The ordering sheet will be picked up each day before noon. The selections you make today will be served to you tomorrow. A movie on how to use your menu can be viewed on Channel 3 at 9:00 a.m. and 4:30 p.m. each day.

Wine is available to enhance your luncheon and dinner meals. Your physician must give written approval for wine service.

Guest trays may be ordered through nursing service and the business office. It is always nice to dine with friends so feel free to ask about this service. We hope the menu includes your personal preferences. Any comments you may have will be appreciated.

HOW TO ORDER

1. Write your name and room number in the space provided at the bottom of the menu ordering sheet.

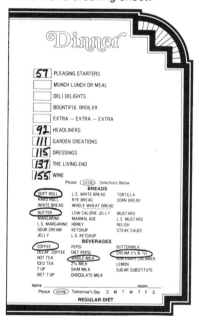

2. Each food item has a group title and a number. Place the number of the food you want for each meal next to the group title indicated on your marking sheet. **Please do not choose** numbers listed under "NOT ALLOWED," on the marking sheet.

3. Please make only **one** selection for luncheon and supper from any **one** of the following food groups: Munch Lunch or Meal, Deli Delights, Bountiful Broiler, or Headliners.

4. The following sample may be helpful as a guide.

ROSE WINE

FRESH FRUIT CUP

CHICKEN ALA KING ON PUFF PASTRY

TOSSED SALAD   FRENCH DRESSING

ANGEL FOOD CAKE

SOFT ROLL — BUTTER

MILK — COFFEE — CREAM

Figure 4-9a. Institutional menu. *(Courtesy of St. Catherine Hospital of East Chicago, IN.)*

Because We Care...

St. Catherine Hospital, East Chicago, Indiana has been surveyed and granted the Certificate of Accreditation as determined by the Joint Commission on Accreditation of Hospitals.

The Joint Commission on Accreditation of Hospitals is administered co-operatively by the American College of Physicians. A board of examiners has inspected the hospital and has determined St. Catherine to be in compliance with the Joint Commission's highest standards.

What does this mean to you our patient?

RECOGNITION — for the quality services provided to our patients through sound principles of medical practice, organization and administration. These are reflections of professional patient care. St. Catherine Hospital has sought and achieved the standards set forth by the Joint Commission.

ASSURANCE — to each patient that qualified medical staff and well-trained nursing personnel complimented by support staff help make St. Catherine Hospital operate at top efficiency.

QUALITY — means a great deal to you. It is like the "sterling" mark on silver . . . a mark of quality in medical and hospital service. WE are proud of our accreditation and assure you, your stay will reflect St. Catherine Hospital's dedication to quality care.

Figure 4-9a. Continued.

Breakfast

ADJUSTMENTS WILL BE MADE FOR MODIFIED DIETS

EYE OPENERS

1. Orange Juice
2. Grapefruit Juice
3. Apple Juice
4. Pineapple Juice
5. Prune Juice
6. Cranberry Juice
7. Pear Nectar
8. Orange Sections
9. Half Grapefruit
10. Fresh Banana
11. Strawberries
12. Applesauce
13. Stewed Prunes
14. Mixed Melon Wedges

HAPPY DAYS

15. Old Fashioned Oatmeal
16. Cream of Wheat
17. Hominy Grits
18. Cream of Rice
19. Frosted Flakes
20. Special K
21. Cocoa Krispies
22. Frosted Rice
23. Cornflakes
24. Rice Krispies
25. Raisin Bran
26. Puffed Rice
27. Shredded Wheat
28. Puffed Wheat

AS YOU LIKE IT

29. Poached Egg
30. Scrambled Egg
31. Low Cholesterol Scrambled Egg
32. Soft Cooked Egg
33. Hard Cooked Egg
34. Fluffy Omelet
35. Low Cholesterol Omelet
36. Egg Easy Up
37. Egg Over Easy
38. Old Fashioned Hot Cakes with Maple Syrup and Butter
39. French Toast with Maple Syrup
40. Low Cholesterol French Toast with Maple Syrup
41. Crisp Bacon Strips
42. Low Cholesterol Bacon
43. Pork Sausage Links
44. Breakfast Ham
45. Hash Brown Potatoes
46. Breakfast Steak

ETC., ETC., ETC.

47. Toast
48. Low Sodium Toast
49. Toasted English Muffin
50. Hot Biscuit
51. Coffee Cake
52. Tortilla
53. Toasted Bagel
54. Fresh Doughnut
55. Danish Pastry
56. Hard Roll

Figure 4-9a. Continued.

Luncheon

PLEASING STARTERS

57. Chilled Fruit Cup
58. Zesty Tomato Juice
59. Low Sodium Tomato Juice
60. Apple Juice
61. Lemonade
62. Savory Fresh Vegetable Soup
63. Low Sodium Savory Vegetable Soup

64. Cream of Chicken Soup
65. Cream of Tomato Soup
66. Beef Consomme
67. Low Sodium Beef Consomme
68. Chicken Consomme
69. Low Sodium Chicken Consomme

MUNCH LUNCH OR MEAL

71. Julienne Salad Bowl — Crisp salad greens, topped with turkey, ham 'n cheese strips, hard cooked egg wedge, olives, and served with a Kaiser roll.
　　Soft-bland · omit olives

72. Tuna Salad 'n Tomato Cup — Presented on lettuce bed, with hard cooked egg wedge and crackers.
　　Soft-bland, fiber restricted · omit tomato.

73. Cottage Cheese—Fresh Fruit Plate Chilled cottage cheese, pineapple spears, strawberries, melon and grapes, served with raisin bread.
　　Soft-bland, fiber restricted · canned fruit.

DELI DELIGHTS

74. The Belt Buster — Lettuce, thin sliced beef 'n turkey, topped with tomato and bacon, served on toast with potato chips.
　　Low fat, fiber restricted, soft-bland · baked french fries. Fiber restricted, soft-bland · omit tomato.

75. Piled High on Rye — Hickory smoked ham 'n Swiss cheese over lettuce on rye bread, garnished with cole slaw and dill pickle spears.
　　Fiber restricted, soft-bland · omit cole slaw, pickle.

76. Super Bird — Swiss cheese and breast of turkey sliced over lettuce, topped with tomato, tucked in a vienna roll, with cranberry relish and 1000 island dressing.
　　Soft-bland, fiber restricted, cranberry sauce; omit tomato.

77. It's Wonderful — Lean sirloin of beef, lettuce, tomato and cucumber on a kaiser roll, french dressing a-side.
　　Soft-bland, fiber restricted · omit tomato, cucumber.

78. Sea 'n See—Tuna salad club sandwich served with lettuce, tomato, pickles and chips.
　　Fiber restricted, low fat, soft-bland · omit chips. Fiber restricted, soft-bland · omit tomato and pickles.

79. Original Style Tacos — A Spanish experience, the works on a soft shell.
　　Fiber restricted, soft-bland · omit tomato.

BOUNTIFUL BROILER

80. Steel City Burger — Broiled lean ground round on a bun, with all the trimmings and french fries.

81. Big Cheese — Broiled lean ground round 'n cheese on a bun, all the trimmings and french fries.

82. Broiled Liver—Tender calf's liver broiled onions, with hash browns and buttered green beans.
　　Fiber restricted, soft-bland · omit onions.

83. Fillet of Beef — Succulent steak au jus, mushrooms, served with oven brown potatoes and asparagus spears.

84. Lamb Chop — Presented with seasoned rice and glazed carrots.

Figure 4-9a. Continued.

and Dinner

HEADLINERS

92. Chicken Ala King — Light chunks of chicken, mushrooms and select vegetables in delicate cream sauce over puff pastry, accompanied by buttered peas.

93. Italian Style Spaghetti — Always a favorite, authentically seasoned and **must** be served with garlic bread. Soft-bland french bread.

94. Rock Cornish Hen 'n Orange—Crisp, golden brown, accented with orange sauce, seasoned rice and savory green beans.

95. Cod Almondine—A delectable combination of broiled fish, almonds, lemon, with baked potato and simmered leaf spinach. Soft-bland - omit almonds.

96. Macaroni and Cheese—Tender macaroni blended with mild cheese sauce, hint of seasoning, broiled tomato and glazed carrots. Fiber restricted, soft-bland - omit tomato.

97. Fried Shrimp — Batter dipped, golden brown, enjoyed with zesty seafood sauce and steak fried potatoes.

98. Steamed Jumbo Shrimp — Tempting shrimp with lemon, baked Julienne potatoes and savory green beans.

99. Roast Loin of Pork—A sumptuous cut of pork, cinnamon apples, au gratin noodles and asparagus spears.

100. Prime Rib of Beef — Needs no introduction, spotlighted by mushrooms, baked potato, and glazed carrots. Low cholesterol - roast beef.

101. Southern Style Chicken — Traditionally American, with sweet potatoes and lightly seasoned greens.

102. Shish Kabob — Tender cuts of beef on a skewer, served with seasoned rice, tomato wedges and green peppers. Soft-bland - asparagus spears.

103. Authentic Chili — From south of the border, a hearty meal. Served with a tortilla.

104. Stuffed Cabbage 'n Tomato Sauce —A zestful blend of beef, rice and spices, wrapped in cabbage leaf and topped with sauce, whipped potatoes and savory green beans.

105. Hearty Meat Loaf — Blended choice ground round 'n spices, complimented by whipped potatoes and glazed carrots.

106. Vegetarian Delight — A delightful change of pace, whole glazed carrots, tender asparagus spears, broiled tomato, baked potato and stuffed mushroom caps - sour cream on the side. Soft-bland, fiber restricted - omit tomato.

EXTRA! EXTRA! EXTRA!

85. French Fried Potatoes — Soft-bland - baked.

86. Potato Chips

87. Baked Potato

88. Hash Brown Potatoes — Soft-bland - baked.

89. Broccoli

90. Whole Glazed Carrots

91. French Bread

GARDEN CREATIONS

107. Fresh Fruit Salad on Endive

108. Parfait Salad on Lettuce

109. Cucumber and Vegetable Salad

110. Pear Halves with Cream Cheese on Lettuce

111. Tossed Crisp Greens Sprinkled with Croutons - Choice of Dressing

112. Cottage Cheese 'n Fruit on Lettuce

113. Sliced Tomato Garnished with Chives - Choice of Dressing

114. Cole Slaw Salad on Endive

SALAD DRESSINGS

115. French Dressing

116. 1000 Island Dressing

117. Italian Dressing

118. Mayonnai e

119. Whip Fruit Dressing

120. Vinegar an Oil

Figure 4-9a. Continued.

THE LIVING END

122. Vanilla Ice Cream	137. Angel Cake
123. Lime Sherbet	138. Baked Custard Pie
124. Rainbow Sherbet	139. Strawberry Viennese
125. Chocolate Pudding	140. Lemon Crunch Pie
126. Gelatin Parfait	141. Warm Deep Dish Apple Pie
127. Vanilla Pudding	142. Frosted Devil's Food Cake
128. Chocolate Sundae	143. Fresh Fruit In Season
129. Cream Puff	144. Chilled Fruit Cup
130. Boston Cream Pie	145. Cinnamon Applesauce
131. Italian Ice	146. Sliced Peaches
132. Sliced Pineapple	147. Baked Apple
133. Old Fashioned Pound Cake	148. Strawberries
134. Chilled Pear Halves	149. Cheese Cake
135. Fresh Banana	150. Sweet Potato Pie
136. Tea Cookies	151. Cherry Pie

152. BURGUNDY
"Full Bodied and Pleasantly Tart"
A red dinner wine, best with red meats and full flavored dishes.

153. CHABLIS
"Light and Sweet"
The wine that enhances all good food.

154. CHENIN BLANC
"Light, Crisp with a Hint of Sweetness"
Preferred with seafood, fowl and other light entrees.

155. ROSE
"Light, Sweet and Fruity"
Best for the more delicate taste — good with all foods.

WINE WILL BE SERVED WITH PHYSICIAN'S WRITTEN ORDER!

Figure 4-9a. Continued.

Daily Specials

In addition to the twenty-nine entree selections in your menu booklet, you may select from our daily specials. To receive a daily special entree, place the number of the entree you want, 200, 300, or 400, in the box next to **Headliners** on your menu marking sheet. The specials are available for lunch and supper. Please remember you will be selecting your meals for the next day, so Sunday specials will be selected on Saturday to be served on Sunday. Bon Apetit!!!

SUNDAY

200. Roast Breast of Turkey — Old fashioned dressing enhanced by giblet gravy, whipped potatoes and broccoli spears.
   (soft, bland - omit dressing, serve potatoes)

300. Hickory Smoked Ham — Served with fresh pineapple spear, whole candied sweet potato, and light, but rich spinach souffle.
   (soft, bland - omit fresh pineapple, serve canned pineapple slice)

400. French Dip — Tender, juicy round of beef thinly sliced and tucked in a French roll ready to be dipped in a mouth watering au jus, so good with steak fries.
   (soft, bland - baked steak fries)

MONDAY

200. Beef Stew — a proud combination of choice pieces of beef, garden vegetables in hearty gravy, flaky biscuit, and crabapple garnish.
   (soft, bland, fiber restricted - omit crabapple)

300. Roast Leg of Veal — Generous slices of veal placed over apple dressing, accompanied by asparagus spears and oven brown potato.

400. Tuna Melt — A unique flavor experience of tuna salad heaped on a tomato slice and English muffin, topped with cheddar cheese, broiled and served with a crisp vegetable kabob.
   (soft, bland - omit tomato)

TUESDAY

200. Breaded Center Cut Pork Chop — Deep fried to golden brown, presented with potato puff au gratin and Italian green beans.
   (soft, bland, low fat - baked pork chop)

300. Swiss Steak — Seasoned perfection, served with green pepper, onion, tomato, completed with whipped potatoes, and butter crumb cauliflower.
   (soft, bland, low fat - steak in seasoned sauce and whole buttered carrots)

400. Grilled Cheese Sandwich — Straight from the grill and best with a mug of tomato soup, served with potato chips and dill pickle spears.
   (soft, bland, low fat, low cholesterol - omit chips and pickles)

REGULAR DIETS

Figure 4-9a. Continued.

WEDNESDAY

200. Bar-B-Que Back Ribs — Broiled in our own sauce, enjoyed with baked potato and buttery corn on the cob.
 (soft, bland, baked back ribs, baked apple)

300. Stuffed Pizza — Deep dish cheese pizza, a thick, rich blend of fine cheeses and seasonings, completed by tossed crisp greens and your choice of dressing.

400. Hot Beef Sandwich — Tender slices of roast beef on fresh baked bread with whipped potatoes, rich gravy, cole slaw a-side.
 (soft, bland - omit cole slaw)

THURSDAY

200. Chicken and Dumplings — Down home flavor! A quarter chicken, parsley dumpling, rich cream gravy, irresistably served with cranberry sauce and glazed whole carrots.

300. Chinese Stir Fried Beef — Marinated beef strips accented with sliced mushrooms and peapods, stir fried and served over fluffy rice, complemented by mandarin oranges and water chestnuts.
 (soft, bland - omit water chestnuts)

400. Hearth Sandwich — A delightful combination of fresh pineapple, broccoli spears, sliced breast of turkey, and tomato all covered with sharp cheese sauce, NEVER served with bread!
 (soft, bland, low fat - canned pineapple, asparagus, omit tomato)

FRIDAY

200. Breaded Perch Filet — Crisply fried, served with fresh lemon wedge, enhanced by macaroni and cheese and julienne green beans.
 (soft, bland - baked perch filet)

300. Veal Parmigian—Veal cutlet glazed with zesty tomato sauce and mozarella cheese featured over spaghetti noodles, served with fresh spinach salad - choice of dressing.
 (soft, bland, low fat, - mild tomato sauce)

400. Cheddar Cheese Omelet — Fluffy and delicious topped with sliced mushrooms, accompanied by hash brown potatoes.
 (low fat, low cholesterol - egg substitute omelet. Soft, bland - baked hash browns.)

SATURDAY

200. Short Ribs of Beef — Lean and meaty in rich brown gravy, presented with oven brown potatoes and butter crumb cauliflower.

300. Vegetable Lasagne—A zesty blend of eight cheeses combined with spinach, carrots and just the right seasonings, great with crisp tossed salad greens and garlic bread.
 (soft, bland, low fat - French bread)

400. Breast of Chicken Filet Sandwich — A pyramid of deep fried chicken filet on a soft roll, crowned with crisp lettuce, tomato slice, Wisconsin cheese, broiled and accented by cranberry relish.
 (low fat, soft, bland, baked filet of chicken, cranberry juice, omit tomato)

Figure 4-9a. Continued.

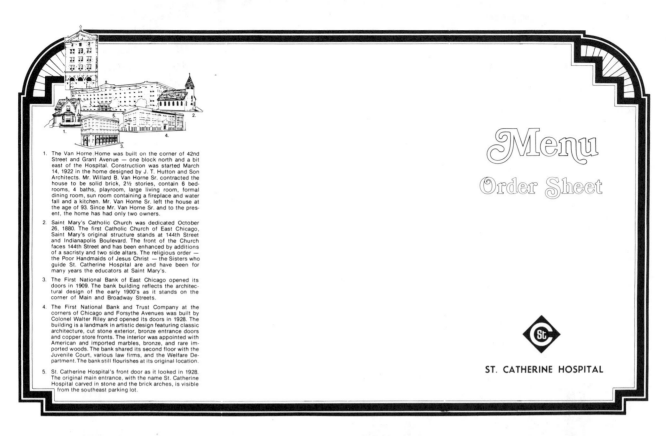

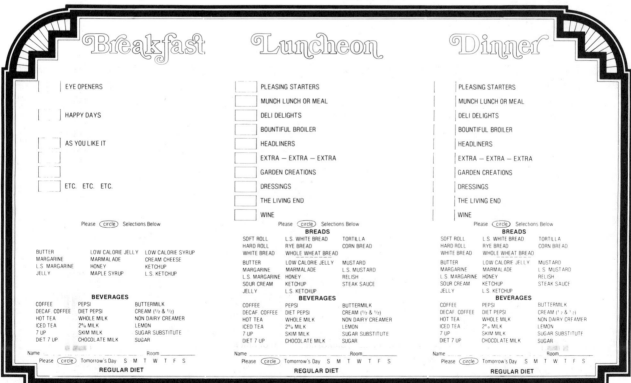

Figure 4-9b. Institutional menu, order sheet. *(Courtesy of St. Catherine Hospital of East Chicago, IN.)*

St. Catherine Hospital

Candle Light Menu

CANDLELIGHT SUPPER
MENU

APPETIZERS
Chilled Shrimp Cocktail

Fresh Fruit Cup

French Onion Soup - Au Gratin

ENTREE
FILET MIGNON OF BEEF
with Sauteed Mushrooms

ROCK CORNISH HEN à l'Orange

Baked Potato served with sour cream	Green Beans Almondine
Rice Pilaf	Broccoli & Cheese Souffle

Hot Baked Bread
on a Board

Tossed Crisp Green Salad
Choice of Dressing

Cheese Cake in Cherry Sauce

Chocolate Bavarian Mint Pie

Coffee	Tea

Champagne for Two

Please ⬭circle Selections

Name _____ Room_____

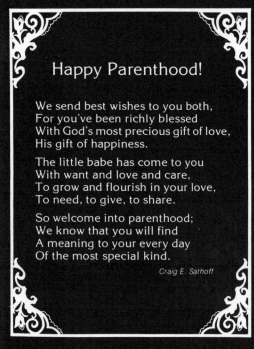

Happy Parenthood!

We send best wishes to you both,
For you've been richly blessed
With God's most precious gift of love,
His gift of happiness.

The little babe has come to you
With want and love and care,
To grow and flourish in your love,
To need, to give, to share.

So welcome into parenthood;
We know that you will find
A meaning to your every day
Of the most special kind.

Craig E. Sathoff

CANDLELIGHT SUPPER
MENU

APPETIZERS
Chilled Shrimp Cocktail
Fresh Fruit Cup
French Onion Soup - Au Gratin

ENTREE
FILET MIGNON OF BEEF
with Sauteed Mushrooms
ROCK CORNISH HEN à l'Orange

Baked Potato served with sour cream	Green Beans Almondine
Rice Pilaf	Broccoli & Cheese Souffle

Hot Baked Bread
on a Board

Tossed Crisp Green Salad
Choice of Dressing

Cheese Cake in Cherry Sauce

Chocolate Bavarian Mint Pie

Coffee	Tea

Champagne for Two

Figure 4-9c.   Institutional menu, candelight menu. *(Courtesy of St. Catherine Hospital of East Chicago, IN.)*

Room Service Menu

MARRIOTT,
Providence, Rhode Island

Type of Menu. The style of menu (Fig. 4-10) is a la carte and semi a la carte. The fruit juices, breakfast bakeries, cereals, side orders, appetizers, salads, desserts, and beverages are a la carte. The complete breakfasts, tortilla flats, sandwiches, and entrees are semi a la carte.

Food Availability. All food items on the room service menu are included on the main dining room menu; therefore, there should be no difficulty in purchasing food items.

Equipment. The room service menu requires a service table with adequate heating units. Since all the room service items are offered in the main dining room, all other equipment is available.

Expense Level. The expense level is moderate to high. The Vegetable Pocket costs $4.50 and the Fresh Swordfish Steak costs $15.25. The Chicken Cashew Salad costs $5.50.

Atmosphere. The gold lettering and maroon menu cover with a gray background and maroon printing denote a gracious and relaxed atmosphere, which the Marriott certainly reflects throughout its operation.

Proficiency. Waiters and waitresses must have some knowledge of how items are prepared and must serve the food items in a courteous manner. The cooks must have a good culinary background in preparing the soups, entrees, and desserts.

Customer Makeup. The customers are business people, families, tourists, and other hotel patrons.

Type of Service. Room service orders are given over the phone. The orders are placed on trays or heating units and delivered to the individual's room. This service is American.

→

ROOM SERVICE IS AVAILABLE
From 6:30 a.m. until 1:00 a.m.
All Orders are subject to a 1.25 Service Charge, plus 15% Gratuity.

FRUITS & JUICES
Fresh Squeezed Orange, Apple
and Grapefruit Juice 2.50
Assorted Chilled Juices 1.50
Seasonal Melon 1.95
Seasonal Berries 2.25
Grapefruit or Pineapple 1.95

BREAKFAST BAKERIES
Bagel with Cream Cheese 1.75
Hot Buttermilk Biscuits 1.50
Breakfast Pastry 1.75
Toasted English Muffins 1.50
Hot Buttered Toast 1.25
Raisin Toast 1.25   Croissants 1.75

CEREALS
Hot or Cold Cereals 1.75
With Milk, Half & Half or Skim Milk
Cereal with Fruit 2.50
Granola 2.50

SIDES
Two Eggs, Any Style 2.95
One Egg, Any Style 2.25
Bacon Strips or Sausage 1.95
Ham Steak 2.95   Canadian Bacon 2.25

BREAKFAST ENTREES
Eggs Benedict 5.50
Ham & Cheese Omelette 5.25
Mushroom Omelette 4.95
Pancake Stack 3.25
Raisin French Toast 3.95

BEVERAGES
Freshly Brewed Coffee and Decaffeinated Coffee
10 oz. 1.95   32 oz. 4.00
Tea 1.25   Hot Chocolate 1.25   Milk 1.25

BREAKFAST
Daily 6:30 a.m. - 11:30 a.m.; Sunday 6:30 a.m. - 12:00 noon

COMPLETE BREAKFASTS

ALL-AMERICAN 6.25
Chilled Juice, Two Eggs Any Style, Bacon Strips or Sausage Links,
Breakfast Potatoes, Buttered Toast and Choice of Beverage.

FAST FARE 5.75
Chilled Juice, Scrambled Eggs with Diced Ham,
Breakfast Potatoes, Hot Biscuits or Buttered Toast
and Choice of Beverage.

THE CONTINENTAL 4.25
Chilled Juice or Fresh Fruit, Breakfast Bakery, English Muffin
or Toasted Bagel with Cream Cheese
and Choice of Beverage.

COUNTRY FAIR 5.95
Chilled Juice, Short Stack of Pancakes topped with an Egg,
Warm Syrup and Whipped Butter, Bacon Strips or
Sausage Links and Choice of Beverage.

NEW ENGLAND HOSPITALITY 4.95
Chilled Juice, Raisin French Toast served with
Choice of Warm Syrup and Whipped Butter or Apple Butter,
Sour Cream and Toasted Nuts and Choice of Beverage.

All Orders are subject to a 1.25 Service Charge, plus 15% Gratuity.

HOT HORS d'OEUVRES
Priced Per Dozen Pieces.

DEEP FRIED ZUCCHINI 4.95   *EGG ROLLS 5.95*

DEEP FRIED ONION RINGS 4.95   *BUFFALO WINGS 4.75*

POTATO SKINS 4.50

CHEESE WEDGES 6.25   *BEEF KNISHES 8.95*

ASSORTMENT of THREE 5.75   *MINI FRANKS 5.95*

RAW BAR
By the Dozen

CLAMS or OYSTERS on the HALF SHELL 11.50

ICED SHRIMP 15.00

SNACKS
For Two or More

CRUDITE PLATTER 5.25
Bleu Cheese Dip accompanied by Fresh Vegetables.

BOWL of CHIPS or PRETZELS 4.95

BOWL of MIXED NUTS 9.50

CHEESE & FRUIT PLATE for TWO 10.95

NACHOS 4.25
Crisp Tortilla Chips with Melted Cheese, Hot Peppers,
Guacamole, Sour Cream and Salsa.

All Orders are subject to a 1.25 Service Charge, plus 15% Gratuity.

HORS d'OEUVRES & SNACKS

Figure 4-10.   Room service menu. *(Courtesy of The Marriott, Providence, RI.)*

APPETIZERS

RAW BAR
Oysters .95   Clams .95   Shrimp 1.25
Pick and choose for your favorite combination.

SAUTE of MARINATED SHRIMP 5.95
Prepared Cajun Style.

BAKED SMOKED SAUSAGE 3.95
With a Honey Mustard Sauce and Poached Apple.

THREE CHEESE PENNE 4.50
Imported Pasta tossed with a Sauce of Three Cheeses and Sun-Dried Tomatoes.

DEEP FRIED CROQUETTES 4.25
Vermont Cheddar and Wild Rice Croquettes, complemented with a Spicy Tomato Sauce.

RHODE ISLAND CLAM CHOWDER 2.25
Brothy with lots of Clams.

NEW ENGLAND CLAM CHOWDER 2.25
Thick and Creamy.

DAILY CHEF'S SELECTION 2.00

ONION SOUP 3.00
Baked with a Crouton and Cheese.

SALADS

FRESH SPINACH 5.95
With a Hot Dressing of Duck Confit, Garlic and Vinegar.

SHRIMP & SCALLOP 5.50
Over Angel Hair Pasta, tossed with a Creamy Peppercorn Dressing.

HOUSE SALAD 2.25
Boston Lettuce with Fresh Tomatoes and a Mustard Chive Dressing.

All Orders are subject to a 1.25 Service Charge, plus 15% Gratuity.

TORTILLA FLATS

HONEY FRIED CHICKEN 6.75
A Half Chicken deep fried and served with Cole Slaw and French Fries.

NARRAGANSETT BASKET 7.25
*Deep Fried Clams, Scallops and Whitefish, served with Cole Slaw,
French Fries and Tartar Sauce.*

SHRIMP TEASE 7.25
*Shrimp in a Coconut Batter nestled in a Bed of French Fries.
Served with Cole Slaw and Cocktail Sauce.*

SENSATIONAL SANDWICHES

MARRIOTT CLUB SANDWICH 5.50
Piled Three High with Turkey, Bacon, Lettuce and Tomato, served with Potato Chips.

CHICKEN CASHEW SALAD 5.50
Served on a Croissant, a mouth-watering and crunchy delight, try it with tuna.

REUBEN 5.50
*A Combination of Corned Beef, Sauerkraut and Russian Dressing
on Dark Rye. Served with French Fries and a Dill Pickle Strip.*

STEAK & BOURSIN 6.25
Thin Sliced Steak served on a Croissant with Boursin Cheese and French Fries.

VEGETABLE POCKET 4.50
*A Pita Pocket filled with Sauteed Broccoli, Cauliflower, Onion, Red and
Green Pepper, Mushrooms and Melted Jack Cheese. Served with French Fries.*

PROVISIONS BURGER 5.25
*Freshly Ground Beef served with or without Cheese
on a Grilled Kaiser Roll, with French Fries.*

ELEGANT BURGER 5.95
*Freshly Ground Beef, covered with Swiss, Bleu and
Cheddar Cheeses and served with French Fries.*

BACON CHEESEBURGER 5.50
*Your Choice of Cheddar, Jack or American Cheese,
topped with Bacon and served with French Fries.*

All Orders are subject to a 1.25 Service Charge, plus 15% Gratuity.

ALL DAY MENU

DINNER
Daily 5:00 p.m. - 11:00 p.m.

ENTREES

Ask the operator for Today's Special Selections.

SCALLOPINE of VEAL SAUTE 15.95
Served with a Pan Sauce of Lemon, White Wine, Butter and Fresh Seasonal Vegetables.

PRIME RIB of BEEF 15.95
Herb Au Jus and Fresh Popovers.

TENDERLOIN of BEEF 16.95
With Confit of Bermuda Onion and Red Wine Butter.

BROILED NEW YORK SIRLOIN STRIP STEAK 16.25
Topped with a Hot Pepper Butter and garnished with Grilled Scallions.

BONELESS BREAST of CHICKEN PICCATA 11.75
With Tagliatelli Pasta, served with a clear Sauce of Butter, Capers and Herbs.

NEW ENGLAND STYLE SCROD 12.95
Baked with Herbed Bread Crumbs and Butter, served with New Potatoes.

FRESH SWORDFISH STEAK 15.25
*Marinated in Olive Oil and Spices, served over
Herbed Diced Tomatoes with New Red Potatoes.*

FETTUCCINE with VIRGINIA HAM and SHRIMP 12.25
In Basil Cream Sauce.

SAUTEED MEDALLIONS of VEAL and SPANISH RED SHRIMP 17.95
With Sauce of Wine, Pernod and Cream.

A SEAFOOD MEDLEY in LOBSTER SAUCE 12.95
Over Tagliatelli Pasta.

SAUTEED CHICKEN and SHRIMP 13.75
With Red Peppers and Bok Choy, served over Rice Noodles.

ROAST RACK of LAMB with WALNUT HERB TOPPING 19.50
Accompanied by Rosemary and Garlic Sauce and Braised Navy Beans.

Specialty Wines Available by the Glass

All Orders are subject to a 1.25 Service Charge, plus 15% Gratuity.

Figure 4-10. Continued.

TWICE A DAY-NEVER ON SUNDAE
Why: Because the Sauces will dazzle you into alpsomania - they are rich and full bodied.

THE SAUCES

Inoui Fudge	*Real Butterscotch*	*Strawberries*
Sticky Bun Pecan	*Pineapple*	*Rum Raisins*

FREEZER FRESH HOMEMADE ICE CREAMS

Vanilla   Strawberry   Coffee   Chocolate   Peppermint   Oreo Cookie

1 Scooper/1 Sauce 2.25

2 Scooper/2 Sauces 2.75

3 Scooper/3 Sauces 3.25

4 Scooper/4 Sauces 3.95

CHOCOLATE SWEET CHOCOLATE 3.75
A Chocolate Chambord Cake set adrift in a pool of tantalizing Chocolate Sauce.

DOUBLE DEVIL DELIGHT 3.95
Your Choice of Ice Cream covered with the Sauce of your taste,
resting on a rich Chocolate Brownie and topped with Whipped Cream.

STRAWBERRY GRAND MARINER CREPE 3.95
Strawberry Ice Cream rolled into a Crepe, covered with a Strawberry
Grand Marnier Sauce, topped with a Strawberry and Whipped Cream.
"For the Strawberry in all of us."

COOKIE MONSTER 3.50
Fresh hot gooey Chocolate Chip Cookie with your favorite
Ice Cream and mounds of Whipped Cream.

THE BIG APPLE 2.75   A la Mode 3.25
The flakiest of Pie Crusts; the sweetest of Apples.
"Grandma would be proud."

FLAVORED CHEESECAKES 3.25
Strawberry   Chocolate Chip   Plain

PECAN PIE 2.75   CARROT CAKE 3.25

All Orders are subject to a 1.25 Service Charge, plus 15% Gratuity.

DESSERTS

BEVERAGE & BAR SELECTIONS

DOMESTIC BEER 2.00   IMPORTED BEER 2.75

YOUR FAVORITE COCKTAIL
House 3.00   Premium 3.50

HOUSE WINE 2.75
Specialty Wines Available by the Glass

Please call Room Service for Bottled Liquor Selections and Prices.

WINE LIST

CHAMPAGNE

Bouvet Brut	*12.00*
Korbel Brut	*19.25*
Freixenet Cordon Negro	*12.75*
Split	*9.50*
Dom Perignon	*95.00*

RED WINES

Louis Jadot Beaujolais Villages	*12.00*
Split	*7.00*
Beaulieu Vineyards Cabernet Sauvignon	*18.75*
Robert Mondavi Pinot Noir	*18.25*
Hidden Cellars Zinfandel	*12.50*

WHITE WINES

Louis Jadot Chardonnay	*18.00*
Glenn Ellen Chardonnay	*12.50*
Hidden Cellar Sauvignon Blanc	*11.25*
Mondavi Fume Blanc	*19.25*
Chapin Landais Vouvray	*14.00*
Santa Sofia Soave	*10.00*
Split	*7.00*

BLUSH WINES

Sutter Home White Zinfandel	*12.75*
Moc-Baril Cabernet	*9.00*
Split	*6.00*

All Orders are subject to a 1.25 Service Charge, plus 15% Gratuity.

Figure 4-10. Continued.

COCKTAILS & WINE

Ethnic Menu

RITZ-CARLTON,
Boston, Massachusetts

Type of Menu. The Ritz-Carlton is a combination of an a la carte and semi a la carte menu (Fig. 4-11). A la carte items include hors d'oeuvres, soup, salads, and beverages. The semi a la carte items come with the entrees. The menu is in its original language, French. The menu explains the food items in English.

Food Availability. French ingredients can be obtained easily through the local purveyors.

Equipment. The salads and vegetables require a slicer. The entrees require ovens, range top, and guéridons for tableside cookery. The scallops, lobster, and swordfish require a broiler.

Expense Level. Expense level is moderate to high for this type of operation. The Chateaubriand Bouquetiere for two is $48.00 and the Foie de Veau Lyonnaise is $17.00.

Atmosphere. The Ritz-Carlton's logo, a lion's head, with the white background and royal blue printing, gives the menu a feeling of richness that the Ritz-Carlton's decor exudes throughout its operation. The headings and subheadings, written in French, give an appearance of a true ethnic restaurant.

Proficiency. The front and back of the house employees have to be skilled. The waiters and waitresses not only have to pronounce the menu items correctly, but need a thorough knowledge of how the food items are prepared. The service personnel and the cooks have to know various cooking techniques such as sautéing for the sole and lobster dishes and sauce cookery for the various veal, beef, and chicken dishes.

Customer Makeup. The customers are French–Americans, business people, families, and couples.

Type of Service. The service is French.

--→

LES HORS D'OEUVRE FROIDS

Caviar Frais Petrossian Fresh Imported Russian Ossetra Caviar	36.00	Huitres ou Palourdes en Saison Oysters or Little Neck Clams in Season	8.00
Saumon Fume de Nouvelle Ecosse Nova Scotia Smoked Salmon	12.25	Terrine de Foie Gras de Strasbourg Imported Strasbourg Foie Gras	20.50
Cocktail de Homard, Sauce Mercedes Lobster Cocktail, Sauce Mercedes	14.50	Jambon de Foret Noire aux Melon ou Asperges Westphalian Ham and Melon or Asparagus	8.00
Saumon Marine Norvegien, Sauce Moutard Marinated Fresh Salmon, Mustard Dill Sauce	8.50	Pate en Croute Maison House Pate in Crust, Cumberland Sauce	9.00
Coupe de Crevettes, Sauce Rouge Gulf Shrimp, Cocktail Sauce	13.25	Terrine de Fruits de Mer, Sauce Aneth Seafood Terrine, Dill Sauce	9.00
L'Avocat Farci au Crabe, Sauce Cognac Avocado Filled with Crabmeat, Cognac Sauce	13.25	Coupe de Crabe Ravigote Native Crabmeat, Sauce Ravigote	12.50

LES HORS D'OEUVRE CHAUDS

Tartelette de Champignons a la Creme Mushrooms, Shallots, Cream, Madeira in Tart Shell	9.00	Nouilles Sautees aux Saumon Fume et Concombre Linguini, Smoked Salmon, Cucumber	13.00
Ragout d'Homard et Ris de Veau Lobster and Sweetbreads in Pastry	14.50	Escargots de Bourgogne French Snails in Garlic Butter	9.50
Coquille de Fruits de Mer au Basilic en Feuilletage Seafood, Basil Cream, Puff Pastry	12.00	Palourdes au Four Casino Baked Clams with Bacon	8.00

LES POTAGES

Chowder de Palourdes du Boston Boston Clam Chowder	3.00	Consomme aux Chanterelles et Xeres Consomme with Chanterelles and Sherry	3.75
Soupe a l'Oignon Gratinee Baked Onion Soup	4.25	Soupe de Tortue Louisiane New Orleans Style Turtle Soup	4.25
Bisque de Homard Americaine Bisque of Lobster with Cognac	4.25	Vichyssoise en Tasse Frappe Chilled Cream of Leeks and Potatoes	3.00

LE BUFFET FROID

Salade de Homard a la Ritz Fresh Lobster Salad	32.00	Salade de Crevettes Oriental Shrimp, Soy, Vegetables, Ginger	29.00
Bifteck Tatare, Facon du Chef Raw Prime Beef, Seasoned Tableside	24.00	Salade de Volaille a la Ritz Breast of Chicken Salad Garnished	17.00

LES POISSONS

Escalope de Saumon Hollandaise Poached Salmon, Hollandaise	25.00	Homard Etuve au Whiskey Sauteed Maine Lobster in Whiskey Sauce	35.00
Filet de Boston Scrod au Naturel Broiled Boston Scrod	19.00	Espadon Grille, Sauce Mousseline au Raifort Grilled Swordfish, Horseradish Mousseline	24.00
Sole du Douvre Saute Meuniere Sauteed Dover Sole	29.00	Scampis Saute au Beurre d'Orange Albert Jumbo Shrimp, Orange Butter Sauce	26.00
Coquille Saint Jacques, Pain Grille Broiled Scallops on Toast	25.00	Supreme de Fletan Poele au Cresson et Orange Poached Halibut, Watercress and Oranges	25.00
Homard Nouvelle Angleterre Etuve ou Grille Steamed or Broiled Lobster	37.00	Saumon Farcie au Crabe, Sauce Champagne Filet of Salmon Stuffed with Crab, Champagne Sauce	27.00

Truite de Riviere, Poele Grand Pere   23.00
Sauteed Trout, Port Wine and Bacon Sauce

Figure 4-11. Ethnic menu. *(Courtesy of Ritz Carlton, Boston, MA.)*

LES ENTREES

Entrecote Saute aux Poivre a la Cognac
    Sauteed Sirloin Steak, Cognac, Peppercorns
	24.50	Caneton Poele Montmorency
		    Roasted Duckling, Cherry Sauce
			23.00

Ris de Veau aux Coeurs d'Artichauts
    Sauteed Sweetbreads, Artichoke Hearts
	23.00	Supreme de Volaille aux Queues de Langoustines
		  et Creme
		    Breast of Chicken, Baby Lobster, Cream Sauce
			21.00

Rognons de Veau Saute Berrichonne
    Veal Kidneys, Red Wine, Onions, Mushrooms,
    Chestnuts
	18.50	Medaillons de Veau Saute Parisien
		    Medallions of Veal, Sauteed
			23.00

Medaillons d'Agneau Saute Delice de Foret
    Medallions of Lamb, Mushrooms
	21.00	Foie de Veau Lyonnaise
		    Calves Liver Sauteed with Onions
			17.00

Cote de Veau Saute aux Morilles
    Sauteed Veal Chop, Morel Sauce
	23.00	Escalope de Veau Saute Viennoise
		    Breaded Veal Cutlet, Capers and Anchovy
			22.50

Cailles Saute aux Peches
    Sauteed Quails, Brandied Peaches
	21.00	Selle de Chevreuil Grand Veneur
		    Medallions of Venison, Game Sauce
			25.00

LES GRILLADES ET ROTIS

Carre d'Agneau Roti Dijonaise (Pour Deux)
    Roast Rack of American Lamb,
    Assorted Vegetables (2 persons)
	48.00	Chateaubriand Bouquetiere (Pour Deux)
		    Chateaubriand, Garnish of Vegetables,
		    Sauce Bearnaise (2 persons)
			48.00

Faisan Roti a la Normande (Pour Deux)
    Pheasant, Apples, Calvados, Crouton (2 persons)
	48.00	Paillarde de Veau aux Ciboulettes
		    Thin Veal Cutlet, Chive Butter
			22.50

Entrecote Grille, Beurre Cafe de Paris
    Broiled Sirloin Steak, Herb Butter
	24.50	Cotelette d'Agneau Vert Pre
		    Lamb Chops, Watercress
			23.50

Filet de Boeuf Wellington
    Individual Beef Wellington
	25.00	Filet Mignon Grille Bearnaise
		    Tenderloin of Beef, Bearnaise Sauce
			24.50

LES LEGUMES ET POMMES DE TERRE

L'Assiette de Legumes Assortis 12.50
Assorted Vegetable Plate

Haricots Verts au Beurre
    Green Beans with Butter
	2.25	Champignons de Paris Sautes
		    Sauteed Mushrooms, Garlic Butter
			2.25

Brocoli Hollandaise
    Broccoli Hollandaise
	2.75	Asperges au Beurre ou Hollandaise en Saison
		    Fresh Asparagus, Butter or Hollandaise Sauce
			5.25

Carottes Vichy Persilles 2.25
Carrots Cooked in Vichy Water

Pommes Delmonico 1.75
  Creamed Potatoes,
  Green Peppers,
  Pimiento
	Pommes Anglaise 1.75
	  Steamed Potatoes,
	  Parsley
		Pommes Lyonnaise 1.75
		  Sauteed Potatoes,
		  Onion
			Pommes Noisettes 1.75
			  Small Roast
			  Potatoes

LES SALADES

Laitue de Boston Nanon
    Boston Lettuce, Sliced Eggs, Walnuts
	3.00	Salade de Celeriac Allemande
		    Marinated Celery Root Salad
			4.00

Endive de Belgique en Saison
    Belgian Endive in Season
	4.00	Coeur de Romaine Vinaigrette
		    Hearts of Romaine
			3.00

Tomates et Cresson
    Tomato and Watercress
	3.00	Salade Compose a la Ritz
		    Boston Lettuce, Sprouts, Marinated Goat Cheese
			4.00

Salade de Cesare (Pour Deux)
    A Traditional Caesar Salad (2 persons)
	11.00	Salade Grande Ferme (Pour Deux)
		    Chickory, Roquefort, Bacon, Croutons (2 persons)
			9.50

LES BOISSONS

Cafe ou Cafe Decafeine	1.50	The 1.75 Ceylon and India, Earl Grey's, Keemun, Darjeeling or Lapsang Souchang
Espresso 2.75	Cappuccino 3.00	

Dessert Souffles and Baked Alaska require 45 minutes
Please consult captain.

Mass. Meals Tax 5%

Specialty Menu

PIRATE'S HOUSE,
Savannah, Georgia

Type of Menu. The style of menu (Fig. 4-12) is a la carte and semi a la carte. The a la carte items include the soups and beverages. The semi a la carte items include the entrees.

The Pirate's House specializes in seafood. Seafood is offered in soups, like Seafood Gumbo, in the specials of the day, like Shrimp-Burgers, in the salads, like Golden Isles Shrimp Salad, and of course in the entrees, like Shrimp and Crabmeat au Gratin.

Food Availability. The location of the Pirates' House in Savannah, Georgia, on the coast, allows the restaurant to purchase fresh seafood daily.

The menu includes nonseafood items such as the Glorified Hamburger for customers who do not want seafood or who may be allergic to seafood.

Equipment. The equipment needed to produce this menu is as follows: Soups require a stockpot on top of a range or a soup kettle; quiche requires an oven; hamburgers and fish fillets require a broiler; fried shrimp requires a fryolator.

Expense Level. The Pirate's House menu is moderately priced with prices ranging from a cup of Seafood Gumbo at $2.75 to the Shrimp and Crabmeat au Gratin at $7.25.

Atmosphere. The light blue background, the name of the restaurant, and the artwork all reflect the restaurant's specialty of seafood.

Proficiency. The waiters and waitresses should be able to explain the items on the menu and how they are prepared.

Customer Makeup. The customer market is predominantly families, tourists, and local business people.

Type of Service. The service is American.

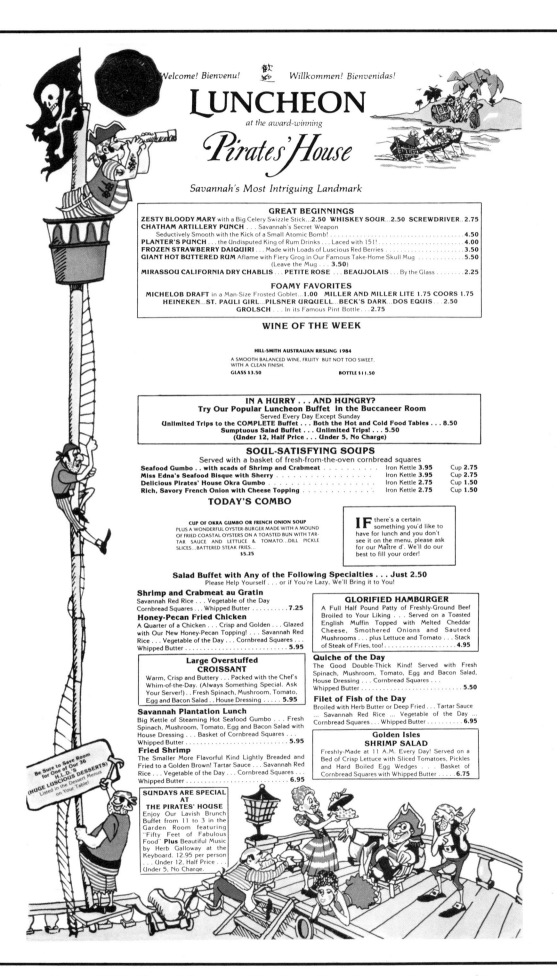

Welcome! Bienvenu! 歓迎 Willkommen! Bienvenidas!

LUNCHEON
at the award-winning
Pirates' House

Savannah's Most Intriguing Landmark

GREAT BEGINNINGS

ZESTY BLOODY MARY with a Big Celery Swizzle Stick...**2.50 WHISKEY SOUR**...**2.50 SCREWDRIVER**...**2.75**
CHATHAM ARTILLERY PUNCH . . . Savannah's Secret Weapon
    Seductively Smooth with the Kick of a Small Atomic Bomb! **4.50**
PLANTER'S PUNCH . . . the Undisputed King of Rum Drinks . . . Laced with 151! **4.00**
FROZEN STRAWBERRY DAIQUIRI . . . Made with Loads of Luscious Red Berries **3.50**
GIANT HOT BUTTERED RUM Aflame with Fiery Grog in Our Famous Take-Home Skull Mug **5.50**
    (Leave the Mug . . . 3.50)
MIRASSOU CALIFORNIA DRY CHABLIS . . . **PETITE ROSE** . . . **BEAUJOLAIS** . . . By the Glass **2.25**

FOAMY FAVORITES

MICHELOB DRAFT in a Man-Size Frosted Goblet...**1.00 MILLER AND MILLER LITE 1.75 COORS 1.75**
HEINEKEN...**ST. PAULI GIRL**...**PILSNER URQUELL**...**BECK'S DARK**...**DOS EQUIS** . . . **2.50**
GROLSCH . . . In its Famous Pint Bottle . . . **2.75**

WINE OF THE WEEK

HILL-SMITH AUSTRALIAN RIESLING 1984

A SMOOTH BALANCED WINE, FRUITY BUT NOT TOO SWEET,
WITH A CLEAN FINISH.
GLASS $3.50   **BOTTLE $11.50**

IN A HURRY . . . AND HUNGRY?
Try Our Popular Luncheon Buffet in the Buccaneer Room
Served Every Day Except Sunday
Unlimited Trips to the COMPLETE Buffet . . . Both the Hot and Cold Food Tables . . . 8.50
Sumptuous Salad Buffet . . . Unlimited Trips! . . . 5.50
(Under 12, Half Price . . . Under 5, No Charge)

SOUL-SATISFYING SOUPS
Served with a basket of fresh-from-the-oven cornbread squares

Seafood Gumbo . . with scads of Shrimp and Crabmeat	Iron Kettle **3.95**	Cup **2.75**
Miss Edna's Seafood Bisque with Sherry	Iron Kettle **3.95**	Cup **2.75**
Delicious Pirates' House Okra Gumbo	Iron Kettle **2.75**	Cup **1.50**
Rich, Savory French Onion with Cheese Topping	Iron Kettle **2.75**	Cup **1.50**

TODAY'S COMBO

CUP OF OKRA GUMBO OR FRENCH ONION SOUP
PLUS A WONDERFUL OYSTER-BURGER MADE WITH A MOUND
OF FRIED COASTAL OYSTERS ON A TOASTED BUN WITH TAR-
TAR SAUCE AND LETTUCE & TOMATO...DILL PICKLE
SLICES...BATTERED STEAK FRIES...
$5.25

IF there's a certain something you'd like to have for lunch and you don't see it on the menu, please ask for our Maître d'. We'll do our best to fill your order!

Salad Buffet with Any of the Following Specialties . . . Just 2.50
Please Help Yourself . . . or if You're Lazy, We'll Bring it to You!

Shrimp and Crabmeat au Gratin
Savannah Red Rice . . . Vegetable of the Day
Cornbread Squares . . . Whipped Butter **7.25**

Honey-Pecan Fried Chicken
A Quarter of a Chicken . . . Crisp and Golden . . . Glazed
with Our New Honey-Pecan Topping! . . . Savannah Red
Rice . . . Vegetable of the Day . . . Cornbread Squares . . .
Whipped Butter **5.95**

GLORIFIED HAMBURGER
A Full Half Pound Patty of Freshly-Ground Beef
Broiled to Your Liking . . . Served on a Toasted
English Muffin Topped with Melted Cheddar
Cheese, Smothered Onions and Sauteed
Mushrooms . . . plus Lettuce and Tomato . . . Stack
of Steak of Fries, too! **4.95**

Large Overstuffed
CROISSANT
Warm, Crisp and Buttery . . . Packed with the Chef's
Whim-of-the-Day. (Always Something Special. Ask
Your Server!) . . . Fresh Spinach, Mushroom, Tomato,
Egg and Bacon Salad . . House Dressing **5.95**

Quiche of the Day
The Good Double-Thick Kind! Served with Fresh
Spinach, Mushroom, Tomato, Egg and Bacon Salad,
House Dressing . . . Cornbread Squares . . .
Whipped Butter **5.50**

Savannah Plantation Lunch
Big Kettle of Steaming Hot Seafood Gumbo . . . Fresh
Spinach, Mushroom, Tomato, Egg and Bacon Salad with
House Dressing . . . Basket of Cornbread Squares . . .
Whipped Butter **5.95**

Filet of Fish of the Day
Broiled with Herb Butter or Deep Fried . . . Tartar Sauce
. . . Savannah Red Rice . . . Vegetable of the Day . . .
Cornbread Squares . . . Whipped Butter **6.95**

Fried Shrimp
The Smaller More Flavorful Kind Lightly Breaded and
Fried to a Golden Brown! Tartar Sauce . . . Savannah Red
Rice . . . Vegetable of the Day . . . Cornbread Squares . . .
Whipped Butter **6.95**

Golden Isles
SHRIMP SALAD
Freshly-Made at 11 A.M. Every Day! Served on a
Bed of Crisp Lettuce with Sliced Tomatoes, Pickles
and Hard Boiled Egg Wedges . . . Basket of
Cornbread Squares with Whipped Butter **6.75**

SUNDAYS ARE SPECIAL AT THE PIRATES' HOUSE
Enjoy Our Lavish Brunch Buffet from 11 to 3 in the Garden Room featuring "Fifty Feet of Fabulous Food" **Plus** Beautiful Music by Herb Galloway at the Keyboard. 12.95 per person . . . Under 12, Half Price . . . Under 5, No Charge.

Be Sure to Save Room for One of Our 36 H.L.D.'S (HUGE LUSCIOUS DESSERTS) Listed in the Dessert Menus on Your Table!

Figure 4-12. Specialty menu. *(Courtesy of Pirate's House, Savannah, GA.)*

Standard Menu

DURGIN PARK OF COPLEY PLACE,
Boston, Massachusetts

Type of Menu. The style of menu (Fig. 4-13) is a combination of a la carte and semi a la carte. A la carte items are represented by the appetizers, soups, salads, desserts, and beverages. The semi a la carte items are represented by the entrees. The menu permits entree selections to be interchangeable for both lunch and dinner.

Food Availability. The location of the Durgin Park Restaurant in Boston, Massachusetts, is conducive to obtaining the items on the menu. Fresh seafood, meats, and produce are available year-round in Boston.

Equipment. The major pieces of equipment needed are as follows: steam kettles for the sauces, stocks, and soups; a broiler for the broiled steaks and lamb chops; fryolators for the fried clams and fried oysters; a baker's oven for the baked beans and desserts; and a steamer pressure cooker for the lobsters and vegetables.

Expense Level. The prices are low, ranging from $3.00 for Frankfort and Beans to $4.50 for the Roast Stuffed Duck Platter to $8.00 for the Boiled Live Two Pound Lobster.

Atmosphere. The decor is relaxing, with plants and a wooden bar.

Proficiency. The skills of the cooks are needed in the areas of sautéing for Chicken Livers Sauté in Wine with Bacon; broiling for Broiled Lamb Chops; braising for Yankee Pot Roast; frying for the Fried Scallops; roasting for Roast Stuffed Turkey; and baking for Hot Fresh Apple Pie. The waiters, waitresses, and cooks have to be organized in their working habits because the menu is predominantly a short-order menu that requires quick service.

Customer Makeup. Tourists, families, shoppers, couples, and local business people are the customers.

Type of Service. The service is predominantly American.

A La Carte Menu

Apple Juice	.25	Tomato Juice	.25

Oysters and Clams

Oysters, Half Doz.	1.25	Oyster Stew	3.00
Oyster Platter, One Doz.	2.25	Half milk-half cream	
Cherry Stone, Half Doz.	1.25	Cherry Stone Stew	3.00
Cherry Stone Platter, One Doz.	2.25	Half milk-half cream	

Soup and Chowder

Cup of Soup or Chowder	.25	Plate of Onion Soup	.75
Plate of Fish Chowder	.75	Cup of Chicken Soup	.25
Plate of Vegetable Soup	.75		

Includes Potato Mashed Baked Potato or French Fried Potatoes Hash Brown

Frankfort and Beans	3.00
Broiled Pork Chop	3.00
Broiled Hamburger Steak	3.00
Yankee Pot Roast	3.00
Roast Leg of Lamb	3.00
Chicken Livers Saute in Wine with Bacon	3.00
Roast Loin of Pork with Fresh Apple Sauce	3.00
Roast Stuffed Duck	3.25
Broiled or Fried Native Chicken	3.25
New England Boiled Dinner	3.25
Roast Stuffed Turkey	3.25
Broiled Calves Liver (Bacon or Onions)	3.25
Broiled Scotch Ham Steak	3.25
Broiled Lamb Steak	3.25
Broiled Hamburg Platter	4.00
Broiled Lamb Chops (2)	4.00
Broiled Pork Chop Platter (3 Chops)	4.00
Broiled or Fried Native Chicken Platter	4.00
Roast Stuffed Duck Platter	4.50
Broiled Lamb Chops, Mixed Grill (2)	4.50
Roast Prime Rib of Beef (with Vegetable)	6.50
Broiled Tenderloin Steak (with Vegetable)	6.50
Broiled Sirloin Steak (with Vegetable)	6.50

We are not responsible for any steak ordered well done.

We use 38 to 40% Whipped Cream on all Desserts

Coffee Jelly (Made from our own Coffee)	.25	Hot Fresh Apple Pan Dowdy with Ice Cream or Whipped Cream	.75
Fresh Apple Sauce	.25	Hot Deep Dish Fresh Apple Pie with Whipped Cream or Ice Cream	.75
Hot Fresh Apple Pie	.50		
Hot Fudge Sundae	.75	Hot Mince Pie	.50
Baked Indian Pudding with Ice Cream or Whipped Cream	.75		

Vanilla	.35	Frozen Pudding	.35
Chocolate	.35	Special	.35

Ice Cream

Coffee, Tea or Milk	.25	Ginger Ale or 7-Up	.25
Iced Tea or Coffee	.25	Coca Cola or Root Beer	.25

Drinks

Also 18 to 20% Cream used for Coffee

All Our Steaks, Chops, Calves Liver and Hamburgers are Charcoal Broiled on our Open Fire Place on the Dining Room Floor with real Wood Charcoal. We do not use Briquettes

Figure 4-13. Standard menu. *(Courtesy of Durgin Park of Copley Place, Boston, MA.)*

YOU ARE INVITED TO VISIT OUR KITCHEN

NOT RESPONSIBLE FOR HATS, COATS OR ANY ARTICLES LEFT IN OUR DINING ROOMS

Salads

Fresh Lobster Salad	6.00	Fresh Lobster Cocktail	6.00
Shrimp Salad	1.50	Shrimp Cocktail	1.25
Lettuce and Tomato Salad	.75		

Vegetables

Cabbage	.35	Boiled Turnip	.35
Boiled Onions	.35	Stewed Tomatoes	.35
Sliced Onions	.35	Cole Slaw	.35
Carrots	.35	Lettuce	.35
Green Peas	.35	Squash	.35
Kernel Corn	.35	Sliced Tomatoes	.35
Sauerkraut	.35	Boston Baked Beans	.35

Fish

Includes Potato Mashed Baked Potato or French Fried Potatoes or Hash Brown

Please allow 20 minutes for all Broiled Fish orders.

We use only Fresh Lobster Meat at all times

French Fried Onion Rings, 75c

Fresh Boston Broiled Schrod	3.00
Fresh Boston Fried Cod	3.00
Broiled Mackerel	3.00
Fried Filet of Sole	3.00
Broiled Halibut	3.00
Ipswich Fried Clams	3.00
Fried Scallops	3.00
Sea Food Plate	3.00
Fried Fresh Oysters	3.00
Oyster Stew, Half Milk, Half Cream	3.00
Cherry Stone Stew, Half Milk, Half Cream	3.00
Fried Shrimp	3.00
Broiled Scallops	3.50
Sea Food Platter	4.00
Fresh Lobster Stew	6.00
Fresh Lobster Saute in Butter and Wine	6.00
Fresh Lobster Newberg	6.00
Fresh Lobster and Shrimp Newberg	6.00
Boiled Live Two Pound Lobster	8.00
Broiled Live Two Pound Lobster	8.00

Please allow thirty minutes for the proper preparation of Live Lobsters.

All our fried foods are cooked in pure vegetable shortening.

Bar Service is now available at your table.

We use only fresh strawberries on our strawberry short cakes and strawberry sundaes.

WE DO NOT SUBSTITUTE

Our desserts, corn bread, and baked beans are baked in our own bakery on the premises.

Our Boston Baked Beans are Baked the Old-Fashioned Way in Stone Crocks in Our Own Bakeshop on the Premises

Massachusetts Old Age Tax of 5% added to all meals amounting to $1.00 or over.

Figure 4-13. Continued.

The Yield Test

Yield tests are an essential part of determining the profit of a menu item. This chapter discusses the types of yield tests, how to do a yield test, and the importance of doing yield tests.

OBJECTIVES

1. To define yield tests.
2. To explain how to use yield tests within the foodservice industry.
3. To discuss how a yield test is used when planning menus.
4. To calculate the costing of yield tests.

DEFINING THE YIELD TEST

A yield test is used to determine the amount of edible product (EP) and the amount of waste product (WP) of a particular food item.

It is essential for the menu planner to know the amount of EP (also referred to as *yield*) in the food items so that the owner does not lose money by purchasing a food item that yields very little EP and produces WP that cannot be used. The higher a food item's yield, the more portions there are to be made into profit.

Yield tests should be done at least three times on every food item that is purchased in your foodservice operation, so that management, the chef, and the cooks will know how much each food item will yield according to the recipes being used in the foodservice operation. Because of the perishability of the food items and the wide variances of uniformity in the food items used, the amount of yield will differ from delivery to delivery. Food items such as meats, poultry, produce, fruits, and seafood that have a high perishability factor should have yield tests done on a regular basis.

Management must be demanding when setting specifications for food items. Specifications are factors that determine a standard of quality in a food product. Examples of such factors are

- Weight
- Color
- Shape
- Grade
- Texture
- Size
- Odor
- Packaging

♦ Product temperature
♦ Yield grade

It is these specifications that will help determine the quality of the food to be served to the guests.

A yield test is to be done under two conditions: in a controlled environment and during actual production time. A controlled environment exists when the person conducting the yield test is not distracted by anything or anyone, is not rushed, and has all the necessary equipment to do the yield test.

The reason for conducting a yield test under both conditions is because results from a yield test under the controlled environment will give management a true count of the amount of yield on the food item. This amount will be the maximum yield the product can be expected to produce. The yield test results done under the actual production period will give management the actual yield being accomplished. This result is always lower until management trains the employees to cut and serve the food items properly to gain a better yield.

TYPES OF YIELD TESTS

There are two basic types of yield tests.

1. Convenience foods yield test
2. Fresh foods yield test

Convenience Foods

The convenience food item yield test is done on food items that have been prepackaged into cans, bags, and boxes. This test consists of cutting open the packaging and weighing the amount of edible product and the amount of packing that comes with the edible product. Packing is the extra filling placed inside a convenience food product to keep its quality. An example is the amount of liquid in most canned products.

This test will determine if the amount of packaging is what management's specifications have requested. If the amount of packing is not what the specifications require, then management is losing money by paying for excess packing. The Food and Drug Administration has set standards for the amount of packing used in all canned products.

Fresh Foods

The fresh food items yield test (see Fig. 5-1 for form) is done on food items that are purchased in an unaltered fresh state. This test consists of weighing the food items before any type of preparation has been started and after the final preparation is completed. This procedure is done in eight steps to calculate the amount of waste products.

1. Weigh the fresh food product as it is received.
2. Weigh the fresh food product after it comes out of storage. (Most foods will lose weight in storage through evaporation.)
3. Trim any undesirable parts such as fat, bones, and outer leaves.
4. Wash and weigh the fresh food product. (At this point the convenience foods yield test can be calculated in the same manner.)
5. Once the food item is prepared for cooking and is cooked, it is weighed to determine the amount of edible product loss caused through shrinkage during the cooking stage.
6. The food product is then cut into portion sizes.
7. The food product is weighed to determine the amount of edible product lost during the portioning or carving stage.
8. Once the food item has been cut into the total number of portions, the amount of waste product is totaled.

CALCULATING A YIELD TEST

Step 1

Establish the AP weight. The AP weight is the as purchased weight of the raw product that is purchased from the purveyor.

Step 2

Calculate the amount of waste. This amount is established by weighing the amount of bones, fat, outer leaves, and so forth. Once this weight has been calculated, subtract the waste from the AP amount. The amount left is the edible product.

AP weight	10 lb
−Waste products	3 lb
Edible product	7 lb

Item _____ Grade _____ Date _____

Pieces _____ Weight _____ lb _____ oz Average Wt. _____ lb _____ oz

Total Cost $ _____ at $ _____ per _____ Purveyor _____

| Breakdown | No. | Weight | | Ratio to Total Weight | Value per Pound | Total Value | Cost of ea. | | Portion | | Cost Factor per | |
		lb	oz				lb	oz	Size	Value	lb	Por.
Total												

$$\text{Cost Factor per lb or Portion} = \frac{\text{Ready-to-Eat Value per lb or Portion}}{\text{Purchase Price per lb}}$$

Cooking Loss
To find ready-to-eat value of cuts at a new market price, multiply new price per lb by the cost factor.

Item _____

Portion Size _____ Cooked _____ hr _____ min at _____ degrees

Portion Cost Factor _____ Cooked _____ hr _____ min at _____ degrees

| Breakdown | No. | Weight | | Ratio to Total Weight | Value per Pound | Total Value | Ready-to-Eat Value per | | Ready-to-Eat Portion | | Cost Factor per | |
		lb	oz				lb	oz	Size	Value	lb	Por.
Original Weight												
Loss in Trimming												
Trimmed Weight												
Loss in Cooking												
Cooked Weight												
Bones and Trim												
Loss in Slicing												
Salable Meat												

$$\text{Cost Factor per lb or Portion} = \frac{\text{Ready-to-Eat Value per lb or Portion}}{\text{Purchase Price per lb}}$$

Figure 5-1. Yield test card.

Step 3

Convert the edible product unit of measurement to the portion size. The portion size unit of measurement is in ounces so the edible product must be converted to ounces. This amount will determine the number of portions.

$$7\,lb \times 16\,oz = 112\,oz$$

Step 4

Divide the portion size into the total converted amount of the edible product.

$$\frac{112}{4}$$

$$\begin{array}{r} 28 \\ 4\,)\overline{112} \\ \underline{8\,0} \\ 32 \\ \underline{32} \\ 0 \end{array}$$

4 oz is the portion size.
112 oz is equivalent to 7 lb.
   28 is the number of portions.

Step 5

To establish the portion cost, divide the total cost by the total number of portions.

$$\begin{array}{r} .7142 \\ 28\,)\overline{20.0000} \\ \underline{19\,6} \\ 40 \\ \underline{28} \\ 120 \\ \underline{112} \\ 80 \\ \underline{56} \\ 24 \end{array}$$

.7142 = .72 portion cost.
28 is the number of portions.
$20.00 is the total cost.
This cost is calculated by multiplying the as purchased price of $2.00 per lb by the as purchased unit weight of 10 lb. The as purchased price is the current market price.

PRACTICE PROBLEMS

1. AP weight   20 lb
   AP price $3.55 lb   Total Extension _____
   Waste   2 lb   Total Number of Portions _____
   Portion size 3 oz   Portion Cost _____

2. AP weight   30 lb
   AP price $4.25 lb   Total Extension _____
   Waste   3 lb   Total Number of Portions _____
   Portion size 5 oz   Portion Cost _____

3. AP weight   8 lb
   AP price $2.10 lb   Total Extension _____
   Waste   3 lb   Total Number of Portions _____
   Portion size 6 oz   Portion Cost _____

4. AP weight   22½ lb
   AP price $1.95 lb   Total Extension _____
   Waste   3 oz   Total Number of Portions _____
   Portion size 4 oz   Portion Cost _____

The AP weight must be converted into ounces before subtracting the waste.

Answers to Practice Problems

1. Total extension is $71.00.
   Total number of portions is 96.
   Portion cost is $0.74.

2. Total extension is $127.50.
   Total number of portions is 86.4.
   Portion cost is $1.48.

3. Total extension is $16.80.
   Total number of portions is 13.3 (= 13).
   Portion cost is $1.26 (= $1.29).

4. Total extension is $43.88.
   Total number of portions is 89.25 (= 89).
   Portion cost is $0.49 (= .4930).

REVIEW QUESTIONS

1. Define yield test.

2. What do the following abbreviations mean: EP, AP, and WP?

3. What is the formula for finding a portion cost?

4. List five types of waste that can be produced during a yield test.

6

Standard Recipes

Standard recipes are needed to produce a standard-quality food product. This chapter discusses the different methods of writing recipes, different techniques for standardizing recipes, and the importance of standardizing recipes.

OBJECTIVES

1. To identify the elements of a recipe card.
2. To give the student an understanding of the importance of using standardized recipes.
3. To show standard recipe card format.
4. To illustrate different methods of recipe creativity.

DEFINING STANDARD RECIPES IN THE INDUSTRY

The objective of writing, maintaining, and using standardized recipes is to consistently guarantee the customer a quality product.

When customers enjoy what they ate at a restaurant they want to experience the enjoyment of eating those foods again. Customers expect the food quality to be the same (or better) than the most recent time they ate at the foodservice operation.

When the foodservice operation does not duplicate the same food quality every time the product is made and served, customers will be disappointed. Customers should not have to second guess the quality of food at a foodservice operation.

In today's competitive society, customers will not tolerate inconsistent food quality from a foodservice operation. Therefore, in terms of profit, a foodservice operation cannot afford to disappoint its customers by serving inconsistent food.

The fast food industry, with its standards of quick service, low prices, and organized systems to produce the same quality of foods, has taught the foodservice industry and the consumer the value of producing a standardized food product.

Not only do customers demand the best quality of food that their money will buy, but also the competition makes a demand on the foodservice operation to meet the demands of customers or be left behind in the competition. By standardizing recipes, the foodservice operation will be able to meet the high quality that is being demanded by customers as well as being competitive in the foodservice industry.

To set a standard means to adapt your food quality to a level or degree of excellence. The standardizing of your recipes is one of the first steps that must be taken to obtain the level of excellence your customers come to expect. Some smaller foodservice operations do not use standardized recipe cards per se. The expense of writing, testing, and recording the recipes on index cards or computer files is too great for most smaller operations.

Some operations can afford the expense and do realize the value of having a standardized recipe card system. Hotels, institutions, foodservice chains, and larger restaurants use standardized recipes and systems.

Not only should chefs and/or cooks know how to produce the items on the menu, but management must also have knowledge of how the food items on the menu are prepared. Many people will argue that it is sufficient for the chefs and/or cooks to know the recipes but this argument simply is not true. Management leaves the door wide open for failure if it does not know how the food items on the menu are prepared. If the chef and/or cooks cannot be at work, management must take over. If management is not familiar with the preparation and cannot fill in for chefs or cooks, the food quality will not be consistent, causing customer dissatisfaction, a loss of sales, and perhaps a damaged reputation.

There are different formats into which recipes can be placed. Recipes can be placed on plain sheets of paper, index cards, or in computer files. The format you select is optional based on what system is going to provide the best support for your operation, but some rules for standardizing recipes are as follows:

1. Use them.
2. Test and retest them to achieve the excellence of food quality desired.
3. Keep them simple to read and to follow.
4. Ensure that there are no errors within the recipe.
5. Check to be sure that the recipes are grammatically correct.

Management should select a standardized recipe card system that is going to fit the operation. A simple system will be more useful and therefore will be more successful than a complex one. Standard recipe cards can be used most effectively during the training period of the cooks and management personnel.

Before they are to be placed on the menu, all food items are to be tested and retested for food quality, cost, and ease of preparation. When these tests are accomplished, the recipe should be recorded in a manner that is grammatically correct, easy to read, and simple to follow.

RECORDING RECIPES

A recipe card (see Fig. 6-1) should include the following:

1. Name of the recipe (item to be made).
2. Yield (total portions and/or number of servings).
3. Portion size.
4. An index number as identification.
5. Ingredients column.

Item _____			Menu No. _____
Portion Size _____			Issue No. _____
Yield _____			
Ingredients	**Weight**	**Measure**	**Method of Preparation**

Recipe Name		Menu No.
Yield:		
Ingredients	**Quantity**	**Directions**

Figure 6-1. Recipe formats.

6. Weight column.

7. Measurement column.

8. Directions/method of preparation column.

9. Picture of the finished product.

It can be expensive to place a picture of the finished product with each recipe. However, the saying that a picture is worth a thousand words carries a lot of truth. It is much easier to train a cook or manager to prepare a recipe when the person has a picture in mind of how the finished product will look. Any presentation mistakes can be identified by referring to the recipe picture before the customer receives the product.

The weight column refers only to ingredients that are expressed by ounces and pounds. The measure column refers to all other terms of measurement. Examples are to taste, pinch, dash, teaspoons, tablespoons, cups, pints, quarts, gallons, number 2 and number 10 cans.

The direction or method of preparation column must be written in a clear, grammatically correct way with simple steps to follow. To save time for the chef/cook, always place information of lengthy tasks first, so they can be done first (for example, preheating the oven). Proceed with a step-by-step method of preparing the recipe (see Figs. 6-2 and 6-3).

Item New England Clam Chowder			Recipe Number S-1
Portion Size 8-oz bowl			Portions 8
Yield ½ gal			

Ingredients	Weight	Measure	Method of Preparation
Shucked clams	1	quart	A. Drain clams, saving the juice. Chop clams.
Chopped bacon	8	tablespoons	
Sliced onions	1	cup	B. Cook bacon in a large sauce-pan until crisp. Do not drain grease. Add onions and brown slightly.
Diced potatoes	3½	cups	
Salt	½	teaspoon	
Pepper		pinch	
Hot water	2	cups	C. Add potatoes, salt, pepper, and water. Cook for 10 minutes.
Milk	1	quart	D. Add clams, milk, Half & Half, and clam juice; cook until the potatoes are tender, about 10 minutes. Do not overcook the potatoes.
Half & Half	1	cup	
Soda crackers	8	each	E. Pour chowder over crackers in serving bowls.

Figure 6-2. New England clam chowder recipe.

Item Swiss Steak in Sour Cream			Recipe Number E-1
Portion Size 8 oz			
Yield 6			
Ingredients	**Weight**	**Measure**	**Method of Preparation**
Round steak, 1-inch thick	3 lbs		A. Wipe steak with a damp cloth.
Salt	½	teaspoon	B. Rub in seasonings.
Pepper	¼	teaspoon	C. Pound with a meat mallet until fibers are well broken, add-
Paprika	1	teaspoon	ing a dusting of flour at a time
Flour	½	cup	and pounding it well into the
Chopped onion	½	cup	steak.
Sour cream	½	cup	D. Brown meat on both sides in
Boiling water (see method of prep.*)			hot fat. E. Add onion, smothering onion around and over the top of the
Chopped parsley	¼	cup	steak. F. Drain off excess fat. *G. Add sour cream and enough boiling water to barely cover steak. H. Cover and let simmer until tender, about 2½ hours. I. Garnish with a sprinkling of parsley.

Figure 6-3. Swiss steak in sour cream recipe.

RECIPE CREATIVITY

To be competitive in the foodservice industry, it is vital that foodservice operations provide the types of foods that customers are demanding. Since customer food preferences are always changing, the foodservice operation must be constantly offering different foods.

Foodservice operations should change their menus often. The more profitable restaurants are arousing their customers' curiosity and tantalizing their taste by creating new and exciting dishes of food, perhaps as often as weekly. The successful foodservice operations are experimenting with recipes on a regular basis, not only when changing the menu.

One method of helping to create sales as well as adding excitement to creating menus is discussed here. The first step is to take a recipe and make the recipe exactly according to directions. Then make it a second time, changing a few ingredients or the amounts of ingredients so it will become your way of making the recipe. Give the recipe to the cooks and tell them to make it.

1. As it is now.
2. Your individual way.
3. The cook's way.

When the process is complete you will have the same recipe but three different variations.

Next have the employees taste the product and evaluate it. Listen to the employees' suggestions and make the changes if necessary.

Once the employees are excited about the product, start giving samples to a few selected customers each night. Ask the customers what they think about the product and how it could be improved. Do this for about a month to get the customers and employees talking about the new food product. After everyone is talking about the product, have your employees verbally suggest it for the night special. *Do not place this product on the menu. Verbal sales only!* You must wait until the product has become a good seller (15 percent to 20 percent sales of the night) to place it on the menu.

The reason for waiting is that management is always trying to create excitement in its foodservice operation to draw people into the operation for more sales. When management allows its employees and customers to get directly involved in the planning and creating of menu items, it gives them a sense of pride to be working or dining at this particular foodservice operation.

Not placing this product on the menu keeps the anticipation level high and this adds to the pride, curiosity, and excitement that we all look forward to in work and in dining.

REVIEW QUESTIONS

1. Why is it important to standardize recipes?

2. What part of the foodservice industry does a particularly good job of producing a standardized food product?

3. Name three rules to make standardized recipes successful.

4. Name the items necessary for a standardized recipe card.

Recipe Costing

Recipe costing is the method to determine a profit on food products. This chapter discusses the importance of costing out recipes, the methodology used to cost out recipes, and examples of costing out recipes.

OBJECTIVES

1. To explain why recipe costing is necessary.
2. To indicate different methods of lowering the food cost percentage.
3. To identify the elements in costing out recipes.
4. To illustrate how to cost out a recipe.

ASSIGNING THE TASK OF RECIPE COSTING

The majority of people who enter the foodservice industry do so for the reason of profit. Profit is why the costing out of recipes is vital.

The task of costing out recipes is not a difficult one to understand. Although it is a very time-consuming task, the expense of costing out recipes is well worth the investment.

To accomplish this task, management needs to assign a person who is to be responsible for overseeing the entire project from start to finish. This individual is not solely responsible for doing the entire project; however, this individual is responsible for having the entire project completed on time and with a complete analysis of the recipe costing system.

It has been found that when a group of people or a committee is assigned the task of costing out the recipes for a foodservice operation, the task rarely gets accomplished. Therefore, assigning one person who has leadership ability and a clear understanding of how recipe costing relates to food costing and profit is a better method of accomplishing the recipe costing.

THE IMPORTANCE OF RECIPE COSTING

Why is recipe costing necessary? To understand the full effect that recipe costing has on the amount of profit a foodservice operation is going to make, one must understand the relationship of how food cost affects profit.

To obtain and maintain the maximum profit, all foodservice operations need to know their expenses. The four major expenses are:

1. Food
2. Labor
3. Overhead
4. Profit

Food expense is the cost of the food being purchased. Some foodservice operations include beverages in this category. Labor expense is the total cost of the labor force a foodservice operation employs.

Overhead is defined as all other expenses except food, labor, and profit. Examples of overhead expenses are the costs of equipment, uniforms, laundry service, water, electricity, rent or mortgage, and taxes. Profit is considered an accrual expense before any cash flow or sales. It takes money to make money. You have to bill yourself to make a profit. Once a sales transaction has taken place and there is money in the cash register, and all the other expenses have been paid, then you have a profit. This profit is no longer considered an expense but is considered an asset to the foodservice operation.

Once a cash flow has been established, the relationship of the three other expenses—food, labor, and overhead—becomes an inverse relation to profit. An inverse relationship means that when one of the expenses increases or decreases, it does the direct opposite to profit. For example when the cost of food, labor, and overhead decreases, profit increases.

On a percentage basis the three expenses plus profit must equal 100%. This percentage represents sales and sales at 100% represents all the money the foodservice operation is going to make.

It is important for the management team to establish an annual forecast of its sales, profit, and expenses. The management team must keep track on a daily, weekly, and monthly basis of how well it is doing in order to obtain its projected annual profit. The management team does not wait three or six months from the opening date to see if it is making a profit. If the management is not making a profit it will not take three months to recognize this fact. But if a profit is being made there is still the question of the profit being the same annual amount that was projected before the opening of the operation.

Most small family and independent foodservice operations are concerned primarily that at the end of the day there is enough money in the cash register to pay the daily bills and still make a profit. There is nothing wrong with this philosophy except that the family could be increasing their daily profits. How? Simply by understanding and implementing more control of the three expenses, for example, control of food costs. How does a foodservice operator control the cost of the food?

♦ One effective method is to do comparative buying. Purchase food from more than two vendors/purveyors. Occasionally purchase your food from regular purveyor's competition. Doing so will keep your relationship with your regular purveyor honest and he or she will try harder to keep you as a satisfied customer.

♦ Do not always purchase a product with the lowest price. Never sacrifice your quality standards. The quality of the food you serve is determined by management. Your customers will appreciate and will pay a higher price for a quality food product. It is when you deviate from that high quality to a lower quality while charging the same price that customers will disapprove.

♦ Pilferage is the biggest culprit in having a high food cost percentage. Employees often times do not understand fully the implication that when they eat a food product without compensating for the cost of that food, it increases the food cost percentage. It is the decision of the management team as to what type of meal policy to implement and how to enforce it.

The real problem is that employees in the foodservice industry eat in the walk-in whenever management lets them do so. Placing a lock on the walk-in when it is not being used and restricting the use of it to the cooks can help control this problem. It is impossible to keep all the employees from snacking or eating in the foodservice operation but management must realize the effect this problem has on profit if it is not controlled.

♦ Proper training of all employees will help reduce the food cost. Another form of wasted food is due to employee accidents. The cook who burns the Newburg, the service personnel who spills the sauce, the bartender who incorrectly mixes a drink are examples of how the food cost percentage is increased.

Proper training will not prevent all accidents. Most accidents occur when people become too careless about what they are doing. A proper training program should teach the employees to take pride and care in their work. The more employees take pride in their work, the more care they are going to take in doing each facet of their jobs. Thus, accidents will be reduced.

♦ Portioning foods in their proper portion size is vital in controlling the food cost percentage. When a cook serves an extra two or three ounces of a food product, it increases the food cost percentage. The customer is getting more food than what management costed out the menu price to be. The customer is receiving more and paying less for it.

♦ Waste of food caused by overproduction is another factor that contributes to less profit. For controls on accurate forecasting, see chapter 9 on Sales History.

These are a few examples of the types of controls management must understand to have a profitable foodservice operation.

HOW TO COST OUT A RECIPE

Once a recipe has been established, it needs to be recorded in a format that is easy to use in costing out recipes (see Fig. 7-1 for an example).
The form contains the following information:

A. Recipe name
B. Recipe identification
C. Portion size
D. Yield or number of portions
E. Ingredients
F. Waste percentage
G. Edible portion
H. As purchased
I. Unit purchase price
J. Conversion measure
K. Ingredient cost
L. Subtotal recipe cost
M. Q factor of 1%
N. Total recipe cost
O. Portion cost
P. Desired overall food cost %
Q. Preliminary selling price (based on food cost percentage of ____)
R. Actual selling price
S. Actual food cost percentage
T. Additional cost

To illustrate how to cost out a recipe, see Figure 7-2.
The first step is to decide mathematically how you will round off your numbers. This author uses the requirement of rounding the number at the third decimal place. We are suggesting that you use the five or greater rule. If the fourth digit is five or greater, then the third digit should be rounded up to the next number. If the fourth digit is four or less, then the third digit will remain the same number.

A. Recipe Name _____   **B.** Recipe I.D. No. ____
C. Portion Size ____
D. Yield _____

E Ingredients	F Waste %	G EP	H AP	I Unit Purchase Price	J Conversion Measure	K Ingredient Cost

L. Subtotal

M. Q Factor

N. Total Recipe Cost

O. Portion Cost

T. Additional Cost

P. Desired Overall Food Cost %

Q. Preliminary Selling Price

R. Actual Selling Price

S. Actual Food Cost %

Figure 7-1.   Recipe costing form.

Recipe Name _Swiss Steak in Sour Cream_ Recipe I.D. No. _E-1_

Portion Size _8 oz_

Yield _6 servings_

Ingredients	A Waste %	B EP	C AP	D Conversion Measure	E Unit Purchase Price	F Ingredient Cost
Round steak	3	3 lb	3.09 lb		$2.59 lb	$8.00
Salt			½ tsp	$\frac{0.50 \text{ tsp}}{96 \text{ tsp}} = 0.005$	$1.85 lb	0.01
Pepper	Q factor		¼ tsp		$1.	Q factor
Paprika			1 tsp	$\frac{1 \text{ tsp}}{96 \text{ tsp}} = 0.010$	$1.80 lb	0.02
Flour			½ cup	$\frac{0.5 \text{ c}}{2 \text{ c}} = 0.25$	$2.00 lb	0.50
Chopped onion	12	½ cup	4.55 oz	$\frac{4.55 \text{ oz}}{16 \text{ oz}} = 0.284$	0.18 lb	0.05
Sour cream			½ cup	$\frac{0.5 \text{ c}}{2 \text{ c}} = 0.25$	0.89 pt	0.23
Boiling water	Q factor					Q factor
Chopped parsley			¼ cup	$\frac{2 \text{ oz}}{16 \text{ oz}} = 0.125$	0.55 lb	0.07

D Conversion Measure

Salt $\frac{0.50 \text{ tsp}}{96 \text{ tsp}} = 0.005$

Paprika $\frac{1 \text{ tsp}}{96 \text{ tsp}} = 0.010$

Flour $\frac{0.50 \text{ cup}}{2 \text{ cups}} = 0.25$

Chopped onions $\frac{4.55 \text{ oz}}{16 \text{ oz}} = 0.284$

Sour cream $\frac{0.50 \text{ cup}}{2 \text{ cups}} = 0.25$

Chopped parsley $\frac{2 \text{ oz}}{16 \text{ oz}} = 0.125$

G. Subtotal $8.88

H. Q factor (1%) multiply the subtotal equals $\frac{\times 0.01}{0.09}$

I. Total recipe cost equals the subtotal plus the $\frac{\begin{array}{r}\$8.88 \\ + \quad 0.09\end{array}}{\$8.97}$

J. Portion cost equals the subtotal cost divided by the recipe yield $8.97 ÷ 6 = $1.50

K. Additional costs are added (there are no additional costs for this recipe)

L. Desired overall food cost % 0.40

M. Preliminary selling price equals portion cost divided by the food cost % $1.50 ÷ .40 = $3.75

N. Actual selling price $3.95

O. Actual food costs % equals portion cost divided by the actual selling price $1.50 ÷ $3.95 = 0.38 (38%)

Figure 7-2. Recipe costing example.

Column A: Waste Percentage

Most recipes call for ingredients that are one hundred percent edible, having no waste. The fact is, however, that most fresh food products, that is, poultry, fish, seafood, beef, fruits, and produce, have a certain percentage of waste.

The cook must calculate the amount of waste a product has so as to be accurate in the amount of food product to be purchased. For example, if a recipe calls for 3 lbs of one hundred percent edible round steak, the cook must take into account the fact that a piece of round steak usually will have excess fat that has to be trimmed. If the cook does not take into consideration the amount of fat to be trimmed before purchasing the meat, then he or she will end up with less than 3 lbs of meat, thus altering the yield of the recipe and leaving the cook six portions short.

To calculate the amount of round steak needed for this recipe to yield six portions, the cook must establish the amount of waste the round steak will produce. This is done by conducting a yield test on the round steak. A yield test will give the amount of edible produce (EP) and the amount of waste product (WP).

Column B: Edible Product Amount (EP)

The EP amount is the amount of the ingredient in the recipe excluding the waste from that ingredient.

Column C: As Purchased Amount (AP)

The AP column is used to indicate the amount of the ingredient in the recipe that includes the waste product. This amount is what is to be purchased from the purveyor.

When only the AP amount is given or needed, it is not necessary to calculate the waste product. An example is the salt amount ½ tsp. There is no waste product in salt.

The round steak has a waste percentage of 3 percent and an EP amount of 3 lbs. To find out how much round steak should be purchased (AP amount) the cook must use the following formula: (W = waste)

$$AP = \frac{EP \times 100}{100\% - W\%}$$

The waste amount is put into the formula as a whole number.

$$AP = \frac{3 \times 100}{100 - 3} = \frac{300}{97} = 3.09 \text{ lbs.}$$

The technical amount of round steak for the cook to purchase is 3.09 lbs. The 0.09 or 9% represents 9% of a pound (16 ozs), which equals $0.09 \times 16 = 1.44$ oz (1½ oz).

When the cook is cutting his or her own round steaks, cutting a 3 lb 1½ oz piece is not a problem. When the cook has to order 3 lbs 1½ ozs from the meat purveyor, however, then the cook has a problem.

The problem is that most meat purveyors will not cut the round steaks at 3 lbs 1½ ozs without charging an additional fee for being exact to the half ounce. The cook should shop around for a meat purveyor who will accept the cook's meat specifications for the round steaks. There are purveyors who will cut meat to any specifications desired. You will pay an additional fee for the service. The cook must figure out which method is more profitable.

One way the cook can recover the extra cost is to use the waste of the round steak in another food product. The fat trimmed from the round steak can be rendered down and used in sautéing other food products, thus cutting down on the amount of oil to be purchased for sautéing.

The point is to recover the additional cost in any way that is possible to help maintain a lower food cost. The last step is to increase menu prices.

Column D: Conversion Measure

The conversion measure column is a place where the conversion formula and the converting factor are to be written.

The AP amount will often be in ounces while the AP price will be expressed in pounds. When there are two different units of measurement being used, one has to be converted into the same unit of measurement as the other. For example, chopped onions require an AP amount of 4.55 ozs but very often are purchased by the pound. In this recipe onions are at a unit price of 0.18 per lb. The question is how much does 4.55 ozs cost if onions are purchased at 0.18 lb? The menu planner cannot divide 0.18 by 4.55 ozs to arrive at the correct answer. The menu planner must find out what percentage 4.55 ozs is of 1 lb (16 ozs). This is done by dividing 4.55 ozs by 16 ozs, which equals a decimal-converting factor of 0.284. This 0.284 is the equivalent of 4.55 ozs.

Now the same units of measurement have been achieved, which are expressed in decimals. The onion conversion factor (0.284) times the unit price 0.18 will equal the ingredient cost of 0.051 (0.05).

Column E: Unit Price Column

This column is what the cook pays the purveyor for an ingredient.

Column F: Ingredient Cost

This column is used to carry out the total cost of the ingredient being used in the recipe by multiplying the conversion measurement factor and the unit price.

Column G: Subtotal of the Recipe Cost

All the ingredients costs in Column F are added together to calculate a subtotal.

Column H: Q Factor 1%

The definition of a Q factor is the price the cook must charge to recover the cost of all the ingredients that are too small to calculate. For example, when a recipe calls for a dash or a pinch of an ingredient, this amount becomes difficult to cost out. The amount a cook uses in a pinch or a dash will differ from time to time.

One method to recover the ingredient cost is to use a percentage factor. Since the amount of the ingredient to be used in this situation is questionable, we call this recovering cost factor a Q factor.

The percentage amount of 1% is based on the following:

1. Most recipes do not have more than three Q factors in them.
2. The cost of these Q factor ingredients do not add up to 1% of the subtotal of the recipe.

Thus it is important that the menu planner be selective when deciding on the Q factor. The exception to using more than 1% of the recipe subtotal would be if the ingredient is expensive such as saffron.

The monetary value of the Q factor is calculated by multiplying 1% by the recipe subtotal.

I: Total Recipe Cost

This amount is calculated by adding the Q factor of 1% to the subtotal of the recipe.

J: Portion Cost

To calculate the portion cost (PC) divide the total recipe cost by the total number of portions the recipe yields.

K: Additional Items

When the food item is to be sold as a semi a la carte item, the portion cost of any additional food items are added to the original portion cost. For example, the swiss steak in sour cream comes with a baked potato and green peas. The menu planner calculates the portion cost of the baked potato and the green peas separately. The cost of the items is added to the portion cost of the swiss steak and the entire plate cost is marked up for a preliminary selling price.

When the customer is given a choice of vegetables or starches, the menu planner must add to the entree the highest-priced vegetable or starch. For example, most menus offer a choice of baked, mashed, or french fried potatoes with an entree. The menu planner must cost out all three potato dishes to establish which one is the most expensive to produce. The most expensive one will be added to the portion cost of the entree. Do not offer the customer a choice of vegetables that vary greatly in cost. Select vegetables that are in similar price ranges to avoid pricing the plate cost too high for the entree to sell.

L: Desired Overall Food Cost Percentage

This amount is established by determining what management would like its food cost to be at the end of the year.

M: Preliminary Selling Price

This selling price is established by dividing the portion cost by the food cost percentage. The selling price is the price at which the food item should be sold to maintain a profit.

N: Actual Selling Price

The actual selling price is the amount at which the product will be sold on the menu. This price will differ from the preliminary selling price because of what the customer is willing to pay for the product. Other factors that influence the actual selling price are

♦ Direct competition's price for the food product
♦ Demand (popularity) of the food product
♦ Availability of the food product

The menu planner must be sure of all three factors before raising the price.

O: Actual Food Cost Percentage

Once the preliminary selling price has been readjusted either up or down, the menu planner must calculate the new food cost percentage on this food product. This process is accomplished by dividing the portion cost by the actual selling price.

The main objective for the menu planner in costing out recipes is to accurately calculate the cost of the food and to mark up the portion cost price to pay for the labor cost and overhead cost, and to make a profit.

The menu planner has to adjust the preliminary selling price to an actual selling price, which sometimes means lowering the profit margin being made on the food product, for example, lowering the preliminary selling price of barbeque chicken wings from $3.50 to $2.95. The chicken wings will not sell at the restaurant at $3.50 because

1. The customers think the price is too high.
2. The competition is selling chicken wings at $3.00.

By lowering the price, the chicken wings are selling and the customers are not complaining. The problem, however, is that this product is not making as much profit as needed to reach the annual projected profit margin. The menu planner must compensate for the lower profit margin on the chicken wings.

The method to recover this $0.55 difference is to spread out the cost throughout the menu, known as *balancing the menu*.

Menus have a certain number of high food cost items and a certain number of low food cost items. Every foodservice operation would like to have just low food cost items on the menu for better profit. Low food cost items are not always what the majority of customers would like, however. Prime rib of beef is not the highest profit item on most menus but it is one of the most popular. By offering some high food cost items on the menu, customers keep patronizing the restaurant. But the menu must maintain a good balance for the menu planner to make up the profit margin on the high food cost items such as the $0.55 difference on the chicken wings.

REVIEW QUESTIONS

1. Define *Q factor* and explain how it is used in the costing out of a recipe.

2. What are three methods of lowering a food cost percentage?

3. Why is recipe costing necessary?

4. What do EP and AP have to do with recipe costing?

5. Explain how *balancing a menu* is done.

8

Marketing Characteristics of a Menu

Once the menu has been costed out and final decisions have been made about food selection, the menu planner can begin to analyze the marketing characteristics of a menu.

Decisions about paper, printing, color, listing of items, size, and cover can be made following discussion with a local printer. It is important that the menu planner have basic knowledge about these menu mechanics to facilitate communication with the printer.

Balance, variety, composition, and descriptive copy for food and beverage items that one wishes to have on the menu should be planned and outlined before the menu planner goes to the printer.

The marketing characteristics of a menu, which are paper, printing, color, balance, variety, composition, descriptive copy, listing of items, size, and cover are discussed in this chapter.

OBJECTIVES

1. To understand the marketing characteristics of a menu, which are paper, printing, color, balance, variety, composition, descriptive copy, listing of items, size, and cover.
2. To understand how marketing characteristics better merchandise menu items.

One must use marketing techniques to design and construct menus to increase the ability to merchandise not only items on the menu but also the restaurant as a whole. The marketing characteristics of a menu are as follows:

- Paper
- Printing
- Color
- Balance
- Variety
- Composition
- Descriptive copy
- Listing of items
- Size
- Cover

PAPER

To begin the process of designing the menu, start with paper characteristics. The menu planner should keep in mind how the menu is going to be used. If the menu is going to be changed daily, the paper can be less expensive and less durable, that is, uncoated and lightweight. For a menu that does not change often, the paper should be durable, coated, heavy stock, water resistant, and stain resistant.

For most menus the outside cover should be durable. Inside pages can be lighter and somewhat less durable.

When selecting paper, the following factors must be considered by the menu planner:

- Strength
- Texture
- Color
- Opacity (Opacity is the substance or property of paper that minimizes the show-through of printing to the back side of the next page of the menu.)

PRINTING

Printing that is difficult to read results in dissatisfied customers. It is vital that the printing on the menu be sufficiently large and easy to read.

Type comes in various forms; we will discuss the three major ones: roman, modern, and script. *Roman type* is characterized by its thin and thick character. It is very readable and is found in newspapers, magazine articles, and books. Roman type should be used in the descriptive copy on the menu (see Fig. 8-1). (Descriptive copy means describing items on the menu in an appetizing way.)

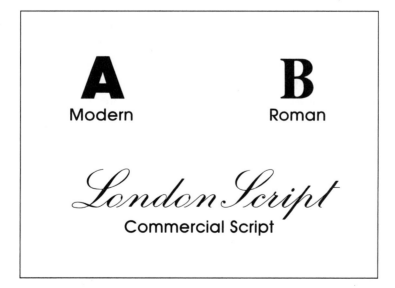

Figure 8-1. Script typefaces: roman, modern, and commercial.

Modern type does not have the thick or thin character like Roman type. It has thick block letters (see Fig. 8-1). Many government buildings have modern type on them.

Script type looks like handwriting. Script is difficult to read and should only be used in subheadings or headings on the menu. Headings on the menu might read Appetizers, Soups, Salads, Entrees, and Desserts. Subheadings would be Stuffed Mushrooms for an appetizer and Sirloin Steak with Hollandaise Sauce for an entree.

The menu planner must also decide on the type size. Type size is measured in points, starting with 6 points and ending up with 192 points (Fig. 8-2a). Most menus should be at least 12 points. Smaller type will be too difficult to read. For descriptive copy, space between lines must be allowed, called *leading*. Leading is also measured in points (Fig. 8-2b). No space between lines is referred to as *set solid*. All menus should have at least 3 points between each line.

It is important that the type is in character with the restaurant. For example, if your restaurant is modern, the type for your menu should be modern as well. Modern type is airy and light in character and can reflect the decor of the restaurant.

Finally, color of the type is a factor. The type on a menu should be dark and the background should be light. For example, light blue background with dark blue type is acceptable. When the type is light and the background is dark, it is called reversed type.

As previously mentioned, there are many variations of typefaces (Figs. 8-3, 8-4, and 8-5). Within these, there are two parts, lowercase and uppercase. Lowercase letters are small letters. Uppercase letters are capital letters. Lowercase should be used in descriptive copy on the menu and uppercase should be used for headings or subheadings on the menu.

Menu planners must also decide on the italic variation of the typeface. Italic variation means that the typeface is designed at an angle or slant, whereas most typeface is usually straight up and down. The menu planner should use caution with regard to italic. This form of type can be difficult to read and should be used only for subheadings or headings and to highlight items on the menu so the customer will look at that item and perhaps select it over other items on the menu.

Avoid reversed type (light or white type on a dark background) on the *inside* of the menu. Reverse type is acceptable on the cover of the menu, however.

(Text continues on page 156.)

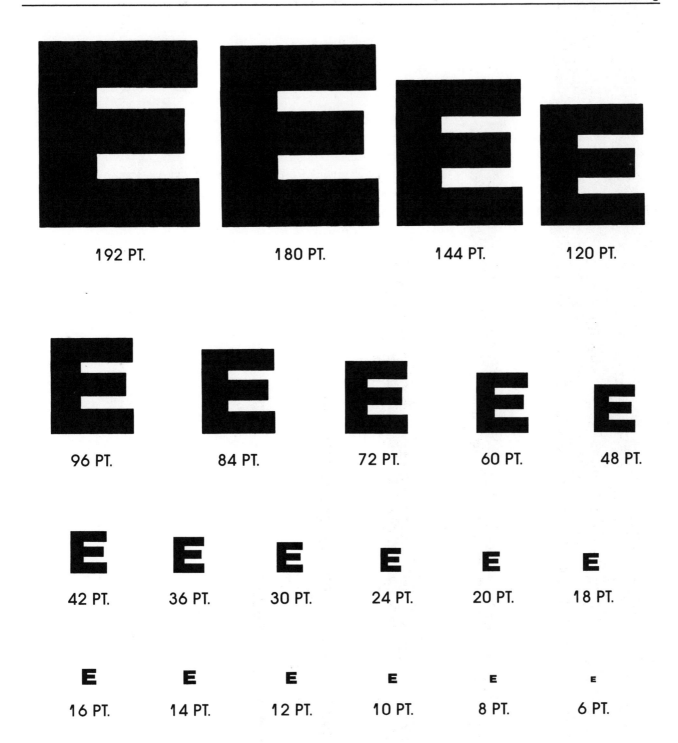

Figure 8-2a. Examples of point sizes.

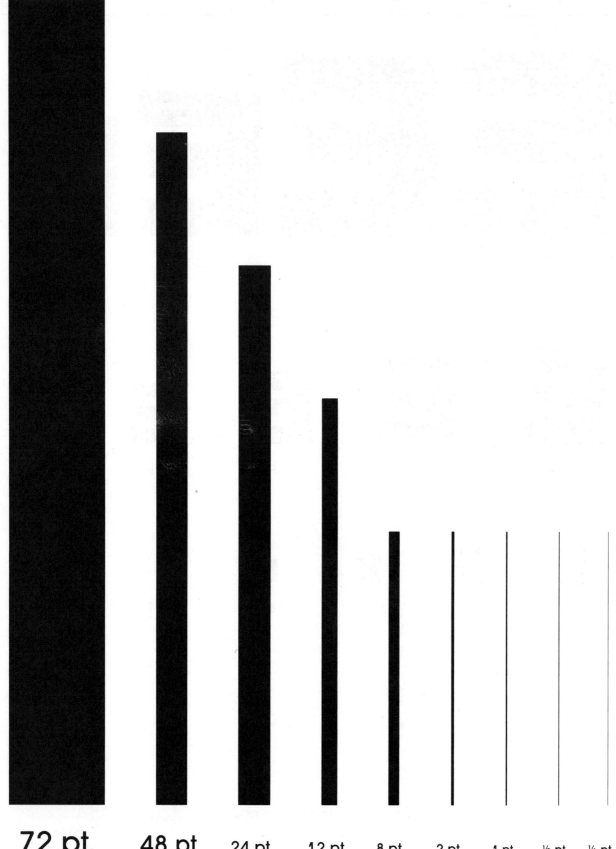

72 pt.   48 pt.   24 pt.   12 pt.   8 pt.   2 pt.   1 pt.   ½ pt.   ¼ pt.

Figure 8-2b.   Sample rules in available point sizes.

A B C D E F G H I J K L M
N O P Q R S T U V W X Y Z
a b c d e f g h i j k l m
n o p q r s t u v w x y z
1 2 3 4 5 6 7 8 9 0 $
1 2 3 4 5 6 7 8 9 0 { & ( )

7 Point Size:

9 Point Size:

10 Point Size:

12 Point Size:

14 Point Size:

16 Point Size:

18 Point Size:

20 Point Size:

24 Point Size:

28 Point Size:

30 Point Size:

36 Point Size:

42 Point Size:

48 Point Size:

54 Point Size:

60 Point Size:

Figure 8-3. Cooper Black typeface.

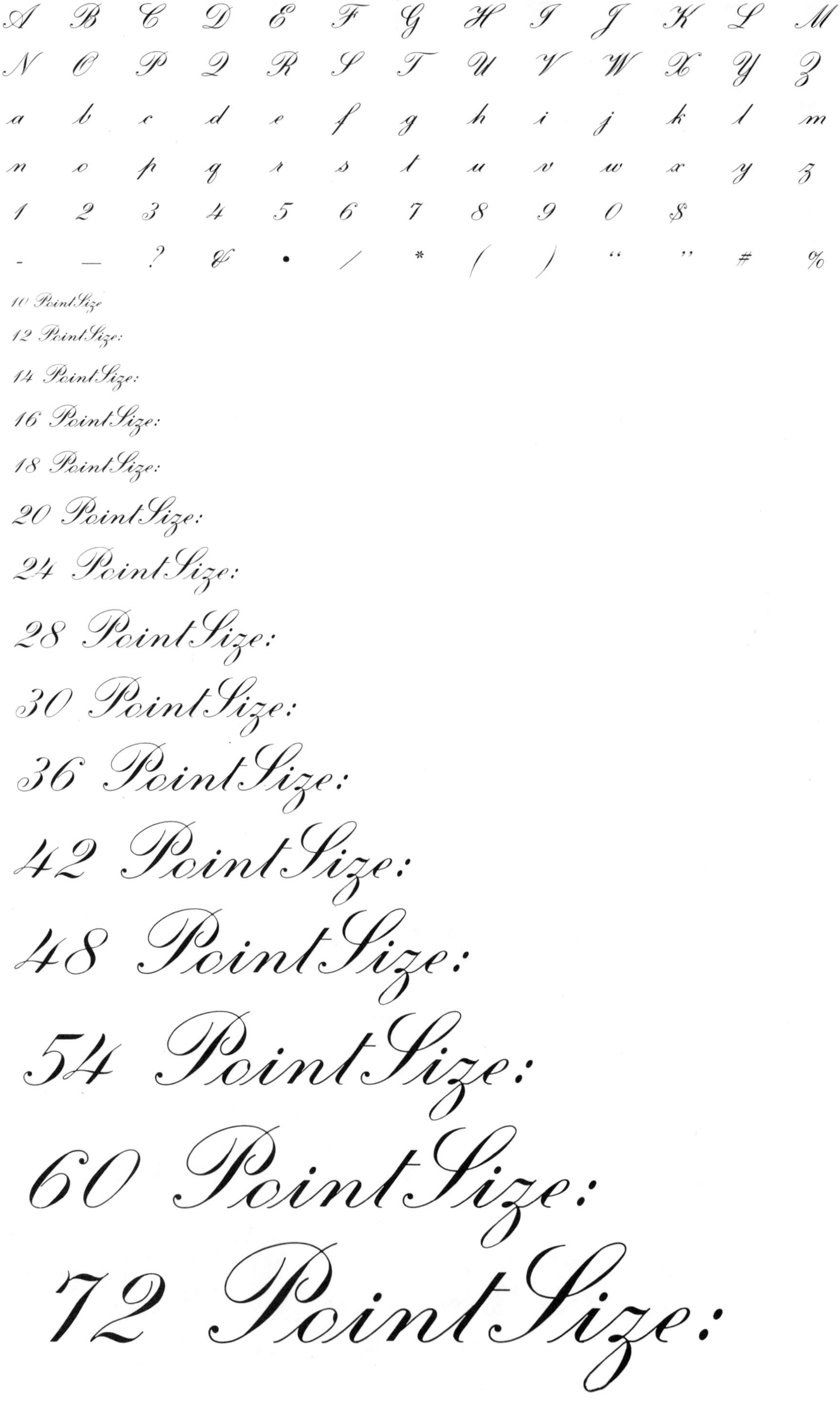

A B C D E F G H I J K L M
N O P Q R S T U V W X Y Z
a b c d e f g h i j k l m
n o p q r s t u v w x y z
1 2 3 4 5 6 7 8 9 0 $
*- — ? & • / * ( ) " " # %*

10 *Point Size*

12 *Point Size:*

14 *Point Size:*

16 *Point Size:*

18 *Point Size:*

20 *Point Size:*

24 *Point Size:*

28 *Point Size:*

30 *Point Size:*

36 *Point Size:*

42 *Point Size:*

48 *Point Size:*

54 *Point Size:*

60 *Point Size:*

72 *Point Size:*

Figure 8-4. London Script typeface.

Eras Light

Eras Medium

Eras Bold

Eras Outline

Eras Contour

Fat Face

Fat Face Condensed

Fortune Bold

Franklin Gothic

Franklin Gothic Extra Cond

FRIEND

Friz Quadrata

Friz Quadrata Bold

Futura Black

Futura Bold

Futura Bold Italic

Futura Demibold

Futura Medium

Futura Medium Italic

GOLD RUSH

Gorilla

Grizzly

Grotesque No. 9

ACCENT

Advertisers Gothic

AKI LINES

Amer. Typewriter Bold

American Typewriter Bold Cond

Amer. Typewriter Medium

American Typewriter Med Cond

Arpad Light

Astur

Avant Garde Bold

Avant Garde Book

Avant Garde *Med.*

Avant Garde Bold Condensed

Avant Garde Medium Condensed

Bauhaus Medium

Bauhaus Heavy

Bauhaus Heavy Outline

BLACKLINE

Blippo Black

Bolt Bold

Bookman Bold

Bookman Bold Italic

Bookman Contour

MACHINE

MANDARIN

Manhattan

Microgramma Bold Extended

Microgramma Extended

MOORE COMPUTER

NEON

Newtext Book

Newtext Demi

Old English

Optima

Palace Script

PEIGNOT Bold

PEIGNOT LIGHT

PIONEER

Playbill

PROFIL

Ronda

RUSTIC

SAPPHIRE

Serif Gothic Black

Serif Gothic Bold

Serif Gothic Ex. Bold

Figure 8-5. Various typefaces.

COLOR

The colors chosen for the paper and type on a menu should match well together. A red background with yellow lettering does not blend, for instance. These colors clash. Pink paper with red type blends. Professional printers or artists can help determine what colors go together and what colors do not.

BALANCE

A menu is said to be balanced if all the food groups are proportioned. For example, if a menu has four appetizers, four soups, four salads, eight entrees, four potatoes, four vegetables, and four desserts, the menu is well balanced. A larger amount of entrees than other items is not only acceptable but also recommended because entrees are the focus of the menu and are the most expensive items.

VARIETY

Variety is crucial to a good menu. Variety is important in the amount of selections within the food groups and in the ways the items are prepared. For example, under the appetizers, the menu might include clams casino, stuffed eggplant, and fettucini Alfredo for a good variety. Entrees can be steamed, broiled, sautéed, poached, braised, boiled, fried, roasted, or simmered. Customers like to see variety on a menu. Variety reflects the chef's creativity.

COMPOSITION

Composition of menu item groupings is important in planning a menu. The menu planner must look at how well certain dishes go with certain entrees. For example, sweet potatoes are excellent with ham, just as popovers go with roast beef. In general, when entrees have lots of flavorings, side dishes should have a less pronounced flavor. For example, beef Stroganoff could be served with peas or carrots. On the other hand, if less rich entrees are served, side dishes should be more pronounced in flavor. For example, if the entree is baked chicken, the vegetable might be zucchini Provençale (zucchini, tomatoes, bread crumbs, parmesan cheese, garlic, and assorted spices).

Another way to address composition is through eye appeal. Colors of foods can hold tremendous eye appeal with proper composition. A plate of white baked haddock, steamed green broccoli, and ruby red stewed tomatoes reflect good color and composition. Remember, eye appeal enhances customer satisfaction.

DESCRIPTIVE COPY

Descriptive copy is an explanation of an item, how it is prepared, and how it is served. It is the descriptive copy that helps sell the item on the menu in most cases. Entrees on the menu should have the most descriptive copy because they are the most expensive items on the menu. One important rule to follow when composing descriptive copy is to avoid using words that describe a killing process, such as "slaughtered" or "butchered." In the United States, ethnic language menus should use English for descriptive copy.

Descriptive copy of all foodservice operations fits into one of three philosophies of profit management. The first one is an exclusive gourmet menu with a high check average. This type of operation wants the customers to wine and dine themselves for a period of one to two hours. There will be a substantial amount of descriptive copy on this type of menu. More descriptive copy on a menu does two things. It gives the customer more information about the food products and it keeps the customers in the restaurant longer by having more to read on the menu.

The second philosophy of profit management is to have a short, limited menu with a low check average. This type of operation wants the customer to stay only fifteen to twenty minutes or less. The menu has little or no descriptive copy. The food selections are limited and simply listed with the price, thus eliminating wasted time in the customer's decision-making process.

The third philosophy is to try to combine the best of the first two. A family-style foodservice operation will just list food items such as appetizers, desserts, and beverages and give descriptive copy to the soups, salads, and entrees. This type of operation wants its customers to eat and enjoy themselves for about forty-five minutes to one hour. The check average is usually between $8.00 and $12.00 per person.

LISTING OF ITEMS

Items should be presented in the order they are consumed. For example, most menus list appetizers, soups, salads, entrees, starches, vegetables, breads, beverages, and then desserts. This listing is the proper one. In other cases, the listing depends on the formality of the cuisine, for example, a French classical menu places the salads immediately before the desserts. It is recommended that the most profitable food items be listed first and last in a particular list. The most popular and least profitable food items should be listed in the middle. When reading a column of any type of listing a person will always look at the first few items on the list first, will skim the middle section if it is a long column, and then read the last few listings before going on to the next column. The most popular items, however, will most likely be ordered no matter where they are placed on the menu.

The best location for the most profitable items is in the top half of the second quadrangle on a single-fold menu (Fig. 8-6). When a person opens a menu from right to left the first page or quadrangle seen is 2 and 4, or the second page. Because we are taught to read from left to right, a customer will start reading at quad 1 but the eye will first see quad 2.

Entrees fall into place nicely on the right after listing appetizers, soups, and salads on the left. Items should be listed in order of profit. High-profit entrees such as chicken and pasta should come first under the entree headings, then lobster, sirloin, and veal.

SIZE

The menu should be large enough to merchandise the food items without appearing crowded. Avoid type that is too small for customers to read. Too large a menu, however, will be awkward to handle. Most menus are four pages. The cover forms pages one and four and the inside with food items forms pages two and three. The most popular menu size is 8½ inches by 11 inches.

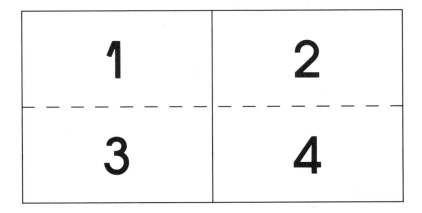

Figure 8-6. Diagram of single-fold menu.

COVER

The front and back of a menu cover can yield tremendous merchandising power. The cover of a menu should reflect the decor and theme of the operation. For example, a specialty restaurant featuring broiled steaks that has red tablecloths and black napkins could have a red menu cover and black print.

The front cover should have the name and recognizable symbol or logo of the restaurant on it. The logo of a seafood restaurant named The White Cap could be an anchor. It is amazing to note that 50 percent of the back of menu covers are never used. The back cover should have the phone number and address of the operation and any information on credit cards accepted. Directions, hours, restaurant history, and banquet and take-out service information are some examples of effective merchandising uses for the back of the menu.

On a more practical note, the menu cover should be durable, water resistant, and stain resistant unless the menu changes daily and is disposable.

REVIEW QUESTIONS

1. What factors must the menu planner take into consideration when selecting paper?

2. How should uppercase and lowercase be used on the menu?

3. What is reverse type?

4. How is type measured?

5. What is leading?

6. What is balance?

7. What are two ways to add variety to a menu?

8. What are two aspects of composition?

9. In what order should items be listed on a menu?

10. What should be on the front and back covers of a menu?

Sales History

In this chapter we discuss the use of the sales history and the value of the computerized goal value program. To plan your future it is wise to take a look at your past.

OBJECTIVES

1. To understand the importance of a sales history report.
2. To be able to complete a sales history report.
3. To be able to complete a goal-value analysis problem.

SALES HISTORY BACKGROUND

The sales history, also known as a scatter sheet mix, is a record kept daily of the menu items that have been sold. The sales history should contain any information that will explain why the sales volume turned out to be what it is for that day. The following is a listing of the uses of the sales history:

- To forecast.
- To keep a daily record of which food items were sold.
- To keep a daily record of how many menu items were sold.
- To predict sales volume.
- To record information that will aid management in forecasting accurately.
- To aid management in predicting a sales analysis.
- To project the annual budget.
- To aid management in determining what the customer is willing to pay.

The purpose of a sales history is to help management be more accurate in forecasting the foodservice operation's needs. It is a difficult task for management to be able to forecast how many customers it will be feeding in the future and to be able to purchase the correct amount of supplies ahead of time to feed these customers. If management purchases too many supplies, then profit is being lost. If it does not purchase enough supplies, the customer will be dissatisfied.

Keeping a daily record of which menu items have been sold and how many have been sold, plus recording information that tells management the reasons for the daily sales, is vital in helping management to predict future needs accurately.

The factor that makes a sales history so worthwhile is based on the theory that history repeats itself. In most cases foodservice management teams will verify that customer sales volumes are predictable to a certain degree of accuracy. For example, let's look at a seasonal foodservice operation located in New England. In the New England area, seasonal foodservice operations will open on the weekends in April. During May, foodservice operations will open on the weekends plus one or two days during the week. After Memorial Day, seasonal foodservice operations will open full-time until Labor Day. Then most foodservice operations will start cutting the number of days they will be opened.

After Memorial Day, sales volume will slowly start to increase week by week because 90 percent of colleges have ended their academic year. In June, sales volume will increase at a greater rate, especially when the elementary and secondary schools end their academic year. During July, sales volume will increase steadily because many people will begin to take their vacations.

In August and September, foodservice operations will reach their peak sales volume. Beginning in April, the sales volume will increase from week to week until mid-September when the sales volume starts to decrease.

August is a favorite month for families to go on vacation because the children are out of school and the weather is at its hottest. In September, once Labor Day arrives, the volume of families traveling is lowered drastically because the children are back in school. However, the foodservice operation does not close for the season. There is a considerable amount of people who do not wish to tolerate the August heat or the crowds and they take their vacations after Labor Day. After September, the sales volume on a weekly basis will decrease enough for a seasonal operation to close its doors. This trend is a seasonal one in New England if the economy and the weather remain stable during the summer months.

Keeping a sales history on the volume of menu items being sold will help management purchase the correct amount of supplies by analyzing sales volume of the past to predict the sales volume of the future. When analyzing the sales history it is important to compare same time periods. Compare a Monday's business with another Monday's business. Never compare a Monday with a Saturday or a Sunday with a Tuesday. Each time period is a separate day of the week, with each day having its own unique characteristics that only that day will be able to produce.

For example, Mondays are usually the lowest day of the week. Customers on Mondays have little disposable income left from the weekend. Also most people are recuperating from weekend activities. Most people are back at work and are putting all of their energy into activities at work.

Saturdays are one of the busiest days of the week because people have the disposable income to spend. Most people do not work on Saturdays; therefore, Saturday becomes a day of relaxation and entertainment.

It is important not to compare a single meal period with another meal period within the same day. Breakfast, lunch, and dinner have their own unique characteristics. Breakfast has a different type of customer, check average, and turnover rate than lunch and dinner. These meals are three different types of businesses under one roof.

For better accuracy in forecasting the number of customers for each meal period, management needs to have information that will influence sales on that particular day. Examples of such information are:

Day of the week.

Date.

Weather

Time of day.

Meal period.

Special events within the community that will produce more sales such as concerts, conventions, meetings, and bus tours.

Employees who were absent from work that day.

It is a difficult task to be one hundred percent accurate with each day's forecasted needs to have a maximum profit for that day. With experience and knowledge of the type of customers and community of the foodservice operation, forecasting can be very accurate and exciting to do.

BENEFITS OF THE SCATTER SHEET

At the end of each meal period the food items that were sold must be recorded into the sales history ledger. This information most likely will be taken from the register slip, as shown in Figure 9-1.

Once this information has been recorded the management team must analyze the results. This analysis should be done on a daily, weekly, and monthly basis. The management team should be looking for which menu items are not selling, and if the sales are in line with the annual sales projection.

When a restaurant is losing sales, the sales history record can be helpful in determining the problem. Most restaurants lose sales because customers do not like the approach the restaurant is taking in one or several of the following areas:

```
DURGIN PARK - COPLY

        SALES ANALYSIS                              SALES ANALYSIS

Z   OO                        40         Z   OO                        40

    ITEM     PRICE  QTY    SALES  %SLS        ITEM     PRICE  QTY    SALES  %SLS
DEPT    1                                PORK LOI    7.95    1     7.95  0.2
                                         LAMB RST    8.95   10    89.50  1.8
1/2 OYST    4.75    3    14.25  0.3       PRM RIB   13.95    6    83.70  1.7
1/2 CHRY    4.75    1     4.75  0.1       HAMB STK   6.95    1     6.95  0.1
1/2 OYST    4.75    3    14.25  0.3       POT RST    6.95    2    13.90  0.3
OYST PLT    9.50    3    28.50  0.6       PORKCHP   12.95    1    12.95  0.3
1/2 CHRY    4.75    3    14.25  0.3       PRK LOIN   7.95   12    95.40  1.9
CLAM CAS    5.95    4    23.80  0.5       LEGLAMB    8.95   18   161.10  3.2
SHP CTL     5.25    8    42.00  0.8       PRM RIB   13.95   51   711.45 14.2
                                         SIRLOIN   16.00    2    32.00  0.6
DEPT    1          25                     HAMB STK   6.95    7    48.65  1.0
TOTALS                  141.80  2.8       MXD GRIL  15.95    4    63.80  1.3
                                         LAMBCHOP  14.95    3    44.85  0.9
DEPT    2                                FILETMGN  18.00    1    18.00  0.4
                                         FRY COD    8.95    3    26.85  0.5
CUPCHOW     1.50    2     3.00  0.1       SEAFD PL  12.95    5    64.75  1.3
CUP CHOW    1.50    1     1.50  0.0       POT RST    6.95   13    90.35  1.8
PLT CHOW    2.25    1     2.25  0.0       PORKCHOP  12.95    2    25.90  0.5
CUPCLAM     1.75    4     7.00  0.1
PLTCLAM     2.95    5    14.75  0.3       DEPT    4         142
CUP CHOW    1.50   17    25.50  0.5       TOTALS                 1598.05 31.9
PLT CHOW    2.25    6    13.50  0.3
CUP CLAM    1.75   39    68.25  1.4      DEPT    5
PLT CLAM    2.95   15    44.25  0.9
                                         TURKEY     8.25    4    33.00  0.7
DEPT    2          90                     HLF DUCK   8.95    1     8.95  0.2
TOTALS                  180.00  3.6       CHIKLIV    6.95    4    27.80  0.6
                                         TURKEY     8.25   21   173.25  3.5
DEPT    3                                CHIKDAY    9.95    1     9.95  0.2
                                         HLF DUCK   8.95    3    26.85  0.5
ANTIPAST    5.95    2    11.90  0.2
ONION RG    2.75    1     2.75  0.1      DEPT    5          34
TOSS SAL    2.95    2     5.90  0.1      TOTALS                  279.80  5.6
BALE HAY    5.75    1     5.75  0.1
VEGGIES     1.25   29    36.25  0.7      DEPT    6
SHP SALD    5.95    7    41.65  0.8
ONION RG    2.75    4    11.00  0.2       FRY SOLE   5.95    1     5.95  0.1
CHEF SAL    5.95    5    29.75  0.6       SEAFD PL  12.95    2    25.90  0.5
TOSSED      2.95   27    79.65  1.6       LOB NEWB  16.95    1    16.95  0.3
SPN SAL     5.95    9    53.55  1.1       SCROD      6.95    1     6.95  0.1
LOBS SAL   16.95    2    33.90  0.7       SWRD STK  14.95    3    44.85  0.9
                                         BKSHRMP   12.95    1    12.95  0.3
DEPT    3          89                     STEAMERS   6.95    2    13.90  0.3
TOTALS                  312.05  6.2       FRY SOLE   7.95    6    47.70  1.0
                                         FRY OYST   8.95    2    17.90  0.4
DEPT    4                                FRY SCLP  12.95    3    38.85  0.8
                                         FRY LOBS  16.95    1    16.95  0.3

                                         0355      25/JUL/88    OO PAGE   2
0355       25/JUL/88    OO PAGE   1
```

Figure 9-1. Computerized register slip. *(Courtesy of Durgin Park of Copley Place, Boston, MA.)*

♦ Sanitation.
♦ Quality of the food.
♦ Quality of the service.
♦ Prices.
♦ Atmosphere and the location of the restaurant.

The sales history will determine which menu items are selling and which ones are not. (It is up to management to determine why the food items are not selling and to correct the problem.) It could be that the price is too high, the portions are too small or too large, the food presentation is not good, or any of several other possibilities. Once management knows the reason behind the poor sales of an item, it should promote the food item or take the item off the menu.

A scatter sheet is used in the annual budgetary projection. Management needs to maintain a daily sales record of how much money was made during the day. Each week should be compared with the annual profit and expense projections. If the sales drops for three consecutive weeks, it is highly unlikely that the sales loss will be regained. Management does not want to wait until three-quarters of the year has passed to check its profits and expense projections. By then it is usually too late to recover losses that have occurred earlier in the year.

It is helpful to determine the potential food cost of a menu and to eliminate items that are not selling, thus aiding management in determining what the customer is willing to pay for the food items on the menu. For example, a restaurant is selling 100 portions of prime rib at $8.95. Management increases the price of the prime rib to $11.95. The number of portions sold decreases to 60 portions. The restaurant is losing money ($178.00). Management reduces the price to $10.95. The number of portions sold increases to 90. The restaurant is now making $90.50 more in profit. Management has established the price its market is willing to pay for the prime rib. The sales history keeps a record of how the prime rib is selling at the different price levels.

HOW A SCATTER SHEET WORKS

The scatter sheet is composed of several elements (see Fig. 9-2). The first column includes the week ending date, the menu item listings, the remarks area, and the meal period space.

Column two includes the name of the restaurant, and a space for the weather and the days of the week. To find out how much of a particular item has been sold, do one of the following:

1. Add from the meal checks the times the item was sold.
2. Program the cash register to keep a tally of each item on the menu so that you can take a reading from the register tape.

Column three is the weekly sum sold of the individual menu item. Column four is the sales price of the individual item. Column five is the item sales column, calculated by multiplying column three by column four.

Column 1				Column 2				Col 3	Col 4	Col 5	Col 6	Col 7
MENU SCATTER SHEET: BRIAN'S RESTAURANT Week Ending: 6/14/85 Weather: clear, 70°F								Weekly No. Sold	Selling Price	Item Sales	Total Weekly Sales	% Contribution to Sales
	TALLY											
Menu Item	Mon	Tue	Wed	Thu	Fri	Sat	Sun					
N.E. Chowder	5	8	10	12	20	30	20	105	$ 0.95	$ 99.75	$16093.65	0.00619
French Onion	7	7	12	11	25	23	29	114	1.25	142.50		0.00885
Tossed Salad	30	40	50	60	70	65	66	381	0.85	323.85		0.02012
Greek Salad	3	4	2	0	1	3	1	14	0.95	13.30		0.00082
Broiled Lobster	15	20	30	31	32	35	50	213	14.95	3184.35		0.19786
Baked Stuff Lobster	16	35	32	40	45	65	55	288	16.95	4881.60		0.30332
Fried Clams	20	25	33	16	10	70	65	239	8.95	2139.05		0.13291
Broiled Scallops	10	15	20	25	30	35	40	175	9.95	1741.25		0.10819
Sirloin Steak	8	10	15	7	20	25	45	130	10.50	1365.00		0.08481
Tenderloin Strip	19	18	17	12	11	13	15	105	12.50	1312.50		0.08155
½ Roast Duck	7	6	4	3	2	0	8	30	11.50	345.00		0.02143
Baked Potato	35	38	40	55	85	90	110	453	0.50	226.50		0.01407
Mashed Potato	20	19	35	20	15	12	20	141	0.50	70.50		0.00438
Peas	15	20	22	23	28	32	45	185	0.35	64.75		0.00402
Corn	20	25	31	38	39	41	46	240	0.35	84.00		0.00521
Carrots	35	39	40	41	42	43	45	285	0.35	99.75		0.00619
											$16093.65	
Etc.												
Etc.												
Remarks:												
Meal Period: Dinner 6:00-10:00 P.M.												

Figure 9-2. Sales history form: scatter sheet.

Column six is the sum of the weekly sales, calculated by adding column five. Column seven, percentage contribution to sales, indicates the contributing percentage of sales by the individual menu item to the total weekly sales of the menu. This amount is calculated by dividing column five by column six.

THE PRODUCTION SHEET

A production sheet is a schedule that indicates the following to the employees:

♦ Who will be doing what task.
♦ When they will be doing this task.
♦ Where they will be doing this task.
♦ What equipment they need.
♦ The quantity needed in doing this task.

The sales history form is extremely helpful in aiding the chef to determine the quantity of food the cooks need to prepare for production. The chef should refer to the sales history when making out the production sheet to see what was sold during the same time frame a week ago. Doing so will give the chef a good guideline of how much to prepare for production.

GOAL-VALUE ANALYSIS

As we have seen, sales history is one way to analyze menu items. Another alternative to menu analysis is goal-value analysis. Goal-value analysis is a simple, comprehensive technique developed by David K. Hayes and Lynn Huffman (Menu Analysis: A Better Way, *The Cornell HRA Quarterly,* February 1985), both employed at Texas Tech University. Goal-value analysis compares the profit contribution of an individual menu item to the average profit performance of the total business.

The business information necessary to do a typical goal-value analysis is presented in Table 9-1, including total sales in dollars, food cost percentage, labor cost percentage, other controllable cost percentage, uncontrollable cost percentage, and profit percentage (see also Table 9-2.)

The goal value (overall standard) is compared to the value of the menu item. If the value is higher than the goal value (overall standard), the menu item is a winner. However, if the value is lower than the

Table 9-1. Information Necessary for Good Value Analysis

Income Statement Information for a Hypothetical Restaurant

Sales for the week	$24,780.00 = 100%
Food cost %	31.4% = Controllable cost = $7,780.92
Labor cost %	34.1% = Controllable cost = $8,449.98
Other controllable cost % (Food, labor, and overhead)	15.6% = Controllable cost = $3,865.68
Uncontrollable cost % (Interest, depreciation, insurance, licenses, real estate taxes, and income taxes)	11.1% = $2,750.58
Profit %	7.8% = $1,932.84

Note: Controllable cost % = food cost % from recipes + labor cost % + other controllable cost %. Total sales = 100% = food cost % + labor cost % + other controllable cost % + uncontrollable cost % + profit %.

Menu Items	Food Cost % (from costed recipes)	% Contribution to Sales (from point of sales cash register)	Selling Price (from menu)	Number Sold
Fried Squid	33.7	0.3	$2.00	372
Pizza	42.1	37.0	$6.85	1338
Egg Plant	31.2	0.7	$0.75	2313
Pepsi	18.6	26.0	$0.75	8590
Amaretto Cheese Cake	28.2	27.0	$3.45	1939

Note: A point of sales cash register is an electronic cash register that can determine the contribution to sales of a food and beverage item as the sale occurs.

Number sold (# sold) = sales × contribution to sales/selling price. For example, number of fried squid sold = (24,780 × 3%) / $2.00 = 372.

Table 9-2. Goal Value Analysis Worksheet

GOAL VALUE (overall standard) =

(1 − FC% 0.686) × (ANS 2910) × (ASP 1.70) × (1 − (LC% 0.341 + OCC% 0.156 + FC% 0.314)) = 0.189

641.398

MENU ITEM VALUE (use all percentages in decimal form)

Menu Item	Food Cost %	Cont. Cost %	Number Sold	×	Selling Price	×	1 − FC%	×	1 − CC%	=	Value
Fried Squid	0.337	0.834	372	×	2.00	×	0.663	×	0.166	=	81.883
Pizza	0.421	0.918	1338	×	6.85	×	0.579	×	0.082	=	435.150
Eggplant	0.312	0.809	2313	×	0.75	×	0.688	×	0.191	=	227.960
Pepsi	0.186	0.683	8590	×	0.75	×	0.814	×	0.317	=	1662.409
Amaretto Cheese Cake	0.282	0.779	1939	×	3.45	×	0.718	×	0.221	=	1061.484

Total number sold   = 14,552

Average number sold = 14,552/5 (number of menu items sold)

Average selling price = 24,780.00 (sales)/14,552 (total number sold)

Number sold   = Sales × % contribution to sales/selling price

Controllable cost % = Food cost % from recipes + labor cost % + other controllable cost %

Value   = Number sold × selling price × (1 − food cost %) × (1 − controllable cost %)

Note: Number sold contributes a popularity factor. *Selling price* contributes a ticket size factor. 1 − *food cost* % contributes a food cost factor. 1 − *controllable cost* contributes a profit factor.

goal value (overall standard), the menu item is a loser. Sometimes, though, a low-value item should not be taken off the menu, because it may be a favorite of loyal customers who, in turn, bring in other customers. Therefore, it is important to remember that goal-value analysis is merely a tool to aid foodservice professionals in analyzing menu items and needs to be considered part of a process of careful analysis.

Goal-value analysis not only demonstrates the profitability of existing menu items, but also can be used for analyzing menu items before they are put on the menu. The following formula shows the sales volume minimum for a new menu item to make a profit.

$$\frac{\text{Goal value} \quad \text{(Overall standard)}}{(1 - \text{actual FC\%}) \times (\text{actual selling price}) \times (1 - \text{CC\%})} = \text{Sales volume goal}$$

Example:
Antipasto, new menu item
Food Cost % = 31.7%
Selling price = $2.50
Labor cost % = 34.1%
Other controllable cost % = 15.6%

$$\frac{641.398}{0.683 \times 2.50 \times 0.186} = \text{Sales volume goal}$$

$$\frac{641.398}{0.318} = \text{Sales volume goal}$$

$$2016.97 = \text{Sales volume goal}$$

This hypothetical restaurant must have a sales volume goal of 2016.97 in order to make antipasto profitable.

REVIEW QUESTIONS

1. Why can't a manager compare the sales of Mondays with the sales of Tuesdays?

2. Which day of the week is usually the slowest for most foodservice operations?

3. What is meant by the term *disposable income*?

4. Define *sales history*.

5. In what two areas is the sales history analysis useful to management?

6. Define goal value analysis.

Marketing and Merchandising the Menu

In order for the menu to be successful, it is not enough to be able to cost it, know the mechanics, and effectively analyze it. Ultimately one must also have a well-merchandised menu.

If a menu planner cannot properly list liquors or wines or does not describe popular entrees such as steak or seafood, this inability can have a devastating effect on sales. The major function of a menu is to sell menu items, but this can only take place if careful marketing and merchandising occurs.

Displaying nonitem information on the menu and listing liquors and wines, appetizers, salads, low-calorie items, steaks, seafood, sandwiches, desserts, take-out service, and specials are analyzed in this chapter.

The final sections demonstrate how to evaluate a sales menu. The evaluating criteria are based on printing, balance, variety, composition, descriptive copy, listing of items, and color of the menu.

OBJECTIVES

1. To have an understanding of how items on a menu are merchandised.
2. To understand the different marketing and merchandising techniques used on a menu.

A well-merchandised menu is a successful menu. The following areas are important for merchandising: displaying other information on the menu and listing liquors, wines, appetizers, salads, low-calorie items, steaks, seafood, sandwiches, desserts, take-out service, and specials.

DISPLAYING NONITEM INFORMATION ON THE MENU

Examples of nonitem information that can help to merchandise a menu are credit cards accepted, history of the operation, a map showing operation's location, a history of certain dishes, catering information, take-out service, management background, information about other locations if part of a chain, AAA accredited, banquet accommodations, tourist attractions in the area, gift shop information, address, phone number, and hours of operation. Many establishments do not put any nonitem information on the menu. The back cover should be used. (*Note:* The back cover should not be used for food items.) Leaving the back cover blank is a waste of space and valuable merchandising power.

LISTING LIQUORS

In most restaurants, management does not list liquors on the menu. It is often the job of the waiter or waitress to take the drink order without the patron seeing a list. Mentioning liquor and wine on the menu often increases sales even if there is also a separate beverage menu.

A separate liquor list or wine list calls attention to the selections available in the operation. A liquor list on the back of the menu is less effective for merchandising because it may be overlooked.

When listing liquors, give brand names. For example, under vodka a recognizable brand name would be Smirnoff's. It is also important to list liquors in the order in which they are consumed at meal time. Before-dinner drinks consisting of scotch, whiskey, bourbon, gin, vodka, and rum should be first, beers may come next, followed by wines (red, white, or rosé) with brandies or liquers. If you do not have a separate after-dinner drink menu, list these drinks after your desserts on a separate page.

WINE LISTS

A large wine selection should be on a separate wine list. A smaller wine selection can be on the menu, but should be listed before the appetizer on the menu, perhaps as part of a beverage list. Wines are listed by the following:

1. Where the wine originates: imported — French, Italian, German, Swiss, Spanish, or Austrian; American — Californian or Eastern.
2. Color of wine: red, white, or rosé.
3. Type of wine: sparkling champagne — Mumm Cordon Rouge, Brut, or sparkling burgundy (Asti Spumante, Martini and Rossi); still wines — Beaujolais, Zinfandel, Mateus, Pouilly Fuisse, Bereich Bernkastel Riesling (Hoch), or Chenin Blanc (Beringer).
4. Style of wine: dry, medium, sweet or semi-sweet, full bodied or light bodied, smooth, fruity flavored.
5. Pricing: on a wine list, display the prices. Wine generally comes by the bottle, half bottle, or glass.
6. Year of production: Château Latour Haut Brion 1979.
7. Bin number: used primarily for inventory purposes.

On a wine list, each wine should have a bin number, which is on the corresponding bottle of wine as well. A bin number serves many purposes. First, it identifies the bottle of wine; second, it aids in the inventory; third, it can make a difficult-to-pronounce French wine easy to order! The customer can simply recite the bin number next to the wine. (A pronouncing glossary or phonetic spelling on the wine list could help also.)

Finally, it is good merchandising to give the wines descriptive copy as well. For example, who could resist Chablis (Drouhin) from the burgundy class made from Chardonnay grapes, very dry, with a rich body?

APPETIZERS

Appetizers should be listed before soups on the menu. Good and easy-to-read descriptive copy will aid in selling appetizers. About four to six appetizers on an a la carte menu provide a good balance. Remember the importance of variety. For example, shrimp cocktail, escargot, stuffed mushroom caps, and stuffed eggplant are a good variety on an a la carte menu.

SALADS

Salads on the menu should be located after the appetizers and the soups. Salads, like appetizers, should be in readable type and be given adequate descriptive copy. For example, chef salad might be described as "a generous portion of romaine, iceberg, and chickory topped with danish ham, genoa salami, smoked turkey, sliced tomatoes, cucumbers, green peppers, and sliced eggs with a side of our own Thousand Island dressing. A complete meal in itself."

Salad dressing can also be an important item on the menu with its own descriptive copy. For example, Thousand Island dressing: "Our own dressing is made with rich mayonnaise, ketchup, Worcestershire sauce, relish, assorted spices, and just a touch of tabasco sauce. A great topping for any salad."

LOW-CALORIE ITEMS

In today's society, people are more aware of what they eat and whether or not it is nutritionally sound. Many customers are eating low-calorie items, the most popular being salad. Low-calorie items can be listed separately or under Salads. An example of a low-calorie item under Salads is a cheeseboard with an assortment of fruits. Again, make sure low-calorie items are in large enough type and are given descriptive copy.

STEAKS

Steak on the menu definitely requires descriptive copy for better merchandising. There are many factors to be considered when describing steaks on the menu, for example, the kind of steak, thickness, size or portion, and the manner in which it is prepared. One example of effective descriptive copy for steaks is as follows: "A 12-oz cut of filet broiled to perfection and topped with a creamy Hollandaise sauce with assorted spices."

Information on what is rare, medium rare, medium, and well done helps the customer. Steaks are one of the most expensive items on the menu. Steak items should be in readable type and be listed on the right side of the menu.

SEAFOOD

Seafood, like steak, should be in large, readable type and should have adequate descriptive copy. It is a good idea to include information such as where the seafood comes from, and how it is prepared and served. An example of descriptive copy for seafood might be "Scrod Bella Vista: A generous portion of baked scrod topped with sliced onions, green peppers, and tomatoes, surrounded by a rich tomato sauce."

SANDWICHES

Sandwiches, like your entrees, should have good descriptive copy and should be in readable type. If sandwiches are a specialty item, they can be listed before the entree. However, it is a common practice to list only the most popular and profitable sandwiches after entrees. Hot sandwiches on your menu can be given more descriptive copy than cold sandwiches if they are the more profitable item.

DESSERTS

Desserts can be listed in two ways. The first method is to list desserts after entrees on the menu in readable type and with descriptive copy. The second method is to have a separate dessert menu that may include after-dinner drinks as well. The separate dessert menu has the advantage of drawing attention to the dessert selections by allowing more room for descriptive copy.

TAKE-OUT SERVICE

Take-out service needs proper merchandising. The best way to merchandise take-out service is to do a separate take-out menu. When listing take-out information, give proper descriptive copy in readable type on the prices, portions, and packaging. Include a phone number if delivery service is available. Some establishments print photographs of their take-out selections, which is a good merchandising tool. Advertise take-out service on the back of the in-house menu.

SPECIALS

There can be two kinds of specials on a menu. The first special may be one for which the restaurant is well known. The second kind of special may be one that is easy to make and a high-profit item. To attract customers to specials, use pictures on the menu like many twenty-four-hour establishments do or set the specials in a box or graphic panel to attract your customers.

EVALUATING THE SALES MENU

The special occasion and dinner menus will be evaluated on the following characteristics: printing, balance, variety, composition, descriptive copy, listing of items, and color.

Evaluating The Inn at Kearsarge Menu—
Special Occasion Menu (see Fig. 10-1)

Printing. The printing is done in a proper manner. The headings are printed in uppercase and the descriptive copy is in lowercase roman typeface. It is not difficult to read this menu.

Balance. Balance is poor because of the limited choices in the selection of entrees and vegetables. There should be a minimum of two vegetable choices along with two potato choices. The entrees should include one other selection, such as Baked Ham with Raisin Sauce.

Variety. The variety within a special occasion menu will be limited because certain foods are traditional for that occasion as on this Thanksgiving menu. Besides the limited selection of vegetables and entrees, the variety of the other food categories is good.

Composition. The eye appeal and aesthetic value of the menu items are good. To have a more colorful plate, a green vegetable is recommended such as broccoli or peas.

Descriptive Copy. The descriptive copy is written in an interesting and appetizing manner. The amount of copy for each item is not too long or overly detailed. The food items are clearly and precisely described.

Listing of Items. The food categories are listed in the proper eating sequence of appetizer, soups, salads, entrees, vegetables, desserts, and beverages. The profit management theory on a modern table d'hôte menu is to include the entire meal for one price. There are choices within the entire selection. Therefore, the order of listing the most profitable food items is a concern.

Color. The color of the menu should be done in fall colors such as browns, oranges, and yellows. The graphics on the menu should relate to the occasion using pilgrims, turkeys, Indians, corn, and corn stalks.

Evaluating the White Cap Menu—
Dinner Menu (see Fig. 10-2)

Printing. Subheadings should be uppercase.

Balance. The menu has five appetizers, five soups, five salads, ten entrees, four vegetables, four potatoes, and four desserts. The menu is somewhat unbalanced in that it has no beverage selection.

Variety. This menu has an excellent variety of cooking techniques. For example, the salmon is poached, the sirloin steak is broiled, the veal is sautéed, the crab legs are steamed, and the chicken is deep fried, then baked.

The Inn at Kearsarge

GREAT BEGINNINGS

Stuffed Mushroom Caps

Mushrooms stuffed with crabmeat, breadcrumbs, sautéed onions, green
peppers, pimentos and just the right amount of sherry and spices.

Apple Cider

This cider comes piping hot with a cinnamon stick to add a special taste.

SOUPS

French Onion Soup

Our soup is simmered slowly and served in a crock dripping with swiss cheese
and topped with croutons.

Potato and Leek Soup

This soup is loaded with potatoes and leeks in a rich creamy base.

SALADS

Fruit Salad

An assortment of oranges, apples, grapefruit, strawberries and blueberries
capped with lime sherbert and served in a chilled cocktail glass.

Garden Salad

This salad is brimming with romaine, iceberg, boston bibb, cherry tomatoes,
cucumbers, radishes, carrots, mushrooms, and chopped eggs. Topped with our
own creamy Italian or Thousand Island Dressing.

THE MAIN COURSE

Roast Turkey and Dressing

Your choice of light or dark meat with our chestnut stuffing and, of course, our homemade cranberry sauce.

Broiled Sirloin Steak with Bordelaise Sauce

Our steak is broiled to perfection and covered with a rich brown sauce with sautéed mushrooms.

FROM THE GARDEN

Acorn Squash

We cook this squash slowly and sprinkle it with brown sugar, butter, cinnamon and a hint of nutmeg.

Sweet Potatoes

This dish is an all-time favorite. We combine pineapple, marshmallows, sweet potatoes and top this side dish with brown sugar and butter.

DESSERTS

Pumpkin Pie

A rich dessert, baked in a whole wheat crust and topped with whipped cream.

Grapenut Pudding

A smooth blend of grapenuts, apples, molasses, brown sugar, with whipped cream. This dessert is a great way to finish any holiday feast.

BEVERAGES

Coffee, tea or milk.

ADULTS — $16.25   CHILDREN — $9.25

(Tax and gratuity included.)

DINNER
THE WHITE CAP

Appetizers

Shrimp Cocktail——4 jumbo shrimp served over ice in a chilled cocktail glass served with a zesty cocktail sauce. **6.00**
Clams Casino——Each is topped with a mixture of breadcrumbs, sautéed onions, pimentos, green peppers, bacon and just the right amount of sherry, herbs and spices. **4.25**
Smoked Salmon——Our salmon is smoked slowly and comes with onions, capers and lemon. **5.25**
Melon with Prosciutto——Slices of melon wrapped in prosciutto ham under iceberg lettuce. **3.50**
Rumaki——Marinated chicken livers wrapped in bacon and then broiled to perfection.
3.25

Soups

Lobster Bisque——A thick creamy soup with tender pieces of lobster meat seasoned with just the right amount of herbs and spices served in a crock and capped with chopped parsley. **4.25**
Bouillabaisse——A seafood stew containing crab, mussels, sea bass, onions, tomatoes, saffron and garlic, assorted herbs with white wine or cognac. Comes with our own homemade French bread. **3.75**
Gazpacho——A cold pureed soup made with tomatoes, green peppers, onions, consommé, garlic and assorted herbs. Garnished with diced cucumbers, tomatoes, and seasoned croutons. **2.75**
Cream of Broccoli——A creamed soup made with broccoli seasoned with ground pepper and paprika. Sprinkled with bacon bits. **2.25**
Chicken Vegetable——Tender pieces of chicken in a rich chicken stock with an array of garden vegetables served with hot biscuits. **2.00**

Salads

Spinach Salad——A generous portion of crispy spinach combined with hard boiled eggs, bacon bits, mushrooms, croutons and our own oil and vinegar dressing. **1.75**
Fruit Salad——Honeydew, cantaloupe, oranges, apples, peaches, strawberries, blueberries, raisins and walnuts on a base of romaine lettuce. Accompanied with Chantilly dressing made with mayonnaise, whipped cream and Grenadine. **1.50**
Tossed Garden Salad——Romaine, iceberg and Boston bibb topped with cherry tomatoes, celery, radishes, green peppers and carrots. With a creamy garlic dressing. **1.50**
Waldorf Salad——A mixture of chopped apples, walnuts, celery and raisins in a mayonnaise dressing over romaine lettuce. **1.50**
Antipasto Salad——Romaine lettuce with sliced red onions, hot peppers, black olives, tomatoes, provolone cheese, salami, and anchovies. With oil and vinegar dressing. **1.75**

Vegetables

Glazed Carrots——Steamed gently then sautéed in butter, honey, and a pinch of nutmeg.
1.00
Broccoli with Hollondaise——Steamed broccoli crowned with a rich creamy lemony egg sauce of Hollondaise. **1.25**
Peas and Mushrooms——Peas lightly steamed then sautéed in butter along with tender mushrooms. **.75**
Baked Tomato——Covered with a mixture of bread crumbs, garlic, oregano, basil, ground pepper, parsley and baked until tender. Then we top this vegetable with cheddar cheese and put it under the broiler. **1.00**

Potatoes

Baby Redskins——Steamed and sautéed in butter and topped with parsley. **.75**
Potato Au Gratin——Layers of thinly sliced potato combined with a rich creamy cheese sauce then covered with buttered bread crumbs. **1.00**
Duchesse Potatoes——Whipped potatoes mixed with eggs, cream, chives, sautéed bacon, on a buttered sheet pan and baked to a golden brown. **1.25**
Rice Pilaf——Rice simmered in a rich chicken stock then sautéed with pimento, bacon, peas, and mushrooms. **.75**

Entrees—Seafood

Seafood Medley——An assortment of sautéed scallops, shrimp and lobster with melted butter. **15.25**
Alaskan King Crab Legs——One pound steamed crab legs served with drawn butter and a lemon wedge. **14.00**
Poached Salmon with Egg Sauce——An 8 oz. portion of salmon poached in a white wine stock with a variety of herbs and covered with a rich egg sauce. **13.25**
Broiled Swordfish——An 8 oz serving of North Atlantic swordfish broiled to perfection and served with a lemon wedge. **13.50**
Stuffed Sole——Two filets of sole stuffed with our special crabmeat stuffing and baked to a golden luster. This dish is then crowned with a Newberg sauce. **11.25**

Entrees—Meats

Sirloin Steak——A 16 oz. prime sirloin broiled to your specifications and topped with a mushroom cap. **12.75**
Veal Picata——Sautéed veal in a white wine, butter and lemon sauce. Garnished with a twist of lemon and chopped parsley. **10.75**
Broiled Lamb Chops——Two lamb chops broiled and served with a mint sauce. **11.25**
Barbecued Pork Chops——Two pork chops broiled over hickory wood and laced with a tangy barbecue sauce. Served with homemade cornbread. **9.75**
Chicken Cordon Bleu——Boneless chicken breast filled with swiss cheese and ham. This dish is deep fried then baked to a golden brown and capped with a Supreme sauce and chopped parsley. **8.75**

Desserts

Strawberries **2.00**
Cheesecake **1.75**
Chocolate Mousse **2.25**
Pecan Pie **1.50**

Composition. The food items on this menu go well together and would appeal to the eye when served to the customer. For instance, if one ordered the Broiled Lamb Chops, Baked Tomato, and Rice Pilaf, the selection would have excellent color and composition.

Descriptive Copy. The dessert section has no descriptive copy. Remember in a fine dining establishment, descriptive copy should be present for all food items. Hollandaise, Picatta, and Newburg are spelled wrong. Remember, it is important for the menu planner to ensure that all words are spelled correctly on the menu. If one word is misspelled, the menu will have to be reprinted.

Listing of Items. The listing of food items is incorrect in this menu. The vegetables and potatoes should be listed after the entrees.

Color. The color of the menu might be a light blue background with dark blue printing to accompany the name of the restaurant, The White Cap, centering around a nautical decor.

REVIEW QUESTIONS

1. Name five pieces of information that could merchandise menus on the back cover.

2. Identify some of the principles of listing liquor.

3. List in order the proper categories of a wine list.

4. What is a bin number?

5. Why is it important for the menu planner to put low-calorie items on the menu?

6. What are some of the factors used to describe steaks?

7. What are some of the factors used to describe seafood?

8. What two important factors affect listing sandwiches on the menu?

9. How can desserts be listed?

10. How can the menu planner attract the customer to specials on the menu?

11

Foodservice Equipment Analysis

Every foodservice operator needs to purchase equipment in order to produce the food products on the menu. This chapter establishes guidelines to selecting equipment and explains how to justify the equipment that the foodservice operator needs to buy.

OBJECTIVES

1. To be able to purchase foodservice equipment without over-purchasing.
2. To be able to complete a foodservice equipment analysis and to establish a listing of foodservice equipment that indicates the capacity of the equipment.
3. To know ten guidelines in purchasing equipment.

GUIDELINES TO SELECTING EQUIPMENT

It is essential for any foodservice operator who wants to stay within budget to be knowledgeable of the types and the volumes of equipment to be purchased. The following are guidelines to purchasing equipment:

> Justify the purchase of the equipment. *If you do not need it, don't buy it!* A lot of equipment is sold each year to foodservice operators who find after the sale that the equipment is of little use or not needed at all.

How does one justify the purchase of equipment? Foodservice operators need to complete a foodservice equipment analysis. The purpose of the foodservice equipment analysis is to establish the type of equipment and the volume of that equipment needed to produce the food product on the menu.

Many foodservice operators rely totally on the sales representative to establish the type of equipment needed to produce their menu. This dependence is harmful because the sales representative does not know the entire foodservice operation. Most foodservice equipment sales representatives do not inflate the type and number of pieces of equipment that are needed. They make recommendations on what to buy based on the needs and desires of the foodservice operators. Always remember, however, that it is the sales representative's job to sell and it is the foodservice operator's job to know what to purchase.

Know when to purchase new equipment.

When do you need to purchase brand new equipment? Always purchase new equipment if the customer is going to be viewing the equipment. The factors that will influence this guideline are the foodservice operator's budget and the image to be portrayed. New equipment is primarily used in the front of the foodservice operation and used equipment is primarily used in the back of the foodservice operation.

Why purchase used equipment? The number one advantage of purchasing used equipment is saving money. Unfortunately, the National Restaurant Association reports that 80 percent of the first-time foodservice operators in a given year fail. Some operators purchase new equipment that has to be liquidated. The life span of a major piece of equipment such as a broiler, fryer, or oven is ten years. Purchasing used equipment that has to be liquidated will save the buyer 60–70 percent off the sticker price of a new piece of equipment. Some disadvantages to purchasing used equipment are that the equipment cannot be one hundred percent depreciated by the second owner, if at all. The second owner may lose the benefits of the dealership guarantee or the manufacturer warranty. The second owner will not know how the liquidated equipment has been maintained.

Where is the best place to purchase used equipment? The best place to purchase used equipment is at a liquidation auction. To be successful at purchasing liquidated equipment, the foodservice operator must not be in a rush to furnish the operation. It takes time, energy, money, and knowledge about the needed equipment and patience. The foodservice operator should contact the nearest auction hall or look in the newspaper to find out when the auction will be held.

It is important before the auction begins to preview the equipment to see if it does operate and if there is damage to see if it is repairable. Another important factor is to establish the amount of money you are willing to pay for each piece of equipment before the auction starts. You do not want to go over your budget during the bidding process. During the preview time find out the procedures on how the auction hall operates. Most places require that the equipment be moved from the hall immediately after the auction. Also inquire on what types of payments the hall accepts. Personal checks and credit cards require a reference check and most halls require you to establish this prior to the start of the auction.

Banks are another source for locating foodservice equipment from places that are being foreclosed. Banks will hold auctions on the site of the foodservice operation. Banks are the first to know if the foodservice operations themselves will be auctioned.

Know about renting versus leasing foodservice equipment.

The term *leasing* means renting with the option to purchase the equipment. When renting equipment there is no option to purchase the equipment. The main reasons for renting and/or leasing equipment are as follows:

1. When something goes wrong with the equipment the foodservice operator does not have to pay for the service charge.
2. If the equipment breaks while in operation, the foodservice operator does not have to pay for the spare parts.
3. When a foodservice operation leases equipment the operating captial that is needed to open the foodservice operation is less. More money is needed to purchase the equipment than to rent or lease the equipment.
4. Unfortunately 80 percent of people going into the foodservice business fail during the first year. If this happens, it is better not to own all of your equipment because you will not be able to retain the total value or return on your investment. When leasing the equipment or renting the equipment the title or ownership is not owned by you. Therefore your loss is not as great.

Consider design of the equipment.

Always purchase equipment that will portray the image you have selected for your customers. Always purchase new equipment for places the customer can see. When the customer is not going to see the area, buy equipment that is operationally good but may not be the best looking.

Purchase equipment that has automation.

Time is money! Purchase equipment that will allow you and your staff to save on the amount of time it takes to do a task. Any automatic device, such as a timer on a fryolator, will allow the fry cook to cook the product and do another job at the same time.

Select self-cleaning and easily cleaned equipment.

Equipment that will clean itself is a miracle in disguise. A ventilation/exhaust hood system that has steam lines within the ducts and has an automatic timing device is an excellent example. The steam lines at a set time will release steam into the ducts (passage ways for air to travel) to clean off the built-up grease. A self-cleaning piece of equipment will save energy and time. Easy-to-clean equipment such as stainless steel tables, counter tops, and shelves are great.

Select equipment that can be sanitized.

Always purchase equipment that has been certified to withstand the harsh chemicals it takes to sanitize a piece of equipment. The National Sanitation Foundation (NSF) is an organization that will test equipment to certify that the finish material on the equipment will withstand the reaction of the abrasive chemicals during the cleaning process. The Board of Health also looks at equipment to see that it can be taken apart easily to be cleaned and sanitized. Look for NSF labels on the equipment.

Know about the guarantee versus the warranty.

A warranty and a guarantee both protect your investment for a certain period of time. A warranty is issued by the manufacturer. It covers a time period of typically five years and protects the major "heart" component(s) of the equipment. A compressor to a walk-in freezer or cooler is an excellent example. If the compressor fails to operate under normal conditions the warranty will allow the owner to get it serviced or replaced without charge. A guarantee is issued through the dealership where the equipment was purchased. It covers a time period of thirty days to two years depending on the type of equipment. It protects the small parts of a piece of equipment. For example, if the door handle to the walk-in freezer or cooler falls off, due to normal use, the owner can have it serviced without being charged.

Guarantees and warranties vary greatly from manufacturers and dealerships so read them carefully. Always make a copy of them and file separately from the originals.

Know about selecting standard equipment and building your own specialized equipment.

Select standard equipment when possible. Standard equipment is equipment that has set a standard in the foodservice industry. It is equipment that comes from a company with a good reputation. Standard equipment is equipment that is readily available and does not cost a lot of money to replace.

Specialized equipment is the opposite. The equipment is designed and built to the foodservice operator's specifications. The equipment is designed to do a particular task in the location of the foodservice operation. The advantages of standard equipment are

The quantity of the equipment is greater.

The price is less expensive.

Spare parts are available at lower prices.

Most foodservice equipment dealers carry the equipment.

The service history has proven that the equipment is durable and has good production.

The warranty and/or guarantee are available and most likely are for a longer time than those for specialized equipment.

One disadvantage of standard equipment is that sometimes the equipment cannot do the production task you want it to do. Specialized equipment will cost more money to obtain and repair, but it is sometimes purchased because it is the only way to accomplish the task at hand.

Check the reputation of the architect, sales dealership, and manufacturer.

Always research the reputation of the person or business from which you will be purchasing equipment. You will be spending thousands of dollars on your equipment. Call the local Better Business Bureau, talk to former customers, get references from the person or business, and check the references. Talk with chefs, managers, and sales representatives to find out who they recommend.

FOODSERVICE EQUIPMENT ANALYSIS

To save money when purchasing equipment, develop a list of equipment that is essential in producing the menu. It is not a wise practice to go shopping for equipment without first establishing your needs. Most people who do shop without a list end up spending more money on equipment than is necessary.

The purpose of a foodservice equipment analysis (see Fig. 11-1) is to establish the type of equipment needed to produce a menu and to establish the volume or capacity of the equipment. The first step is to establish a menu. The second step is to establish the number of portions to be prepared. This number is based on the foodservice

FOODSERVICE EQUIPMENT ANALYSIS SHEET

Meal <u>Dinner</u>
Day <u>Saturday</u>
Peak Period <u>7:00 P.M. to 9:00 P.M.</u>

Meal Item	Portion to Prepare	Weight or Volume per Portion	Total Amount Produced	Items per Hour	Usage Time Range	EQUIPMENT: Including Size and Number			
						Preparation	Production	Holding	Service
Sirloin Steak	120	16 ozs	120 lbs	40	5-9 P.M.	walk-in cooler table reach-in cooler	broiler	reach-in cooler	

Figure 11-1. Foodservice equipment analysis sheet.

operation's capacity times the turnover rate plus a 10 percent growth rate. For example, a 100-seat foodservice operation times a three turnover rate per peak period hour (three hours) equals 300 customers. Add a 10 percent growth rate to plan for the future capacity of the equipment, thus allowing for 330 customers to be served during the peak period. A peak period is the time period a foodservice operation will be very busy. Peak periods for breakfast are usually two hours, between 7:00 A.M. and 9:00 A.M., for lunch, between 11:00 A.M. and 2:00 P.M., and for dinner, between 6:00 P.M. and 9:00 P.M. Peak periods will vary from operation to operation. The peak period in our example is from 7:00 P.M. to 9:00 P.M. on Saturday night.

It is very important to forecast the number of customers the operation will be serving on a typical busy night or peak period. When a chef does not forecast accurately, food cost due to overproduction or underproduction will be high and the end result will be a lower profit.

Once you have established the total customer count, you must forecast how many portions of a menu product will be sold. For example, how many customers out of 330 will purchase the entree sirloin steak? A few factors that will influence your forecasted number are

Total number of steaks offered

Popularity of the food product

Price of the food product

Amount of advertising or marketing done on the food product

Quality of flavor (taste)

Appearance

Effort that the service staff is willing to make to sell the food product

Rarity of the food product

Order in which the menu item is listed

Placement of the item on the menu

Amount of time it takes to produce the food product

In our example, we will sell 120 portions during the peak period only. Once you have forecasted the number of portions to prepare, each portion is given a weight in ounces or pounds or a volume measurement such as cups, pints, quarts, or gallons. The portion size of the sirloin steak is 16 ozs (1 lb). To find the total amount produced multiply the number of portions to prepare times the portion size, 120 × 16 ozs = 1,920 ozs or 120 lbs.

The total amount produced column can also assist the chef in knowing how much food product to purchase. It is important to note that the total amount produced column calculates foods in a one hundred percent (edible) as served quantity. The chef would not purchase 120 lbs of sirloin steak exactly if the chef wanted to end up with 120 lbs. The chef would take into consideration the yield of the sirloin steak. The total amount of sirloin steak to be produced is 120 portions, which equals 120 lbs during the peak period.

The items per hour column indicates how many items need to be produced during one hour. To find this amount, divide the number of peak period hours into the total amount produced column.

$$3 \overline{)120}^{\,40}$$

$$3 \text{ hr} \overline{)120 \text{ sirloin steak portions}}^{\,40 \text{ sirloin steaks per hour}}$$

The reason for finding the production per hour is most equipment and equipment catalogs indicate the production capacity by the hour. A typical broiler catalog will indicate several models. The one you will select will depend on your budget and on your quantity need. In our example, we need 40 portions of sirloin steak per hour. If you were to only broil sirloin steaks on the broiler, which is highly unlikely, you would select a broiler that would broil 40 or as close to 40 sirloin steaks as possible.

The usage time column indicates the amount of time needed to produce the food product. This time range includes the preparation and production time. In our example, the sirloin steaks will be cut from the whole sirloin strip and cooked to order. The time range to prep the steaks is from 5:00 P.M. to 7:00 P.M. and the cooked-to-order time range is the same as the peak period, from 7:00 P.M. to 9:00 P.M. The total time range is 4 hours, 5:00 P.M. to 9:00 P.M. Indicating the four hours will assist the chef in developing a production schedule.

A production schedule indicates who will be cooking, when the food products are to be prepared and produced, and with what equipment. The sirloin steaks will be produced from 5:00 P.M. to 7:00 P.M., cooked to order from 7:00 P.M. to 9:00 P.M., and cooked on a broiler.

The remaining columns refer to the actual equipment needs to prepare, produce, hold, and serve the food products. The preparation column indicates the equipment that is necessary to prepare the sirloin steaks. It is at this point in your thought process that you should get your food product from the storage area. In our example, the sirloin is fresh and stored in the walk-in cooler. From storage, the sirloin strip is placed on a table for cutting. A knife and a tray or pan are also necessary. Next the portioned steaks are either placed back into the walk-in cooler or into a reach-in cooler near the broiler. The reach-in cooler should be indicated in the preparation column and the broiler should be listed in the production column. The difference between the two columns is that the production equipment will indicate the major hot equipment during the production phase of the food product. Hot equipment is normally equipment such as convenction ovens, fryolators, grills, steam equipment, and stoves. The holding column indicates where the food product will be held during the peak period. Cook-to-order items are usually held in a dry or refrigerated state while pre-prepared foods are held in a warm or hot state. The sirloin steaks are held in a refrigerated state. Other holding equipment items are steam tables, food warmers, and ovens.

The service column indicates the equipment that is needed to serve the food product to the customer. The sirloin steaks do not need any additional equipment to be served to the customer if the style of service is American. If the sirloins were done at tableside, you would need a réchaud and a guéridon or a portable carving cart.

The last step in analyzing your equipment needs is to determine the capacity of your equipment. First total the quantities of food that need to be produced by the individual piece of equipment. The broiler is the major piece of equipment to produce the sirloin steaks. What size broiler do you need? You have to count all the food products that will require the broiler during the peak period. In our example, we need 120 portions of sirloin steak. What other food products will be using the broiler? If our menu had broiled fish, chicken, or pork products we would add their portions to be produced to the sirloin steaks. Let us say we need 50 orders of broiled pork chops to be added to the 120 orders of sirloin steaks. The total broiler production is 170 food items.

The next step is to research foodservice equipment catalogs or talk to a salesperson to find out which broiler model will come close to producing 170 food products per hour. Through careful study of the menu and how to produce the menu you have a better idea now of the equipment and the needed equipment capacity. This exercise is to be used as a guide to help you save money in your purchasing of foodservice equipment.

HELPFUL HINTS TO COMPLETING THE FOODSERVICE EQUIPMENT ANALYSIS

- ♦ The foodservice equipment analysis is used as a guideline only.
- ♦ The foodservice equipment analysis purpose is to establish the type of foodservice equipment and the capacity of the equipment that is needed to produce the menu.
- ♦ The foodservice equipment analysis will establish a shopping list for the major heavy-duty cooking equip-

ment. Smaller pieces of equipment such as plates, knives, and cups should be placed on an independent list.

♦ The end results will vary greatly depending on how the chef decides to purchase, prepare, store, produce, and serve the food products.

♦ Not all the columns have to be used in every food product. A tossed salad does not need equipment in the production column.

♦ Soups, sauces, gravies, and other products with volume are usually made prior to the peak period and will not use the production column.

♦ Forecasting portions is a difficult task in the real job market.

♦ The amount of money and floor space the chef has will greatly influence the type of equipment to be purchased.

♦ It is easier to use letters or numbers to represent a piece of equipment, such as the letter D represents a mixer, than it is to write out the word mixer every time you need to indicate it.

♦ Always indicate the equipment when you use it in your planning. Some food products will use two or three pieces of equipment in the production column.

REVIEW QUESTIONS

1. What is the difference between a guarantee and a warranty?

2. What are three guidelines to selecting equipment?

3. What is the purpose of the foodservice equipment analysis?

4. What are four factors that will influence the number of forecasted portions to sell in the foodservice equipment analysis?

5. Why is it important to do a foodservice equipment analysis before purchasing equipment for a foodservice operation?

Appendixes

APPENDIX A

DESCRIPTIVE COPY EXERCISE

From the following list, choose twenty-five menu items and describe each selection using four adjectives for each item. Once an adjective has been used, it cannot be repeated again.

Breakfast Appetizers

Orange Juice
Mixed Fruit
Honeydew
Grapefruit

Breakfast Entrees

Scrambled Eggs
Western Omelette
Denver Omelette
Mushroom Omelette
Eggs Benedict
Apple Pancakes with Syrup
French Toast with Syrup
Sirloin Steak with Choice of Eggs
Corned Beef Hash with Poached Eggs
Waffles with Syrup
Cheese Blintzes with Fruit

Luncheon Appetizers

Nova Scotia Salmon
Oysters on the Half Shell
Antipasto
Fruit Cup with Sherbert
Marinated Herring with Sour Cream

Luncheon Soups

Seafood Bisque with Sherry
French Onion Soup with Cheese
Okra Chowder
Broccoli and Cheese
Minestrone
Cream of Spinch

Luncheon Salads

Chef Salad
Spinach Salad
Waldorf Salad
Crabmeat Salad
Cole Slaw

Luncheon Entrees

Shrimp and Crabmeat au Gratin
Baked Stuffed Sole with Newburg Sauce
Shrimp Scampi
Salmon with Egg Sauce
Sautéed Brook Trout
Filet Mignon with Onion Rings
Beef Stroganoff
Beef Stew with Biscuit
Ground Sirloin Steak

Chicken Divan
Chicken Cordon Bleu
Chicken Kiev
Veal Parmesan
Veal Marsala
Veal Gruyere
Roast Turkey with Dressing

Luncheon Vegetables and Potatoes

Carrots with Dill
Corn Mexican
Broccoli Polonaise
Peas Forestiere
Green Beans Almandine
Eggplant Parmesan
Mashed Potatoes
Scalloped Potatoes
O'Brien Potatoes
Delmonico Potatoes

Luncheon Desserts

Pound Cake with Ice Cream
Blueberry Pie with Ice Cream
Pecan Pie with Whipped Cream
Boston Cream Pie
Lemon Meringue Pie
Strawberry Shortcake
Apple Crisp with Ice Cream
Chocolate Layer Cake
Chocolate Mousse Cake
Sundaes

Dinner Appetizers

Shrimp Cocktail
Escargot
Shrimp Pernod
Clams on the Half Shell
Stuffed Mushroom Caps
Liver Paté
Smoked Salmon

Dinner Soups

Clam Chowder
Cream of Asparagus
Leek and Potato
Scallop Bisque
Gazpacho

Dinner Salads

Caesar Salad
Tossed Greens
Hearts of Palm
Boston Bibb with Crabmeat

Dinner Entrees

Fettucini Alfredo
Veal Dijonnaise
Veal Picatta
Veal a la Holstein
Breast of Chicken Estragon
Roast Beef with Popovers
Chateaubriand
Broiled Lamb Chops with Mint Jelly
Broiled Swordfish
Baked Stuffed Shrimp
Baked Stuffed Lobster
Braised Pheasant
Roast Duckling with Cherry Sauce
Sautéed Liver with Onions and Bacon
Scrod Bella Vista
Lobster Thermidor
Shrimp Teriyaki
Sole Rockefeller
Seafood Brochette

(List continues.)

Dinner Vegetables and Potatoes

Asparagus with Hollandaise Sauce
Glazed Carrots
Peas in Cream Sauce
Baked Stuffed Tomato
Acorn Squash
Cauliflower au Gratin
Fried Eggplant
Duchess Potatoes
Rissole Potatoes
Potato Pancakes
Sweet Potatoes
Baked Stuffed Potato

Dinner Desserts

Strawberries and Cream
Banana Cream Pie
Black Forest Cake
Lemon Chiffon Pie
Cherry Pie with Ice Cream
Rum Cake
Indian Pudding with Whipped Cream
Baked Alaska
Carrot Cake
Angel Food Cake

APPENDIX B

DESCRIPTIVE TERMS FOR MENUS

A deliciously seasoned
A fragrant mixture
An assortment of
And extraordinary ingredients
Artfully seasoned
As you prefer it
A thick generous portion
A thick generous treat
At its delightful perfection
Baked golden brown
Blazed in cognac
Blended with a distinctive sauce
Choice center cut
Cooked in an artistically seasoned sherry sauce
Craftily marinated
Delicate wine sauce
Delicately boiled and served with savory herbs
Delightfully different
Fluffy tenderness
Generous portion
Gourmet's delight

In an intriguing blend
In a traditional manner
Nappe with a piquante sauce
Nationally famous
Prepared by the authentic version
Prepared to your epicurean taste
Roasted to a turn
Sauce enlivened with onions and herbs
Served in a distinctive sauce
Served steaming in a casserole
Served with a lavish hand from a bowl tossed well to your taste
Simmered in it's own juice
Taste enriched with a perky piquante sauce
Tender bite-size flakes
Tender flakes
Tender sweet
Tenderly sautéed in butter
This classic french sauce
To make a meal a feast
Truly delightful
With a natural flavor

APPENDIX C

WORDS FREQUENTLY MISSPELLED ON STUDENTS' MENUS

accompaniment
avocado
bacon
banquet
barbecue sauce
béarnaise
blueberries
broccoli
burgundy
cantaloupe
cinnamon
cocktail
combination
croutons
delicate
delicious
diner
dining

fettuccini, fettucine
filet mignon
flambéed, flambé
fried
fryolator
hollandaise
iceberg lettuce
lasagne
linguine
manicotti
mayonnaise
mozzarella
occasion
omelette, omelet
parmesan
parsley
pimiento, (pimento)

potato
prosciutto
provolone
purveyor
raisins
restaurant
ricotta
romaine
romano
roquefort
sprig
syrup
tabasco
vinaigrette
vinegar
Worcestershire sauce
zucchini

APPENDIX D

CULINARY TERMS

à la CREOLE—In the style of Louisiana cookery; with onions, tomatoes, green peppers, and sometimes okra.

à la FLORENTINE—Foods that have a spinach base such as cream soup with spinach.

à la KING—A white cream sauce with green peppers, pimento, and mushrooms.

à la MODE—With ice cream.

AMANDINE or ALMANDINE—With almonds.

au GRATIN—Topped with bread crumbs and cheese and browned.

au JUS—Served in its own juices.

BABA—Spongy yeast cake soaked in rum.

BÉARNAISE—An egg butter sauce in which tarragon, chervil, shallots, and meat

juices have been added. Sometimes served with tenderloin.

BEAUJOLAIS—Region in the southern part of Bourgogne known for its red wines.

BÉCHAMEL—White cream sauce made with butter, flour, and milk.

BENEDICT—Poached eggs with hollandaise sauce and ham or bacon served on an English muffin.

BISQUE—Creamy soup made with shellfish, usually shrimp and lobster.

BORDEAUX—The most important area in France for the production of wine.

BORDELAISE—Brown sauce that contains shallots, red wine, tarragon, thyme, and sometimes bone marrow.

BORTSCH or *BORSCHT*—Vegetable soup that contains cabbage and red beets or beef base. Originated in Russia.

BOUILLABAISSE—Seafood stew containing crab, mussels, sea bass, onions, tomatoes, saffron, garlic, and assorted herbs with white wine and Cognac.

BOUILLON—Plain white stock originally. In today's restaurants it is a clear soup made from fish, meat, or vegetables.

BOUQUET GARNI—Assortment of herbs to flavor soups, stews, or sauces.

BOURSIN—Cream cheese flavored with herbs and garlic. This cheese is factory made.

BRIE—French cheese characterized by its white rind and rich, creamy, yellow color.

BROCHETTE—Foods that are grilled on a skewer, for example, beef or chicken with onions, green peppers, tomatoes, and mushrooms.

CAMEMBERT—Mild, creamy flavored cheese from France.

CANAPÉ—Small piece of bread, plain or toasted, and topped with seafood, meats, and sometimes eggs.

CAPERS—Pickled bud of a plant that grows in southern California and the Mediterranean Sea area, used in sauces, butter, and salads.

CAVIAR—The eggs of sturgeon, salmon, whitefish, and lumpfish, usually salted. The best caviar comes from Russia and Iran.

CHABLIS—One of the most famous dry, white wines from France.

CHANTILLY—Salad dressing consisting of whipped cream and mayonnaise, flavored with liqueur or vanilla.

CHASSEUR—Garnish containing shallots, white wine, and sliced mushrooms.

CHATEAUBRIAND—Double cut of tenderloin served to two people. Served with a variety of vegetables and a border of duchess potatoes.

CHERRIES JUBILEE—French dessert of vanilla ice cream covered with flamed Bing cherries.

CHIVES—Plant that has a distinctive onion flavor used in salads, soups, and sour cream.

CLAIRET—Light red wine made in Bordeaux and Bourgogne.

COINTREAU—Orange-flavored liqueur.

COMPOTE—Stewed fruits, usually served cold.

CONCASSÉ—Tomato that has been skinned, deseeded, and chopped coarsely. Used as a garnish for entrees and salads.

CONSOMMÉ—Clear soup, usually beef, poultry, or game garnished with an assortment of vegetables and herbs.

COQUILLE SAINT JACQUES—Shell or shell-shaped dish that contains seafood, often with a cream sauce, topped with breadcrumbs, grated cheese, and then browned.

CRÊPE—Thin pancake stuffed with fruits or various meats.

CROISSANT—Crescent-shaped pastry usually served at breakfast.

CROQUETTES—Usually contain fish or meat that has been chopped up and mixed with a white sauce. They are then shaped oblong, breaded, and deep fried.

CROUTONS—Dried pieces of bread that are cut into cubes and flavored with an array of herbs and spices. Served in salads or soups.

DEMI-GLACE—Rich brown sauce that has been reduced.

DEMI-TASSE—Small cup of black coffee.

DRAWN BUTTER—Butter that has been seasoned, usually served with fish.

DUCHESSE POTATOES—Mashed potatoes seasoned with nutmeg, butter, and egg yolk. Shaped and piped onto a buttered baking sheet pan.

ÉCLAIR—Oblong pastry filled with custard for dessert or with creamed food for an entree.

ESCALOPES—Thinly sliced pieces of veal sautéed in fortified butter.

ESPAGNOLE—Brown sauce.

FINES HERBES—Assortment of chopped herbs, consisting of parsley, chives, chervil, and tarragon.

FRICASSÉE—Diced veal or chicken in a white sauce.

GALANTINE—Dish of forcemeat, for example, galantine of duck.

GOULASH—Rich beef stew that contains paprika and onions.

HOLLANDAISE—Sauce consisting of egg yolks, butter, lemon juice, white wine, and paprika.

HORS D'OEUVRE—French word for appetizer.

JULIENNE—Vegetable that is cut in a matchlike fashion, like julienne of carrots.

KIRSCH—Liqueur distilled from fermented cherries. Used in desserts for extra flavor.

LASAGNE—Italian dish made with pasta, tomato sauce, and various cheeses.

LONDON BROIL—Marinated flank steak that is cut across the grain.

LYONNAISE—Sautéed sliced potatoes with onions.

MACEDOINE—Mixture of various fruits or vegetables.

MAITRE D'HOTEL—Butter that contains lemon juice, white wine, parsley, and Worcestershire sauce.

MARMITE—Clear broth served in an earthenware pot that usually has beef and vegetables in it.

MÉDAILLON or MEDALLION—Small cuts of pork tenderloin or beef.

MILANAISE—In the style of Milan cookery. A dish that is dipped in egg, bread crumbs, cheese, and then fried.

MINESTRONE—Rich Italian vegetable and pasta soup.

MIREPOIX—Combination of onion, carrots, and celery. Used as a basis for sauces.

MORNAY—White cream sauce where cheese has been added.

MOUSSELINE—Hollandaise sauce in which whipped cream has been added.

NAPOLEON—Squares cut from puff pastry filled with cream.

NEWBURG—Cream sauce where egg yolk and sherry have been added to enrich the taste.

NORMANDE—Sauce made from white wine and cream, served with fish.

O'BRIEN POTATOES—Potatoes that are diced and cooked, then sautéed with green peppers, pimentos, and bacon.

(à la) PARISIENNE—Garnish for chicken or fish consisting of mushroom, asparagus, truffles, with a white wine sauce.

PÂTÉ—Mixture of meat, usually pork, fish, or game. Baked in an earthenware dish or in a pastry case, usually served cold.

PETIT FOUR—Small cake or pastry.

PROVENÇALE—Cooking style of the southern province of France, consisting of tomato sauce, garlic, herbs, and olives.

RAGOUT—Brown or white stew usually with a small amount of red sauce.

RAVIOLI—Italian pasta dish filled with meat, vegetables, or cheese.

ROBERT—Sauce made with onions, mustard, white wine, and vinegar. Often served with roast pork.

ROULADE—Rolled meat or fish stuffed with vegetables.

SHALLOT—Member of the onion family.

SHISH KABOB, or SHISH KEBAB—Beef, lamb, chicken, or fish roasted on a skewer served with tomatoes, green peppers, onions, and mushrooms.

SMITANE—Sauce made of white wine and sour cream.

SOLE—Delicate tasting fish that is flat. The true sole, English Dover sole, is found in Europe only.

SPUMONI—Ice cream that is flavored with fruit, originated in Italy.

STEAK TARTARE—Tenderloin that has been minced, seasoned, and reshaped. It is often served with raw onions, capers, and egg yolk. The meat is served raw.

TORTE—Rich cake layered with cream.

TOURNEDOS—Small rounded steak from the thickest part of the fillet.

TRUFFE or TRUFFLE—Black fungus that is similar to a mushroom grown underground. It is used as a garnish for the most part because of its high price.

TURBOT—Fish that is similar to halibut. It is flat in nature.

VACHERIN—Dessert that has meringue and whipped cream on a pastry.

VELOUTÉ—Creamy white sauce made from white stock.

VERMICELLI—Thin pasta used in consommé.

VICHYSSOISE—Soup made consisting of potatoes or leeks, from France.

VINAIGRETTE—Cold dressing made of oil and vinegar, herbs, spices and lemon juice.

VOL-AU-VENT—Puff pastry filled with an array of creamed foods.

WIENER SCHNITZEL—Veal that has been breaded and sautéed, garnished with anchovy, caper, and a lemon slice.

YORKSHIRE PUDDING—Popover pastry usually served with roast beef. Originated in England.

APPENDIX E

MEASUREMENTS

General Equivalents

16 tablespoons	=	1 cup
1 cup (standard measure)	=	½ pint (8 fluid ounces)
2 cups	=	1 pint
16 ounces	=	1 pound
3 quarts (dry)	=	1 peck
4 pecks	=	1 bushel
32 ounces	=	1 fluid quart
128 ounces = 8 pounds	=	1 fluid gallon
1 No. 10 can	=	13 cups
1 pound margarine	=	2 cups
1 pound flour	=	4 cups

The number of the scoop determines the number of servings in each quart of a mixture, that is, with a No. 16 scoop, one quart of mixture will yield 16 servings.

Decimal Equivalents of Fractions

0.25	=	¼	0.66	=	⅔
0.33	=	⅓	0.75	=	¾
0.5	=	½			

The abbreviation beside the fraction tells what unit of measure to use.

APPENDIX F

TRUTH OF MENU

1. Brand names must be represented accurately. Examples of brand names of products on a menu are: Perdue Chicken, Hunt's Ketchup, Hellman's Mayonnaise, Green Giant Frozen Vegetables, B and M Baked Beans, and Butterball Turkey.

2. Dietary and nutritional claims must be accurate. To protect customers from potential health hazards, the dietary structure of food must be correctly stated. For example, low-sodium or fat-free foods must be correctly prepared to ensure the protection of all customers. All nutritional claims must be supported with statistical data.

3. The preservation of food must be accurate. The preservation of food is as follows: frozen, chilling, dehydration, drying, such as, sun or smoking, bottled, and canned. If a menu planner wishes to use the above terms, they must be used correctly on the menu. For example, fresh fish is not frozen.

4. Quantity must be accurate. If a sirloin is 16 oz, it must be stated on the menu that this is the weight prior to cooking.

5. Location of ingredients must be accurate. If Dover Sole is on the menu, it must be from Dover and not from New England. Pancakes with Vermont maple syrup must be Vermont syrup, not New Hampshire syrup.

6. Quality or grade must be accurate. When listing quality or grade for meats, dairy products, poultry, and vegetables or fruits, accuracy is critical. For example, if you state *prime sirloin*, it must be exactly that. You cannot use *choice* and say *prime* on a menu.

7. Proper cooking techniques must be accurate. If broiled swordfish is on your menu, it must be cooked exactly that way. You cannot serve the swordfish baked.

8. Pictures must be accurate. For example, apple pie a la mode must be apple pie *with* ice cream.

9. Descriptions of food products must be accurate. On a menu, for example, shrimp cocktail is described as four jumbo shrimp on a bed of crushed ice with a zesty cocktail sauce with a lemon wedge. If the shrimp cocktail comes with medium-size shrimp, the description is incorrect.

APPENDIX G

SAMPLES OF MENUS

Figure G-1. Institutional menu. *(Courtesy of Mr. William Hall, DHCFA, Director of Food Service, North Miami Medical Center.)*

NAME   ROOM

WELCOME

to North Miami Medical Center. The Food Service Department is here to serve you and make your stay with us a pleasant and healthy experience.

This is your menu for tomorrow. Please CIRCLE your selections for each meal. A Food Service Representative will collect your menu by 11:00 A.M. each day. If you do not wish to select your menu items, our staff will make a selection for you.

Your diet, like your medications and treatment, is prescribed by your physician.If you are on a modified diet certain food items, seasonings and spices may be restricted. A Dietitian will visit and explain these limitations to you.

Your total satisfaction is our objective and we welcome your comments and suggestions.

The following additional services are available upon request:

Kosher Meals
Guest Trays
Gourmet Menu
Wine Service (with Physician's approval)

Bon Appetit!

Please (CIRCLE) your selections

Breakfast

Fruits and Juices

Apple Juice

Orange Juice

Applesauce

Citrus Sections

Fresh Fruit

Breakfast Entrees

Soft Cooked Egg

Breakfast—On—A—Bun

Scrambled Egg

Cheese Blintz

Omelet

Cottage Cheese

Bacon

Sausage

Hot Cereals

Oatmeal

Farina

Cold Cereals

Cornflakes

Special K

Bran Flakes

Rice Krispies

Shredded Wheat

Puffed Rice

Breads

White Bread

Wheat Bread

Rye Bread

Bagel

Bran Muffin

Breakfast Roll

Beverages and Condiments

Whole Milk

Skim Milk

Coffee

Decaffeinated Coffee

Tea

Margarine

Butter

Salt

Pepper

Sugar Substitute

Creamer

Diet Syrup

Diet Jelly

Cream Cheese

Catsup

Lemon

CALORIE CONTROLLED   **Wednesday 3**

NAME _____ ROOM _____

Please (CIRCLE) your selections

Lunch

Appetizers

Fruit Cup

Marinated Broccoli Salad

Broth

Chicken Noodle Soup

Orange Juice

Entrees

Beef Burgundy

Diet Sliced Turkey Plate

Garden Stuffed Flounder

Diet Cottage Cheese & Fruit

Starches & Vegetables

Wax Beans

Seasoned Noodles

Peas w/Pearl Onions

Whipped Potatoes

Desserts

Diet Jello

Pineapple

Fresh Fruit

Breads

White Bread

Wheat Bread

Rye Bread

Roll

Crackers

Beverages and Condiments

Whole Milk

Skim Milk

Coffee

Decaffeinated Coffee

Tea

Margarine

Butter

Salt

Pepper

Sugar Substitute

Creamer

Lemon

Catsup

Diet Mayonnaise

Mustard

CALORIE CONTROLLED   **Wednesday 3**

NAME _____ ROOM _____

Please (CIRCLE) your selections

Dinner

Appetizers

Fruit Cup

Tossed Salad

Broth

Orange Juice

Vegetable Soup

Entrees

Chicken & Rice

Hot Roast Beef Sandwich

Diet Cottage Cheese & Fruit

Italian Lasagna

Vegetarian Platter

Starches & Vegetables

Mixed Vegetables

Baked Potato

Carrots

Garden Rice

Desserts

Diet Custard

Fresh Fruit

Diet Jello

Peaches

Breads

White Bread

Wheat Bread

Rye Bread

Roll

Crackers

Beverages and Condiments

Whole Milk

Skim Milk

Coffee

Decaffeinated Coffee

Tea

Margarine

Butter

Salt

Pepper

Sugar Substitute

Creamer

Lemon

Catsup

Diet Mayonnaise

Mustard

CALORIE CONTROLLED   **Wednesday 3**

Figure G-2. Breakfast menu—Chardonnay Restaurant. *(Courtesy of Radisson Park Terrace Hotel, Washington, DC.)*

CONTINENTAL BREAKFAST

Choice of Fresh Juices, Croissant, Danish, Toast or Brioche, Fresh Ground Coffee, Tea or Milk $6.00

JUICES AND FRUITS

Fresh Orange, Grapefruit or Fresh Seasonal Juice $2.00

Fresh Berries $3.50

Half Grapefruit 2.00

Seasonal Melon 3.00

CEREALS AND CAKES

Dry Cereal, Oatmeal or Cream of Wheat with Cream or Milk $2.00

Danish Style Waffle $4.50

Pumpkin Yogurt Pancakes with Harrington Bacon served with Vermont Maple Syrup or Clover Honey $6.50

LITE BREAKFAST

Yogurt with Fresh Fruit and Honey $4.50

Whole Wheat Crepes with Farmers and Ricotta Cheeses, Fresh Fruit and Yogurt Fruit Sauce $5.75

EGGS SERVED WITH TOAST

Two Eggs any style $3.00

With Bacon, Sausage or Harrington Ham $5.00

Eggs Benedict with Smoked Salmon or Harrington Ham $7.25

Chesapeake Crab Omelette $7.00

SIDE ORDERS

Sausage, Bacon or Harrington Ham $2.50

Choice of Croissants, Danish, Brioche or Honeybuns $3.25

English Muffins, Bagels or Toast $1.75

BEVERAGES

Fresh Ground Coffee and Decaffeinated Coffee, Cocoa, Milk or Varietal Teas $1.00

Mineral Waters $2.00

Figure G-3. Seasonal menu: summer I—Chardonnay Restaurant.
(Courtesy of Radisson Park Terrace Hotel, Washington, DC.)

SUMMER 1987

MINI CRAB CAKES $7.50

CHESAPEAKE SEAFOOD STUFFED ARTICHOKE BOTTOM $8.25

SCALLOP CEVICHE WITH MEXICAN SQUASHES $7.25

STIR FRY GINGER DUCK WITH PLUM SAUCE $6.50

TRADITIONAL SHRIMP COCKTAIL $8.25

OYSTERS ON THE HALF SHELL $7.50

CHILLED AVOCADO SOUP WITH BAY SHRIMP $5.75

CHICKEN CONSOMME WITH CELLOPHANE NOODLES $4.50

HEARTS OF BUTTER LETTUCE $4.50

CHILLED SEASONAL ASPARAGUS $4.75

CHARDONNAY HOUSE SALAD $4.25

GRILLED NEW YORK SIRLOIN, BABY BAKED POTATO,
ROAST SHALLOTS $18.50

WHOLE POACHED MAINE LOBSTER, LIME AND GINGER SAUCE,
SUMMER PASTAS $21.95

LAMB BROCHETTE WITH WILD RICE $18.00

SAUTEED MAHI MAHI BREADED WITH MACADAMIA NUTS $17.75

POACHED COHO SALMON WITH CHILI PASTA $18.75

GRILLED SEA SCALLOPS WITH SMOKED SALMON SAUCE $16.95

VEAL LOIN WITH SPINACH AND SHALLOTS, SERVED WITH CRAB
AND MOREL HASH $18.75

MARYLAND CRAB CAKES $18.95

GRILLED SWORDFISH WITH MARINATED BASIL TOMATOES,
SPINACH FETTUCINE AND LEMON BUTTER $18.25

LUMP CRAB AND MANGO SALAD, TROPICAL
FRUIT VINAIGRETTE $14.25

ROAST MARINATED DUCK WITH SUN-DRIED CHERRIES $16.75

SAUTEED CALVES LIVER WITH FIVE ONION RELISH $18.25

Figure G-4. Children's menu. *(Courtesy of Midland Hospital Center, Midland, MI.)*

BREAKFAST

Entrees

SUNDAY   **Breakfast Pie** . . . eggs, cheese, bacon and milk baked in a flaky pie crust until golden brown.

French Toast . . .thickly sliced French bread dipped in egg batter and baked until golden, served with crisp bacon.

MONDAY   **Scrambled Eggs** . . . classic breakfast fare served with sausage links.

Pancakes . . . two buttermilk cakes served with maple syrup and sausage links.

TUESDAY   **Egg M**HC**Midland** . . . scrambled egg atop a grilled slice of Canadian bacon with American cheese served on a toasted English muffin.

Cheese Strata . . . layers of bakery bread smothered with eggs and cheese and baked to a golden puff.

WEDNESDAY   **Cheese Omelet** . . .eggs and cheese combined to create an American classic.

Danish Pastry . . . flaky pastry with fruit filling served with crisp bacon.

THURSDAY   **Egg M**HC**Midland** . . . scrambled egg atop a grilled slice of Canadian bacon with American cheese served on a toasted English muffin.

French Toast . . . thickly sliced French bread dipped in egg batter and baked until golden brown, served with Canadian bacon.

FRIDAY   **Scrambled Eggs** . . . classic breakfast fare served with crisp bacon.

Breakfast Casserole . . . eggs, cheese and sausage topped with delicate puff pastry and baked to a golden brown.

SATURDAY   **Oatmeal** . . . the all-time favorite topped with brown sugar and raisins.

Scrambled Egg . . . the classic that stands alone.

Accompaniments
(available each day)

Chilled Fruits & Juices	Cereals	Breakfast Breads
Orange Juice	Cornflakes	English Muffin and Jelly
Grapefruit Juice	Wheaties	Danish Pastry
Prune Juice	Rice Krispies	Bagel with Cream Cheese
Orange Sections	Raisin Bran	Coffee Cake
Strawberries	Puffed Rice	Cinnamon Roll
Warm Applesauce	Shredded Wheat	Fresh Muffin
	Cherrios	**Toast available by request only**
	Special K	
	All Bran	
	Hot Cereal of the Day	

Figure G-4. Continued.

LUNCH

Entrees

SUNDAY   Chicken strips and tater tots.

Glazed ham with yams and apples and buttered rice.

MONDAY   Grilled cheese triangles with apple sticks.

Popeye Pie . . . spinach quiche with an orange muffin.

TUESDAY   Macaroni and cheese with mini hot dogs.

Charley's Choice . . . all white meat tuna finger sandwiches with tomato wedges, hard boiled egg wedge and fresh veggies.

WEDNESDAY   Drumstix . . . fried chicken drumstick served with mashed potatoes, green peas and a biscuit.

Tacos . . . the Mexican favorite featuring seasoned ground beef in a crisp corn tortilla.

THURSDAY   Meat Loaf served with broccoli spears.

Cheese and Fruit . . . creamy cottage cheese served with fresh fruits and corn bread.

FRIDAY   All American burger with tater tots.

Egg salad sandwich.

SATURDAY   Sloppy Joes served with potato chips.

Chunks and Chips . . . ham, cheese and raw veggies served with potato chips.

Select from the "extra stuff" on page 4 to complete your meal.

ALWAYS

Cottage Cheese

Peanut Butter and/or Jelly Sandwich

Figure G-4. Continued.

Entrees

SUNDAY	Cheeseburger and French fries.
	Tuna noodle casserole.
MONDAY	Roast turkey breast with mashed potatoes and gravy served with buttered green beans.
	Spaghetti and meat sauce.
TUESDAY	Peanut butter and jelly sandwich with cucumber spears and cherry tomatoes.
	Patty Melt with buttered carrots.
WEDNESDAY	Hot dog on a bun with escalloped apples and French cut green beans.
	Swiss steak with baked potato and French cut green beans.
THURSDAY	MHC Chicken Burger with vegetable sticks.
	Bologna sandwich with raw veggies.
FRIDAY	Pizza.
	Pepper steak over rice.
SATURDAY	Ravioli in spaghetti sauce with Italian green beans.
	Roast beef with mashed potatoes and small whole carrots.

**Select from the "extra stuff" on page 4
to complete your meal.**

AVAILABLE:

Chicken Strips

Hot Dog on a Bun

Figure G-4. Continued.

Select from the following to complete your meal

SUNDAY
Apple Juice
Chilled Punch
Sliced Tomatoes
Peas and Peanuts
Molded Bananas
Fresh Fruit Cup
Chocolate Cupcake
Surprise
Tapioca Pudding

MONDAY
Tomato Soup
Pineapple Juice
Ants on a Log
Creamy Fruit Parfait
Seven Layer Salad
Cherry Crisp
Cookie

TUESDAY
Beef & Barley Soup
Grape Juice
Fruit Punch
Spinach Salad
Carrot & Celery Sticks
Canned Fruit
Orangy Yogurt Cake
Chocolate Pudding
Cookie

WEDNESDAY
Bean Soup
Apple Juice
Pineapple Juice
Peachy Ginger Mold
Cukes 'n Cream
Fruity Upside Down Cake
Butterscotch Pudding

THURSDAY
Vegetable Soup
Fruit Punch
Grape Juice
Carrot & Raisin Salad
Molded Cherry Salad
Fruit Cocktail Cake
Coconut Cream Pudding
Cookie

FRIDAY
Pea Soup
Pineapple Juice
Cran-Apple Juice
Cucumber Robots
Tomato Rings
Molded Citrus Salad
Peach Cobbler
Cherry Cupcake

SATURDAY
Chicken Noodle Soup
Grape Juice
Relish Plate
Blushing Pear
Brownie
Bread Pudding
Rice Krispie Treat

ALWAYS AVAILABLE:

Fresh or Canned Fruit	MHC-Made Cookie	Tossed Salad
Jello Cubes	Assorted Juices	Fruit Flavored Yogurt

Figure G-4. Continued.

Figure G-4. Continued.

Figure G-5.   Room service menu—Chardonnay Restaurant. *(Courtesy of Radisson Park Terrace Hotel, Washington, DC.)*

BREAKFAST

Continental Breakfast 6:30 AM to 11:00 AM
Full Breakfast 7:00 AM to 10:30 AM

CONTINENTAL BREAKFAST

Includes your choice of Freshly Squeezed Juices, Croissant, Danish, Toast or Brioche, Served with Butter and Preserves, Your choice of Freshly Brewed Coffee or Decaffeinated Coffee, Tea, Milk, or Hot Chocolate
$7.25

THE CHARDONNAY BREAKFAST

Includes the Continental Breakfast and Two Eggs Served any Style, served with your choice of Bacon, Sausage or Harrington Ham
$8.95

A LA CARTE

Choice of Croissants, Danish, or Brioche, Served with Butter and Preserves
$3.00

Choice of English Muffins, Bagels or Toast, Served with Butter and Preserves
$2.00

Two Eggs Prepared any Style, Served with Toast	$4.50
Two Eggs Prepared any Style, Served with Toast and choice of Bacon, Sausage or Harrington Ham	$7.00
Dry Cereal, Oatmeal or Cream of Wheat, Served with Cream or Milk	$3.75
Half Grapefruit	$3.00
Seasonal Melon	$3.50
Fresh Berries of your Choice	$6.00

BREAKFAST SPECIALTIES

Belgian Style Waffle with Vermont Maple Syrup	$5.25
Pancakes with Bacon, Served with Vermont Maple Syrup or Clover Honey	$7.25
Eggs Benedict with Smoked Salmon or Virginia Ham	$9.95

BEVERAGES

Freshly Brewed Coffee or Decaffeinated Coffee, Hot Chocolate, Milk or Varietal Teas	Large Pot	$4.00
	Small Pot	$2.50
Expresso		$2.50
Capuccino		$2.75
Freshly Squeezed Juices		$2.95
Chilled Juices		$2.25

ALL DAY MENU
Served 11:00 AM to Midnight

SOUPS

Onion Soup	$4.95
Soup of the Day	$4.50

SALADS

Tossed Green Salad	$4.25
Caesar Salad with Garlic Croutons	$5.25
Spinach Salad with Hot Bacon Dressing	$5.25

SANDWICHES

Deluxe Hamburger with choice of Cheddar, Swiss or Bleu Cheese Lettuce, Tomato, and Onion. Served with French Fries	$8.95
Club Sandwich: Choice of Roast Beef, Turkey, or Ham Served with Potato Chips and Kosher Dill Pickle	$8.50
Open-Face Crab Melt Sandwich	$10.75
Rueben	$8.25

SPECIALTIES

Fettucine with Scallops and Plum Tomatoes	$11.25
Maryland Crab Cakes	$17.95
Grilled Swordfish with Roasted Red Pepper and Saffron Sauce	$18.95
Grilled Filet Mignon with Bearnaise Sauce	$19.95
Grilled Veal Chop with Sage Butter	$20.95
Roast Chicken with Lemon and Rosemary	$13.50

DESSERTS

Chocolate Terrine with Raspberry Sauce	$5.75
With a glass of Late Harvest Zinfandel	$8.25
Creme Caramel	$4.50
Homemade Ice Cream Sandwich with Chocolate Sauce	$5.25
Selection of Homemade Cakes	$5.25
Fresh Berries in Season	$6.00
Milk and Cookies	$5.95
(Our cookies are baked to order, please allow 20 minutes)	

BEVERAGES

Freshly Brewed Coffee or Decaffeinated Coffee, Hot Chocolate, Milk, or Varietal Teas	Large Pot	$4.00
	Small Pot	$2.50
Expresso		$2.50
Capuccino		$2.75
Mineral Water		$2.50

Figure G-5. Continued.

SNACKS   SPIRITS   COCKTAILS

Bowl of Mixed Nuts		$6.95
Potato Chips		$5.00
Pretzels		$5.00
Nacho Chips and Salsa		$5.95

GIN	BOTTLE	COCKTAIL
Beefeater	$40.00	$3.50
Tanqueray	$45.00	$3.75
VODKA		
Finlandia	$40.00	$3.50
Stolichnaya	$45.00	$3.75
SCOTCH		
Dewars	$40.00	$3.50
Cutty Sark	$40.00	$3.50
J & B	$40.00	$3.50
Chivas Regal	$50.00	$3.75
Glenlivet	$55.00	$4.00
BOURBON		
Old Grand Dad	$40.00	$3.50
Jack Daniels	$45.00	$3.75
CANADIAN WHISKEY		
Seagrams V.O.	$40.00	$3.50
Crown Royal	$45.00	$3.75
RUM		
Bacardi	$40.00	$3.50
Aperitifs	$30.00	$3.50
Cognacs, Armagnacs	$60.00	$5.75
Imported Cordials	$55.00	$4.50
Micro Brewery Beer		$3.50
Domestic Beer		$3.00
Sodas & Mixes		$2.00

Other Brands are Available on Request.

Figure G-5.   Continued.

CHEESE

Plate of Domestic Cheeses with Seasonal Fruits	$12.50
Also available with glass of Warres Nimrod Port	$15.95

From our "Award Winning" Wine List of All-American Wines
may we suggest the following selections:

SPARKLING WINES

Domaine Chandon Brut
Napa N.V. — $22.00

Shadow Creek Brut
Sonoma N.V. — $20.00

Shramsberg "Reserve"
Napa 1979 — $45.00

WHITE WINES

Frogs Leap Sauvignon Blanc
Napa 1986 — $18.00 Full / $9.00 Half

Cakebread Sauvignon Blanc
Napa 1986 — $22.00

Jekel Johannisberg Riesling
Monterey 1985 — $24.00 Full / $12.00 Half

Sonoma Cutrer "Russian River Ranches" Chardonnay
Sonoma 1985 — $24.00 Full / $12.00 Half

William Hill Gold Label "Reserve" Chardonnay
Napa 1985 — $25.00 Full / $13.00 Half

Raymond Chardonnay
Napa 1986 — $24.00

Mondavi "Reserve" Chardonnay
Napa 1984 — $32.00

RED WINES

Saintsbury Pinot Noir
Napa 1984 — $14.00 Half

Knudsen Erath Pinot Noir
Williametta Valley Oregon 1982 — $23.00

Franciscan Merlot
Napa 1983 — $18.00 Full / $10.00 Half

Lytton Springs "Reserve" Zinfandel
Sonoma 1983 — $25.00

Dunn Vineyards Cabernet Sauvignon
Napa 1982 — $26.00

Jordan Cabernet Sauvignon
Sonoma 1983 — $29.00

Heitz Cellars "Martha's Vineyard" Cabernet Sauvignon
Napa 1978 — $60.00

Please ask your order taker for other varietal
selections from our extensive list of American Wines.

Figure G-5. Continued.

BUFFALO CHIPS MENU

ALL BURGERS ARE ¼ LB. FRESH GROUND AND SERVED MEDIUM RARE WITH FRIES UNLESS OTHERWISE SPECIFIED.

OUR BURGERS ARE GARNISHED WITH LETTUCE, TOMATO, ONION, AND A SWEET TREAT FOR LATER.

OUR BURGERS ARE FRESH GROUND

Shackburger
THIS UNIQUE SANDWICH WAS STOLEN BY US FROM THE FAMOUS SHACK RESTAURANT IN PLAYA DEL REY, CALIFORNIA. IT'S WEESIANA SAUSAGE TOPPED WITH A BURGER AND ALL THE TRIMMIN'S.
$3.09

Mighty Doubleburger
HUNGER IS THE MOST IMPORTANT INGREDIENT IN THIS BURGER. IT'S OUR FAMOUS MIGHTYBURGER, ONLY IN DOUBLETIME! ALWAYS WITH THOSE GOLDEN FRIES! HUM ALONG!
$3.49

Thunder Humper
SMOTHERED WITH MOUTH-WATERING CHILI, CHEESE, ONIONS AND SERVED WITH FRIES. A FORK MAY COME IN HANDY TO CONQUER THIS GIANT!
$3.09

Mightyburger
IT'S THE BEST BY ANYONE'S STANDARD! IT'S HEAPED HIGH WITH ALL THE TRIMMIN'S AND SERVED WITH FRIES, BBQ SAUCE AND MAYO! FUN FOR THE ENTIRE FAMILY!
$2.49

Ava Burger
ALSO KNOWN AS "THE GREEN GIANT" THIS BURGER IS HEAPED HIGH WITH FRESH AVOCADO, ALONG WITH ALL THE TRIMMIN'S AND SERVED WITH FRIES AND MAYO!
$3.09

Swiss & Shrooms
EATING THIS BURGER IS LIKE PUTTING YOUR MOOLA IN A SWISS BANK! WITH SWISS CHEESE, SHROOMS & FRIES! THIS BURGER IS AS GOOD AS GOLD!
$3.09

All-American Bacon Burger
WE AIN'T FAKIN', WE GOT THE BACON FOR THE TAKIN', CRISP AND LEAN TOO! TOPPED WITH AMERICAN CHEESE, ALL THE TRIMMIN'S AND SERVED WITH GOLDEN FRIES! HONK IF YOU LOVE OINKERS!
$3.09

Pat E. Melt
THIS BURGER IS GUARANTEED TO MELT IN YOUR MOUTH. SERVED ON GOLDEN BROWN RYE BREAD WITH LOTSA SWISS CHEESE AND ONIONS TOO! ACCOMPANIED BY FRIES!
$2.79

Other Stuff

Peep
A LARGE BONELESS CHICKEN BREAST, ON AN ONION ROLL, MARINATED IN YOUR CHOICE OF TERIYAKI OR B-B-Q SAUCE AND GRILLED, WE ADD ALL THE TRIMMIN'S AND FRIES TO THIS FEAST!
$3.69

Hawt Dawg
OUR WONDER WEENIES ARE AS THICK AS A BRICK!!
#0~HO HUM DOG~PLAIN
#86~AMERICAN DOG~RELISH & MUSTARD
#69~MODIFIED AMERICAN DOG~RELISH ONIONS & CHEESE
#17~CHINGA DOG~CHILI, ONIONS & CHEESE
#47½~KRAUT DOG~MUSTARD, SAUERKRAUT
$2.19
ALL THE ABOVE INCLUDE FRIES!

French Dip
A MOUND OF ROAST BEEF ACCOMPANIED BY A CUP OF AU JUS, THE FRENCH ROLL IS SUPERB AS ARE THE FRIES, OUI, OUI... ALL THE WAY HOME!
$3.29

Tuna Melt
ON RYE WITH SWISS CHEESE AND FRIES! IT'S GREAT - JUST ASK ANY MERMAID YOU HAPPEN TO SEE!
$2.89

A.B.L.&T.
AVOCADO, BACON, LETTUCE AND TOMATO WITH FRIES! A GREAT TWIST ON THE NORM!
$2.99

Tuna Sand
TUNA ON SOURDOUGH WITH LETTUCE, TOMATO AND FRIES. TELL 'EM CHARLIE SENT YA!
$2.49

Ask the Cook
ASK ANYONE ABOUT OUR DAILY SPECIALS. THEY'RE ALWAYS DELECTABLE!!!

Garden of Eatin'
A CHEF'S SALAD THAT OUR CHEF IS VERY PROUD OF. IT INCLUDES TOMATOES, CUCUMBERS, FRESH AVOCADO, CHEESE, EGGS, GREEN GREENS, CROUTONS AND AT THE LEAST IT'S A FEAST!
$2.99

On the Side
BETTER THAN MOST AND AS GOOD AS THE BEST! FRENCH FRIES, MUG O' SOUP OR DINNER SALAD~MMM!!
99¢

Try our daily specials! Service to go: 396-4725

WE DO NOT ACCEPT ANY CREDIT CARDS. CASH ONLY. NO CHECKS. PLEASE PAY WHEN ORDERING. FOOD PRICES PLUS TAX~THANK YOU.

ICE COLD
～ Budweiser ～
"KING OF BEERS"
89¢

PREMIUM BOTTLED BEER AVAILABLE

PIER AVENUE

TO DRINK $1.49

Chivas Regal
Cuervo Gold
Smirnoff
Tanqueray
Seagram's V.O.
Remy Martin V.S.
Bacardi
Jack Daniels
BLACK LABEL

The selling price of alcoholic beverages includes
sales tax computed to the nearest mil.

Friends Don't Let FRIENDS Drive Drunk!

WE SERVE
Fine French Wines $1.49
PARTAGER

69¢

COFFEE   ICE TEA   SODA   MILK

OUR KITCHEN STAFF

BUFFALO CHIPS AT **2941 MAIN STREET** IN OCEAN PARK, **SANTA MONICA, CALIFORNIA** IS A DELIGHTFUL AND INTRIGUING PLACE FOR LUNCH, DINNER OR A LATE EVENING RENDEZVOUS. IT'S ADJACENT TO THE OAR HOUSE AND THERE'S NO HORSES SERVED AT THE MAIN BAR. RESERVATIONS REQUIRED FOR PARTIES LARGER THAN NINETY AT: **EX**CITE 6~4725. DOORS OPEN AT 11:30 A.M., 369 DAYS PER YEAR!

POST CARD

STAMP

Genuine, nearly-finished menu by Promotional Services of Grand American Fare, made in U.S.A. Photos courtesy Santa Monica Library.

This space for writing messages

This space for address only

Figure G-7. Specialty brunch menu—Sandalwood Restaurants. *(Courtesy of Prime Motor Inns, Inc., Fairfield, NJ.)*

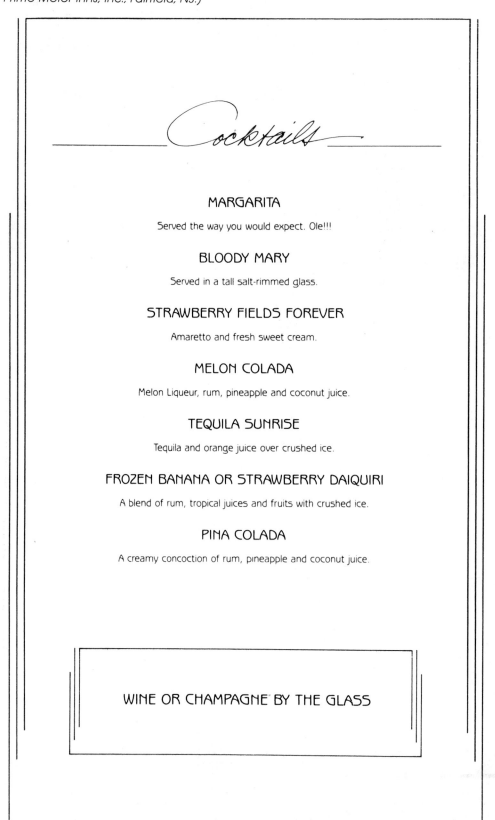

Cocktails

MARGARITA

Served the way you would expect. Ole!!!

BLOODY MARY

Served in a tall salt-rimmed glass.

STRAWBERRY FIELDS FOREVER

Amaretto and fresh sweet cream.

MELON COLADA

Melon Liqueur, rum, pineapple and coconut juice.

TEQUILA SUNRISE

Tequila and orange juice over crushed ice.

FROZEN BANANA OR STRAWBERRY DAIQUIRI

A blend of rum, tropical juices and fruits with crushed ice.

PINA COLADA

A creamy concoction of rum, pineapple and coconut juice.

WINE OR CHAMPAGNE BY THE GLASS

Brunch Fare

SERVED FROM 11:00 A.M. TO 3:00 P.M.

$12.95

ALL ENTREES INCLUDE OUR SALAD BAR, CHAMPAGNE OR FRUIT PUNCH,
JUICE OR HALF GRAPEFRUIT, INTERMEZZO, DESSERT AND BEVERAGE.

❧

CHOOSE FROM ANY ENTREE
WAFFLES OR SPECIALTY EGGS OR BRUNCH SPECIALTIES

Sandalwood Brunch Salad Bar

INCLUDED WITH ALL ENTREES
Return as often as you like creating your own brunch selections.
Variety of salads plus fruits, muffins, sweet rolls, croissants, bagels,
cream cheese and lox.

Homemade Waffles

• PLAIN   • WITH EGGS   • WITH FRESH FRUIT
• WITH EGGS AND YOUR CHOICE OF BACON, HAM OR SAUSAGE

Specialty Eggs

BENEDICT OR FLORENTINE,
Served with
tomato au gratin

CORNED BEEF HASH
Home style, served with
your choice of eggs

Brunch Specialties

MONTE CRISTO, served with honey for dipping
SKILLET OMELETTES, Cheese, Mushroom, Italian or Western
HONEY FRIED CHICKEN, with fries
EGGS As You Like with ham, bacon or sausage, served
  with home fries
CHICKEN OSKAR chicken breast & asparagus over toast points,
  glazed with hollandaise
POACHED SALMON, glazed with hollandaise
SANDALWOOD'S SKILLET OF CHILI, served with rice
CAVETELLI With Broccoli
PANCAKES with ham, bacon or sausage
STEAK AND EGGS, a juicy club steak served with your
  choice of eggs

Desserts

LAYER CAKE OR ICE CREAM

BEVERAGES: COFFEE • TEA • SANKA • MILK

Cocktails

Margarita
Served the way you would expect. Ole!!!

Bloody Mary
Served in a tall salt-rimmed glass.

Strawberry Fields Forever
Amaretto and fresh sweet cream.

Melon Colada
Melon Liqueur, rum, pineapple
and coconut juice.

Tequila Sunrise
Tequila and orange juice over crushed ice.

Frozen Banana or
Strawberry Daiquiri
A blend of rum, tropical juices
and fruits with crushed ice.

Pina Colada
A creamy concoction of rum, pineapple
and coconut juice.

Wine or Champagne
by the Glass

A Tradition of Excellence...

We take great pleasure in presenting a fine selection
of continental cuisine. All meals are cooked to order
using the finest ingredients available, by trained chefs
who take pride in their work. Sit back and enjoy . . . we
will do our best to make your dinner a memorable one.

Sandalwood Management and Staff

Sandalwood's Fare

All entrees include "OUR ANTIPASTO, SALAD & FRUIT DESSERT BAR"

Antipasti & Minestre

Escargot Stuffed Mushrooms 6.95	Shrimp Cocktail 7.50
Clams Casino 6.95	Clam Cocktail 6.95
Clams Oreganata 6.50	Crab Stuffed Mushrooms 6.25
Mussels Marinara 4.95	Pasta, your choice of sauce & pasta 7.50
Shrimp Scampi 7.95	Vegetable Soup of the Season 2.25

Soup Du Jour 2.50

Pasta Importata

Your Selection Includes Our Antipasto, Salad and Fruit
Dessert Bar and Your Choice of Soup.

14.95

Fettuccini Alfredo   Spaghetti Carbonara

Cavatelli with Broccoli   Rigatoni Amatriciana

Linguine alla Pescatore
red or white

Pesce

Filet of Sole Francese
Sauteed in wine, lemon and butter 15.95

Broiled Flounder Amandine
Broiled in butter and wine sauce 16.50

Scallops Genovese
Sauteed scallops in an herb butter with
white wine and served with rice 17.50

Stuffed Shrimp Mare Atlantico
Crab stuffed shrimp over spinach. Served with
a delicate butter sauce 17.95

Shrimp Scampi "Michele"
Sauteed in butter, garlic and wine 18.95

Scrod Livornese
With butter, ripe olives, capers and
marinara sauce 16.50

Lobster Tails Fra Diavolo
OR BUTTER SAUCE OR OREGANATO 22.50

Seafood Marechiaro
Shrimp, clams, lobster tail, mussels, scallops and
calamari 22.95

Fish Du Jour
CHEF'S FANTASY OF THE DAY

Today's Creations

Ask your server what chef delights have been prepared today.

"Soup, Salad & Antipasto Bar"

Over 60 Items

It's an Antipasto Bar! It's a Salad Bar! And It's a Fruit Dessert Bar!

Return as often as you like creating your own selections.
Includes your choice of soup.

18.95

For a lighter meal, we suggest our Soup, Salad & Antipasto Bar and
selections from our appetizer section.

Vitello

Veal Francese
Sauteed in wine, lemon and butter 17.95

Veal Parmigiana
Veal cutlet breaded and sauteed, baked with
mozzarella cheese and marinara sauce 16.95

Veal Florentine
Cheese and prosciutto stuffed
medallions of veal, over spinach 18.95

Veal Sorrentina
Veal sauteed in butter and white wine with
prosciutto 18.95

Veal Marcantonio
Sauteed veal and eggplant topped with
provolone cheese 18.95

Veal Vennini
Medallions of veal and shrimp sauteed in seasoned
butter and glazed with a basil hollandaise 19.95

Veal Piccata
Sauteed in butter and lemon sauce 16.95

Veal Marsala
Sauteed with mushrooms and marsala
wine sauce 17.95

Pollo

"Primavera"
Quick fried chicken breast with fresh seasonal
vegetables, served over rice 14.95

Chicken Marsala
Sauteed with mushrooms in marsala wine sauce . . . 16.95

Giambotta
Chicken pieces sauteed with potatoes, sausage,
mushrooms, peppers and onions 15.50

Chicken Rossini
Chicken breast sauteed and baked with mozzarella
cheese, tomato, ham and marinara sauce 15.95

Chicken Francese
Sauteed in wine, lemon and butter 15.95

Saltimbocca Alla Romama
Chicken sauteed with prosciutto ham and
sauteed spinach 16.95

Manzo

Filet Mignon
Broiled to order with sauteed mushroom caps 19.95

Sirloin Steak Pizzaiola
Sauteed with mushrooms and capers in a
light marinara sauce, baked with cheese 19.95

Tornedos A La Michele
Sliced filet mignon sauteed with bordelaise
sauce and mushrooms 19.50

New York Sirloin Steak
Served with sauteed mushroom caps 19.95

The Perfect Finish

Espresso	1.25
Cappuccino	2.25
Ice Cream	1.95
Sherbet	1.95
Chocolate Mousse	2.50
Pastries	2.50
Assorted Cakes	2.25
Chocolate Amaretto Cheesecake	2.95

Cordials

Sandalwood
RESTAURANTS AND LOUNGES

Figure G-8. Continued.

APPENDIX H

MENU MARKETING CHARACTERISTICS

Marketing Characteristics	Good Menus	Common Mistakes
Size	Large enough to read; small enough to handle	Too small; too large
Descriptive copy	For each item	Not enough descriptive copy
Printing	*No reverse type; large enough to read; uppercase for headings and subheadings*	Headings and subheadings not in uppercase; too small; too much type; too crowded
Listing	Items listed in order eaten; profitable items first and last in a column	Clip-ons cover other specials; omission of liquor or desserts; in wrong order; listing entrees on left; low-profit items listed first
Cover	Fits decor	Back cover not used
Visibility	Proper lighting	Not enough light

APPENDIX I

MENU MAKING PRINCIPLES

Before a menu is made, the following should be analyzed:

Type of customer	Adequacy of equipment
Location	Sales volume
Hours of service	Markets
Type of operation	Competition
Capacity and condition of kitchen	Season
Skill and capability of kitchen crew	Occasion
Skill and experience of foodservice crew	Cost and profits

Know your foods. Get acquainted with grades, varieties, and differences between one kind or another in the following classifications:

Meats—fresh and processed
Poultry—fresh and frozen
Vegetables—canned, fresh, and frozen
Fruits—fresh preserved, frozen, and canned
Dairy products—pasteurized and graded
Condiments and relishes
Flour—cereals and mixes
Beverages—coffee, tea, and cocoa
Groceries—spices and seasonings

To satisfy guests the menu maker must take into consideration the following principles:

Quick turnover	Texture
Leftovers	Color
Make-overs	Arrangement
On-hand supplies	Speed of service
Variety	Merchandising
Balance	Temperature
Temperature	Weather
Season	

Know the operation of your kitchen as related to equipment, personnel, and their functions:

Chef = manager
Sous chef = principal assistant
Saucier = sauce cook
Garde-Manager = cold cook
Poissonier = seafood cook
Rotisseur = roasting cook
Entremetier = vegetable cook
Boucher = butcher
Potager = soup cook

Understand their work and do not make a menu that will overwork a station.

APPENDIX J

STRAIGHT-LINE FLOWCHART

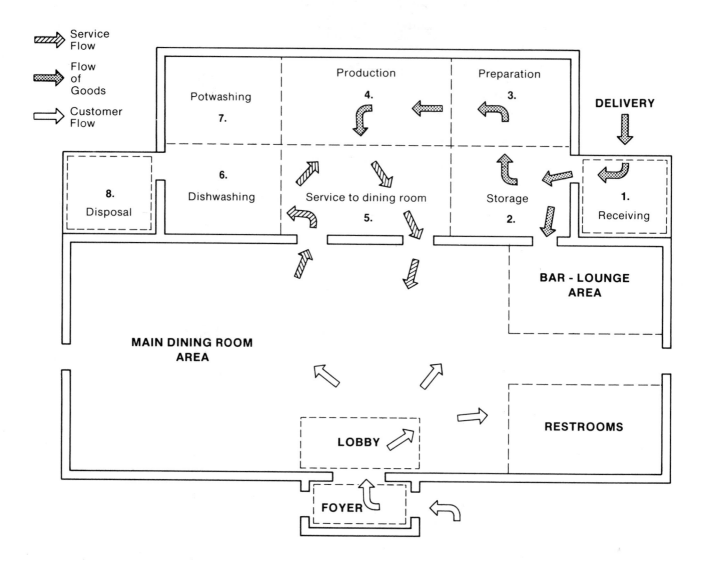

Straight line flow is defined as starting work on a product or task at point **A** and continuously working on the product or task until it reaches point **Z**. You must eliminate the following as much as possible: wasted steps, wasted motions, backtracking, and crisscrossing. Straight line flow does not mean the work flows in a straight line.

SUGGESTED READINGS

Klaus Boehm, Brian Chadwick, and Fay Sharman. 1982. *The Taste of France*. Houghton Mifflin, Boston.

Edward A. Kazarian. 1983. *Foodservice Facilities Planning*, 2d ed. Van Nostrand Reinhold, New York.

Lendal H. Kotschevar. 1975. *Management by Menu*, 1st ed. Wm. C. Brown Publishers, in cooperation with the National Institute for the Foodservice Industry.

Lendal H. Kotschevar and Margaret E. Terrell. 1977. *Food Service Planning: Layout and Planning*, 2d ed. Wiley, New York.

A. Lothar Kreck. 1979. *Menu: Analysis and Planning*. CBI Publishing Co.

A. Lothar Kreck. 1984. *Menu: Analysis and Planning*, 2d ed. Van Nostrand Reinhold, New York.

E. Donald Lundberg. 1985. *The Restaurant from Concept to Operation*. Wiley, New York.

Peter E. Van Kleek and Hubert E. Visick. 1974. *Menu Planning: A Blueprint for Profit*. McGraw-Hill, New York.

Index